Mary Mellor was born in Cornwall in 1946. She is Senior Lecturer in Sociology at Newcastle upon Tyne Polytechnic. She has had a long-term interest in co-operative development work in England and Portugal and for the past six years has been doing research into socialism, feminism, ecology, economics and anthropology for *Breaking the Boundaries*. She has published and presented many papers on this subject, most recently to the annual conferences of Socialist Scholars of America and Australia. Her articles have appeared in *Catalyst, New Ground, Science as Culture, Argument, Capitalism, Nature, Socialism* and *Environmental Politics*.

Mary Mellor lives in Newcastle with her partner and two children.

BREAKING THE BOUNDARIES

*Towards a Feminist
Green Socialism*

Mary Mellor

Published by VIRAGO PRESS Limited 1992
20–23 Mandela Street, Camden Town,
London NW1 0HQ

*A CIP catalogue record for this book
is available from the British Library*

Typeset by Falcon Typographic Art Ltd,
Edinburgh
Printed in Great Britain on recycled paper by
Cox and Wyman Ltd, Reading, Berkshire

For Kate and Joe, that they might share
    this beautiful planet with all
the peoples and creatures of the world

Men and women are sprung from the
Earth which gave substance to the
Son of God.

The ultimate sin that man is
committing is a sin against God's
creation. If we injure the Earth we
will destroy all life including our
own; if we illtreat the elements of
the cosmos, misuse the privilege that
is ours; then God's justice will permit
creation to punish humanity.

Hildegard of Bingen [AD 1098–1178]
Composer, scholar, healer and mystic

A feminist world is a community where . . . women are safe anywhere any time; people treasure the earth, air and all the creatures we live with; women are free to love one another; all people have decent housing, nutritious food, and good health care; older people are respected and the wisdom of their experience sought after; children are not separated from adults, and all share the joy of knowing them; individual, ethnic and racial differences are celebrated; all can teach and all can learn; girls and boys are taught the value of caring for others; work is no longer separate from play, and all people are seen as creative beings; the weapons of war and other wasteful and destructive toys of technology have disappeared; people of the world work together to develop an economy that benefits all of us and conserves the planet; trust replaces fear, love replaces violence, and these hateful times are relics in the archives of patriarchy.
(Statement issued by Women's Pentagon Action, 1980)

Contents

natural boundaries: Global politics · Living
naturally?

Grateful Thanks

My thanks go firstly to Nige, Kate and Joe Mellor for putting up with this obsession for so long. To Yvonne Simpson for her unfailing domestic support. To Muriel and Bill Mellor for their love and care over many years. I am very sad that Bill did not live to see this book published. I also owe thanks to the people who kept me fit and sane despite my lack of exercise and terrible work patterns: my T'ai Chi teachers Alison Melabie and Raymond Towers, who never seemed to despair at my slow progress, and Joan Stewart who pummelled my muscles back into life.

I could not have written this book without the space and resources to write provided by my colleagues at Newcastle Polytechnic. Nor could I have written it without the many people, including several generations of students, who have read and commented on the text or listened endlessly to my ramblings. Particular thanks to Nigel Mellor, Hilary Roberts and Wendy Ranade, who have read every word, often several times! I have gathered ideas from many people in many contexts but in particular those who attended the 1988, 1990 and 1991 Red-Green conferences. I have also had helpful discussions with members of the Red-Green network, the Association of Socialist Greens, Women for Socialism, Socialist Movement, Women's Environmental Network and Socialist Environmental and Resources Association.

I would particularly like to thank Hazel Henderson for giving me permission to publish the diagram on page 210 and for the inspiration I found in her two pathbreaking books, *Creating Alternative Futures* and *The Politics of the Solar Age*. It was really those two books that started me off on this path and I would like to thank Mike Jamieson for introducing me to Hazel's work and for not minding that I never returned his book!

Finally, thanks to the editors of *New Ground, Science as Culture, Argument* and *Capitalism Nature Socialism* for helpful comments on my work, and to Virago for propelling me into print.

A Personal and Political Introduction

When the rush of living stops, I confess to myself that a
great change is coming. What the nature of this change
will be I do not know.
(Susan Griffin, in Caldecott and Leland, 1983, p. 1)

First Thoughts
This book began in 1983 at the women's peace camp outside
the American Air Base on Greenham Common. As I climbed
through the perimeter fence for the first time I realised that
I knew what I was fighting *against*, but not what I was fighting
for. I had no vision, no dream; many years of commitment
to a male-dominated socialism had stripped me of hope. At
Greenham awareness of the collective strength of women allowed
my arrested feminism to be born. Stripped of all the remnants
of the 'feminine mystique', women walked with their feet flat
to the ground, rooted, solid, immovable, a force for life. They
were supported by the magnificent Common which dwarfed
the ugliness of the fence, the razor wire and the weapons of
destruction they enclosed.

As women talked, danced, ate, slept and laughed on the
earth I realised that there was a wonderful peace in following
diurnal rhythms. Materially and spiritually I felt in touch with
the natural world, and this pushed me towards the green
movement. Motherhood and awareness of my responsibility for
my children's children in the face of the threat of war, waste and
wanton destruction made it imperative that I recover my faith

in the future. I needed a vision that was both woman-centred and Earth-centred, that would recover and restore constructive relationships within human societies and between humanity and the natural world. My socialist vision had been crushed by a socialism preoccupied with industrial and economic systems. Feminists and greens had developed new or, perhaps more accurately, very old dreams of their own. But dreams are not enough; I also felt the need to have a clear understanding of the reality we face. For me, the path to the future lay in confronting that reality in the light of my dreams.

As I write this book I have in my mind an image of the Earth as a tiny sphere of life and beauty hurtling through space surrounded (as far as we know) by billions of lifeless stars and planets. That image is followed by anger at the destruction, waste and inhumanity that ravages this unique world. Deforestation, desertification and the tragedy of famine; the homeless children and shantytowns alongside privilege and affluence in cities around the world; poor people living and scavenging on garbage tips, while richer communities pile up mountains of waste; women living in fear of men both outside and inside their homes; the human and ecological ravages of war, strutting militarism and the constant threat of nuclear holocaust; the human error, neglect or worse that caused disasters such as Chernobyl, Seveso, Bhopal, the poisoning of the Rhine and the Alaskan oil spill; the huge drift nets across our oceans endlessly catching and killing fish, birds and sea mammals; factory farming and animal experimentation; hunting whales in the name of 'science'; poaching elephants for their ivory; the trapping and shooting of hundreds of millions of songbirds as they cross southern Europe.

This book was conceived in protest against the threat of nuclear holocaust and born in the shadow of the genocide and ecocide of the Gulf War. Economic, political and military 'logic' dictated that a war should be fought in which neither side would compromise, threatening the use of biological, chemical and nuclear weapons. In the event the war was a conventional but one-sided 'turkey-shoot', in which the US-led allies unleashed more explosive power upon Iraq than was dropped in the whole of the Second World War. Iraq responded to such overwhelming odds by firing oil wells, pouring millions of gallons of oil into the waters of the Gulf, and persecuting its minorities. The war resolved none of the economic and political complexities of the Middle East while adding the tragedy of the Kurds. Such destructive intransigence on all sides must lead us to wonder on what diplomatic hair-trigger the world's stockpile of 50,000 nuclear weapons rests. Our sense of proportion and priority has become so distorted that hundreds of billions of dollars can be squandered in war and 'collateral' damage in the Middle East while twenty-seven million people in Africa topple over the brink of starvation. Just a fraction of the money and organisation that went into the Gulf War could save their lives. One thing is clear: our world is not in safe hands. The 'new world order' has put the Earth under a death sentence.

Anger and frustration in the face of such stupidity and injustice lead easily to hate for all those who threaten the Earth and its people. Not just systems and governments but individuals: soldiers, politicians, businessmen, rapists, the vigilantes who kill the street children of Latin America, huntsmen, loggers, ranchers. I use the male form because they are mostly men. To hate is not helpful; it is part of the problem and cannot lead us to a solution. The majority of the world's people, men and women, are trapped into destructive and harmful forms of behaviour and can see no way out. They are disempowered through being economically, socially, politically and geographically separated from centres of power and decision-making. The future of the planet is being threatened in the interests of very few people. Four-fifths of the world's peoples have had little or no share in the benefits of a way of life for which we and the planet may all die.

I am not searching for a blueprint for the future, nor for a correct 'line'. We cannot wait for the right revolutionary 'moment', the situation is too immediate and serious for that. In the face of economic, military and ecological threats to the survival of both people and the natural world, we need to draw upon the inspiration and insights of political and social movements for peace, justice and sustainability as well as the struggles of oppressed and exploited peoples worldwide. I believe that those ideas and struggles can be drawn together into a feminist green socialism.

Greening the future

Solutions to global problems will not be found if we ignore the interconnectedness of all life – ourselves and the creatures and plants with whom we share the earth, and with whom we are losing touch.
(Meg Beresford, 1988, p. 53)

The world was dying and the world deserved it. This was the shocked fatalistic attitude of the final generation ... 'If only,' people sighed, 'if only we had *done* something. Acted when we still had time, even just ten years ago.'
(Ben Elton, 1989, p. 451)

This book starts from the assumption that there is an ecological crisis. Experts may disagree about how, when and why it has, or will, come about, but to most people the evidence is all around us – not only in tangible effects such as global warming, pollution, doubts about the safety of food and water, soil depletion and deforestation but in the social and psychological effects of the 'rush of living'. Many of us who have had the benefits of the European scientific and industrial revolutions feel depleted within our lives as well as in our environment, while many more people have suffered those same depletions without gaining any of the 'benefits'.

The human spirit has become so debased that human satisfaction is often seen solely in terms of material wealth. Happiness is having the latest electronic gadget or the newest model car. Individual and cultural identities are swallowed up as standardised products and televised images circle the globe to embrace those of us who can afford it in a false unity of consumption. People make 'products' of themselves by pummelling and starving their bodies into a commercially acceptable form. The promise of industrial capitalism is that anyone can join the consumer society if they undergo the process of 'development'. This, together with the vast unmet desire for consumer goods worldwide and the constant search for new and 'improved' products, means that industrial growth is a built-in assumption of the modern global economy. Socialist economies are no less committed to industrial expansion. In Eastern Europe the people have lost faith in their economic and political systems, not in their dreams of the consumer society.

The green movement has warned us that human development has outstripped the planet's capacity to sustain us. The great technologies of industrialism – transport and communication, mass production and mass consumption, industrialised agriculture and military technology – are threatening the survival of the human race, other species and the planet itself.

Modern industrial societies developed with no reverence for the Earth. Nature was seen as 'valueless' and 'dead' unless developed by 'man'. Greens are challenging this view of nature and the assumption that it is a horn of plenty to feed the limitless material demands of humanity. They are asking whether the quality of human life should be measured in terms of quantity of material wealth. Is there any point in owning one, two or three cars if we cannot move on the roads? Is it worth living off the fat of the land if we die of a coronary? Greens are arguing that we have sacrificed part of our humanity, part of ourselves, in a one-dimensional search for material goods. Far from treating nature as a resource for humanity, we should be maintaining the diversity of the biosphere as an end in itself.

There is little evidence that the green message of the end of the bonanza has been taken on board. Despite the growing evidence of ecological crisis, the scientific, political, economic and military institutions that have brought it upon us still form ever greater global networks of power. Individuals and organisations whose actions have threatened the environment are often charged with finding solutions to the problems they themselves have created. The Gulf War is only one example of the way in which the interests of both people and planet are discounted in the 'scenarios' developed by politicians, business and military strategists. Having queued up to obtain the 'spoils of war' by selling weapons to the Middle East, Western companies and governments are now lining up to bid for the 'spoils of peace' in contracts to rearm, rebuild and decontaminate the region.

While the greens have alerted us to the ecological limits to human development, do they offer us a way out of the system that has brought a good deal of benefit to a minority of humanity, but little more than empty promises to the majority? A common declaration within the green movement is that they are 'neither right nor left but in front'. For many greens this means leading us to a new world of small, ecologically sustainable, self-governing communities embodying 'feminine' values. Less clear is the route for our political journey – will the ecological crisis necessarily produce a 'green' response? Capitalism has proved itself to be a remarkably resilient system over the past two hundred years – could it 'go green' and ride the ecological crisis? Why should an ecologically constrained future be 'feminine' and small-scale rather than masculinist and large-scale – a land-grabbing military empire, perhaps? Conflicts over water and oil have played a key role in the maelstrom of the Middle East.

What is the best route to a green future – is there a parlia-mentary road to sustainability, or will we need an eco-revolution? Will it be a revolution of ideas or action? Will there be a vanguard of that revolution? If so, will it be led, once again, by white men from the North? One thing is certain: the ecological crisis will fall, and has fallen, most heavily on the poorest and most vulnerable members of the human community. Among these groups it is women who suffer most; they are the poorest of the poor. A political movement for an egalitarian and sustainable future must start from the perspective of those who are worst affected by the present system and from the planet's ability to sustain them. It is therefore with women that we must begin to build the green path to the future.

Starting again with Women

The rape of the earth in all its forms becomes a
metaphor for the rape of woman.
(Judith Plant, 1989, p. 5)

For women the present 'world order' represents perhaps the ultimate manifestation of male power over both women and nature. The long history of patriarchy goes back much further than the industrial and scientific revolutions of the sixteenth to nineteenth centuries. Patriarchy means literally rule by the father, but the word is generally used more loosely to describe a system which prioritises men and male interests and subordinates women and women's interests.

Throughout history women have struggled against the power of men. Sometimes they have broken through individually or collectively, but male power has never been finally broken. Woman are fighting a many-headed monster that exerts physical, economic, ideological and emotional control over them. In Britain and France the political revolutions of the eighteenth and nineteenth centuries seemed to offer women a way out through the demand for individual political rights. Women need no longer be the chattels of fathers and husbands. Many women identified with the demands of the new social movements for equality and liberty. Unfortunately, the third cry of the French Revolution, 'fraternity', became the reality. The new collective struggle in the trades unions and socialist movements turned out to be for men, for brotherhood, with women as also-rans.

As well as not playing a part in the political systems of the newly industrialising societies, women became detached from the system of production as the rural agricultural tradition gave way to urban industrial society. While urban life broke down some of the social boundaries that constrained women, it effectively divided their lives. Industrial society made women socially schizophrenic, divided between the public world of employment, commerce, politics and culture and the private world of family, sexuality and domestic work. Men dominated the public world while being serviced by women's work in the private world. Women entered the public world only by denying the responsibilities of their private world: by being 'honorary men'.

Nineteenth-century 'first-wave' feminists had struggled to enter the public world on an equal basis. By the second half of the twentieth century women had realised that it would be necessary to break down the divisions in their lives, to reunite the private with the public world. The increasing dangers of ecological and military conflagration make it clear that women must go even further. It is not a case of repairing the damage produced by a society divided on the basis of sex but of overthrowing the economic, political, military and sexual structures of domination that men have created. However, these structures have put barriers around and between women. Women's struggles have been fractured by divisions of class, race, ethnicity and sexuality. Women also differ in their relationship to the means of survival. In industrial economies women have indirect and unequal access to the productive process, while women in non-industrialised societies are directly responsible for sustaining the existence of themselves and their families. Throughout the South, as the market has invaded subsistence economies, women find their land devoured by industrialised agriculture and the pressure to grow cash crops rather than food.

The economic, military and political systems that have produced the ecological crisis were not created by women, although some participated in and benefited from them. Despite the fact that many men have shared the exploitation and oppression that women have suffered, these structures of power start from male interests and priorities. A sustainable society for the future must start from the interests and priorities of women. It is women who are responsible for creating and sustaining the means of life. It is women who nurse the people who are most vulnerable to poverty and environmental squalor – the young, the old and the sick. It is women who bear damaged children and whose bodies are subjected to reproductive engineering. In market economies it is women at whom most advertising is directed and upon whom the pressure to consume is immense; where a woman's worth is judged by the brand name she uses and whether she can afford the latest designer outfit for her children from her domestic budget.

Feminists and greens offer a profound critique of modern society. In contrast, socialism appears to be part of the malaise of the present social order. What can it offer for the future?

Why Socialist?

A careful reading of the historical experience of socialist societies indicates that they better satisfy the basic requirements of life.
(Gita Sen and Caren Grown, 1987, p. 25)

It is ironic that when a global response to an overwhelmingly powerful capitalism is needed, its traditional opponent, socialism, is in confusion and retreat. The collapse of 'communism' in disarray, disillusion and environmental squalor in Eastern Europe, the massacre of protesters in China's Tiananmen Square, the marginalisation of the Left in the West and the capitulation to the 'market' of Western 'socialist' parties have made socialism/communism dirty words. Over the years it had become old-fashioned among socialists to talk about principles or ideals, and socialist movements became preoccupied with organisational structures – whether the state, the party or the trades union. As a result, 'socialist' organisations became increasingly detached from their principles and their roots, and in extreme cases were undermined and distorted through injustices and atrocities committed in the name of socialism.

Socialism was born in the struggle against the divisive and destructive effects of the Industrial Revolution. As people were thrown off the land they crowded into towns and cities and were reluctantly driven to take work in the new factories. As the industrial system developed, socialism remained attached to those same workers through the generations even when, in the West, they in turn became the beneficiaries of the exploitation of new waves of dispossessed and deprived peoples. Many socialist women in the West found themselves being called upon to support the interests of the white, male working class, no matter how racist, sexist or chauvinist. It was a socialism that ignored the unpaid work of women, the exploitation and oppression of colonised peoples and the exploitation of the 'free' resources of the planet.

The economic success of industrial capitalism tempted socialists to take the seemingly easy route to equality and social justice via state welfarism. Economic and industrial growth and rising standards of living meant that they did not need to tackle the fundamental questions of the ownership and control of resources, wealth and privilege. Instead successive Labour and Social Democratic governments 'milked' industrial capitalism through taxation, much of it levied on workers' wages. The 'workers' states of Eastern Europe were equally seduced by the blandishments of industrialism, and eventually, as we have seen, of capitalism. If women or greens look to socialists for a path to the future, they find many of them busy transmogrifying into market socialists or social marketeers, or celebrating the politics of style. Women, the poor, marginalised workers, Black and South peoples have been trampled in the stampede to the right.

The background against which I write this book is the triumph of patriarchal capitalism. Its most vociferous supporters have proudly declared that 'there is no alternative': there is no longer any society, any social rights or needs, only the individual worker/consumer, (his) family and the market. Women are urged to bear the burden of 'family values' while receiving no independent right to economic resources. The services that make their lives easier are available only if capitalism deems them 'affordable' or if there is a profit to be had. Women, as the worst paid and most marginal workers, suffer under the continual pressure on workers to reduce their wages and standard of living. Transnational corporations stalk the globe looking for new markets, tax havens, cheap labour and resources, and somewhere to carry out environmentally sensitive production without too many questions being asked.

It would be foolish to mount a defence of the indefensible and, as a woman, I do not feel constrained by the failures of male-dominated socialism. The sea of men in grey suits who fill the Parliaments of the new 'democracies' of Eastern Europe shows how little state socialism did to undermine male domination of the public world. Socialist societies have also been as militaristic and warmongering as capitalist ones. Socialism has also lost its way in attaching itself exclusively to struggle around 'production'. It is a movement in crisis:

> The crisis is unique. It is not simply about socialism's historical record, economic weakness or even political rejection. There is a less tangible problem which is that its imaginative force has been drained. (Sheila Rowbotham and Hilary Wainwright, *Socialist*, 11 April 1991)

It is that imaginative force in socialism that I want to rescue, and for me it lies in a very simple and perhaps even limited principle. The imaginative force in socialism lies in its dream of a society in which all members have a mutual responsibility to ensure that everyone achieves their creative potential by having an equal share in the resources of that society. It is a commitment that transcends all boundaries, whether of nation, race, ethnicity, sex, sexuality, ability or capacity.

This socialist vision rejects the liberal argument that equal access to human potential can be achieved solely by the guarantee of an individual's political rights and/or economic freedom. Socialism recognises the interdependence of human existence so that the socialist route to freedom must be collective and mutual, with social rights as necessary as political rights. To the interdependence of human society, greens would want to add our interdependence with the planet and other species. This interdependence may limit human potential in a material sense, but in a socialist society those limitations would be experienced equally.

While I accept the environmental limitations to human action, I cannot share the confidence of many greens that the way forward lies in the re-establishment of self-reliant, informal, primary groups. Much green thinking hovers uncomfortably between anarchism and liberalism, both assuming that individual and/or communal self-reliance will be globally constructive. I will argue that this assumption is unwarranted; more appropriate is a social- ist perspective that sees the need to create and sustain *politically* the conditions of mutuality and ecological sustainability.

It may seem that it would be appropriate to find a new word to describe the principles I have set out. I think that would be both dishonest and wrong. It would diminish and undermine the struggles of people over many generations and in many countries, in the name of socialism, for justice, equality, and freedom from want and fear. It would also imply that socialism's traditional struggle against industrial capitalism is no longer necessary, when in the face of the ecological crisis and in the interests of women it is more necessary than ever. What we need, however, is a socialism that breaks free of the constraints of both men and capitalism.

Breaking and Making Boundaries

> Building bridges between our divisions,
> I reach out to you as you reach out to me.
> All of our voices and all of our visions,
> Sisters, we can make such sweet harmony.
> (Greenham Peace Camp song)

If we are to find a path to the future that will create a sustainable egalitarian society, it must be feminist, green and socialist. This does not mean annexing the insights and struggles of feminists and greens to traditional male-dominated socialism. It is not even a case of building a 'rainbow coalition'. The present malaise of socialism will not be overcome by adding the environment, women or the struggles of Black and South peoples on to a flawed base. The reconstruction has to be much more fundamental; it must *start* from women and the natural world to build a vision for the future.

If we are to go 'beyond the fragments' of existing social and political struggles, we must begin by breaking the boundaries that disempower us. Those boundaries are between our movements, within ourselves, within the human community and between the human community and the natural world. Those boundaries have been created by the domination of our systems of knowledge by science and technology; by the economic systems that constrain our lives; by the militarised nation-states and divisions of race, culture, ethnicity and sex. These boundaries limit our understanding and our capacity for action and prevent us from reaching out to each other and thereby gaining collective strength. However, not all boundaries are barriers to action; we need some boundaries as barriers between us and the powerful global forces that invade our lives. A feminist green socialism must enable us to break down destructive and divisive boundaries while building constructive ones.

Some boundaries can be used destructively or constructively. Science and technology, for example, have traditionally developed in a way that sees nature as passive, infinite and available for exploitation. However, the science of ecology sees nature as an interconnected and limited system. A green view of the relationship between humanity and the natural world would seek to break down the human-centred division between ourselves and other species, while at the same time putting up boundaries around our exploitation of nature. The boundaries between the sexes and different ethnic and racially defined seem at present to be entirely destructive, but it may prove possible to construct relations of difference that are not exploitative or oppressive. The boundaries of the economy reflect both human-centred and patriarchal assumptions about what is to be accorded 'value', ignoring much of women's work and the real cost of natural resources for present and future generations.

Both greens and feminists have pointed out that when breaking down the boundaries that exploit and oppress us on the basis of sex, nationalism, race and ethnicity, we must not assume a spurious universalism. Our unity must embrace our diversity; we need to uphold and respect the boundaries of our differences. They have also emphasised the need to break down the boundaries within ourselves, between mind and body, that modern science has created. This has been most clearly demonstrated in the sphere of health. We are also constrained by the competitive relationships of modern society, where one person's success is another person's failure, and external judgements of our worth undermine our ability to value ourselves. We need to find a way of putting around ourselves a constructive boundary that will enable us to take control of our lives both individually and collectively.

Feminists, greens and socialists have all, in their different ways, been challenging the boundaries that constrain us. Feminists have shown the way human relationships have been distorted by heterosexuality and patriarchy. Greens have undermined the false boundary between human society and nature. Socialists have exposed the exploitative reality of economic relationships. These boundaries exist not only in reality but in our minds, and we must confront them at both levels. Repressive military regimes and multinational conglomerates cannot be 'thought away', although we can liberate our thinking from their forms of reasoning. None of the present structures of economic, military and political power will abandon that power willingly. Nor will men willingly abandon their control over women. Landowners will not redistribute their land to the poor, and dictatorial regimes will not recognise human rights. However, breaking through the boundaries they have created in our minds will empower us to begin the struggle to confront them in reality. This was the strength of feminist consciousness-raising and Paulo Freire's movement for popular education.

In building the case for a feminist green socialism I will look first at the potential and limitations of the green movement. From there I will look at the impact on women and the natural world of patriarchal capitalism and the ways in which male-dominated socialism has failed to confront it. Finally, building on an analysis of women's lives and work and the constraints of ecological limits, I will construct the elements of a feminist green socialism.

This book will raise more questions than it answers, and I hope it will stimulate debate. All criticisms are welcome, for only that way will we move forward.

A Word about Words

I have used no capitals when talking about feminism, green thinking or socialism, except when I am referring to a political party or parties by name. Instead of Third World I have tended to refer to the South, as Third World implies that the West/North is a First World, which I cannot accept. In this context I am using

North to mean those capitalist industrial nations that economically, politically, and/or militarily dominate the rest of the world, centred upon North America, Western Europe and Japan.

Although in many green writings indigenous peoples are referred to as tribal, I prefer to use the word 'clan' as I feel that it has fewer connotations of the 'primitive', given the colonial heritage of the English language. On many occasions I have used the word 'struggle'. Some people may find this too militaristic and violent a concept. I accept their concerns, but I can find no other word to describe a very real process people are going through every day of their lives. Finally, despite the considerable theoretical work that has gone into distinguishing the concepts of sex and gender, I have used them fairly interchangeably in my discussion of the sexual division of labour. When I am referring to biological sex, I will make this clear.

Postscript

It is ironic that values that I support in this book have had to be contravened in order to get it written. It has meant long hours in front of a (very fast) word processor that was built, in all probability, by the exploited labour of other women. During those long hours I have neglected family, friends and exercise. I find it fairly hypocritical to write a book that stresses the importance of caring and nurturing when my children have to shout to get my attention away from the computer screen, even when they are ill. As a feminist I am aware that the life of myself and my partner is made possible only through the domestic and caring work of another woman. The book is the worse for all of that. Finally – and perhaps most importantly – as a white, middle-class woman, I am aware that this book is a form of power; it claims space that is not readily available to Black and working-class women, or women of the South. I can only hope that what I have to say here will help those who are oppressed and exploited and undermine those who claim power over them.

CHAPTER 1

The Prophets of Doom and the Politics of Hope: The Coming of the Greens

Humankind's real wealth lies in the health of the planet
– if it dies, so do we all.
(Jean Lambert, 1988, p. 137)

Are we all Green now?

For many people in Britain, the green movement is symbolised by televised images of orange-suited Greenpeace activists in minuscule rubber boats bobbing perilously beneath the towering bows of a whaling ship or struggling to block a nuclear waste pipe. In America it is more likely to be a blockade against logging, in Germany a protest against nuclear power, in India the women of the Himalayan Chipko movement hugging their trees. Across the globe, support for environmental pressure groups is burgeoning. Green Parties have found their political voice, while other political parties hastily cobble together policies on 'the environment'. Political and scientific heads nod with environmental concern at numerous international conferences, and the heir to the British throne appears on television to plead for conservation and organic farming. In June 1989 15 per cent of the British electorate voted Green in elections to the European Parliament, the largest national vote for any Green Party. In 1991, following intense national and international political pressure, Britain and America were finally persuaded to agree to a fifty-year moratorium on mining in Antarctica, and Japan agreed to limit its drift-netting. Are we all green now?

The green movement embraces a wide range of individuals and

organisations, politically, socially and geographically. The largest group are the conservationists, who run from self-interested NIMBYS (Not In My Back Yard) to organisations like the World Wide Fund for Nature in Britain or the Wilderness Society or the Sierra Club in the USA. Next come the more activist campaigning groups, such as Greenpeace or Friends of the Earth, which have emerged across the globe from Ghana to Japan. Greenpeace, founded originally in Canada in 1971, has two million supporters worldwide, more than 300,000 of them in Britain. Friends of the Earth embraces thirty-five organisations, several in countries of the South. Women's environmental movements include DAWN (Development Alternatives for Women in a New Era), formed in Bangalore, India, in 1984, and WorldWIDE (World Women Working for Women dedicated to the Environment), formed in 1982. In Britain there is both a Women's Environmental Network and a Black Environmental Network.

At the most radical end of the campaigning spectrum are groups like the Animal Liberation Front, the American deep ecology group Earth First!, and the Canadian Sea Shepherd Conservation Society, whose members practise 'ecotage'. Both the latter emerged from other pressure groups such as the Wilderness Society and Greenpeace. Members of these groups could be described as 'eco-revolutionaries' willing to pay the price for 'defending the Earth'. Equally, peoples of the South fighting to save their land from Africa to the Amazon are paying the price for the environment even if they are not members of a 'movement'. Many – like Chico Mendes, the Brazilian rubber-tappers' leader – have died for that cause.

In the richer countries of the North, the green movement attracts mainly young – and at least potentially prosperous – people with strong links to the peace movement, women's movement and countercultural groups. In Spain, on the other hand, a good deal of support is drawn from older people, largely as a legacy of the Civil War. In the South, green campaigns are based in the struggles of indigenous peoples such as COICA

(Centre for the Indigenous Organisations of the Amazon Basin). In around twenty countries, from Sweden to Tasmania, political parties have been formed and Green Members of Parliament elected. The dissolution of Eastern Europe has also produced a number of new green groupings, such as the Social Ecological Union of the USSR. Although 'ecoglasnost' played an important role in the collapse of Eastern Europe, environmental issues have subsequently been overwhelmed by the wider political and economic crisis.

Despite all this activity, the seriousness of the ecological situation did not hit home in the major economies and governments of the world until the universality of the crisis became clear – or to be more precise, until the crisis hit the dominant groups in the dominant nations of the North. Ecological crisis is nothing new for the poor and the South; they have always lived with uncaring industrial and agricultural production, poor sanitation, the depletion of poverty and the possibility that their young will have no future. Industrial poisoning and toxic waste dumps in the South or among the poor of the North did not alarm the rich North, unlike the crisis over the disposal and storage of nuclear waste. Climate-induced problems that had killed or displaced many millions of people in the South did not become an issue until global warming threatened to affect the northern hemisphere. Ozone depletion rocketed up the political agenda when it was shown to be dangerous for those with fair skin.

What is unique about the present crisis is that it *is* geographically and socially universal – not even the rich and powerful can escape its effects. People may try to insulate themselves, but the ultraviolet rays that pass through the ozone-depleted air, the sulphurous acid rain and the dust of Chernobyl fall upon the rich as well as the poor. Global warming will flood both Florida and Bangladesh. Pollutants that enter soil and water find their way into every stomach; even bottled Perrier water had to be withdrawn from sale at one point because of contamination by benzine. It is not surprising, therefore, that royal families, industrialists and world leaders are boarding the green bandwagon. But a common bandwagon does not mean a common interest or a common solution. At a superficial level environmentalism unites people of all political persuasions and levels of privilege. At a more fundamental level the environmental movement is an attack on the underbelly of dominant economic, military and national interests, as the blowing up of Greenpeace's ship *Rainbow Warrior* in Auckland harbour showed.

Sounding the Alarm

For the first time in the history of the world, every
human being is now subjected to contact with dangerous
chemicals, from the moment of conception until death.
(Rachel Carson, 1962, p. 31)

Public awareness and concern about the environment came thirty years after Rachel Carson first warned of a 'silent spring' if the accumulation of poisonous pesticides in the food chain destroyed the 'web of life'. Even this was hundreds of years after the Romans prohibited coal burning in London or John Evelyn's warnings of the dangers of deforestation and air pollution in the seventeenth century. It was one hundred years after the German zoologist Ernst Haeckel gave the new science of ecology its name and Ellen Swallow studied ecological issues as the first woman to enter the Massachusetts Institute of Technology (MIT) (Paehlke, 1989). By a quirk of history it was MIT that carried out the 'limits to growth' study in 1970 that helped to launch the present wave of ecological activism (Meadows, 1972).

Throughout the 1960s concern had mounted that there could be a planetary limit to human development on 'space-ship earth' (Ward and Dubos, 1972; Boulding, 1973). Its main focus was population growth and resource depletion, particularly of food and energy (Hardin, 1968; Erlich and Erlich, 1970; Herman

Daly, 1973). The question of population control has remained a difficult issue for the green movement with its totalitarian, if not fascist, overtones – as in Garrett Hardin's declaration that the 'freedom to breed' is intolerable (1977, p. 23).

In 1970 the Club of Rome, an informal group of industrialists and scientists, asked MIT to run a computer projection of future ecological developments in five areas: human population, agricultural production, natural resources, industrial production, and pollution. Despite criticism about the way in which the study was conducted, 'limits to growth' became a clarion call of the emerging green movement. In 1974 Lester Brown founded the Worldwatch Institute, which has issued seven 'State of the World' reports translated into all the world's major languages. The latest Report warns that 'only a monumental effort can reverse the deterioration of the planet' (Brown, 1990). In 1980 another ecological assessment, the Global 2000 Report commissioned by President Jimmy Carter, was shelved by Ronald Reagan, while its doom-laden contents were once more challenged (Simon, 1981; Simon and Kahn, 1984).

The apocalyptic warnings of the scientific ecologists were accompanied by a gentler message of hope in Fritz Schumacher's appeal for a change in political and spiritual values. Schumacher argued for a new form of economics based on Buddhist principles, and his *Small is Beautiful* became a virtual bible of the green movement (Schumacher, 1968, 1973). The tides of doom were also temporarily assuaged by scientific and technological developments, the Green Revolution in agriculture, new industrial processes and materials and the seeming ability of industrial nations to adapt to the oil price shocks of the early 1970s (Paehlke, 1989). With a sigh of relief the richer nations continued their pattern of high consumption interrupted only by occasional appeals on behalf of starving people in drought-ridden countries, majestic sea mammals or cuddly animals.

It took another ten years before it became clear that deforestation and desertification were not faraway problems in faraway countries caused by bad development practices but represented a threat to the whole global climate. The planet was slowly warming up. Burning fossil fuels for industry, transport and heating buildings was putting more carbon dioxide and other 'greenhouse gases' into the air than the plants of the planet could absorb. The remaining 'lungs' of the world, the tropical rainforests, were being destroyed at such a rate that they would all be gone by the year 2050, with an equivalent amount of the world's surface turning to desert (Shiva, 1989). Since 1940 logging and land clearance had destroyed rainforests equivalent in size to North America. Forty per cent of topsoil had been eroded in the same period. By 1990 the 'death of nature' had been declared (McKibben, 1990).

At the present rate of emission, greenhouse gases in the atmosphere will double by 2050. Between 1977 and 1987 chlorofluorocarbons (CFCs) destroyed half of the ozone layer and there is now a hole half the size of Canada over the Antarctic. The problems of the atmosphere finally put the green issue on the desks of world leaders. In 1987 the Montreal Protocol committed governments to phase out CFCs, and in 1988 politicians and scientists at a 'Changing Atmosphere' conference in Toronto predicted severe economic and social dislocation for present and future generations and international tension and conflict if the situation was not addressed. In 1990 the scientists of the United Nations Intergovernmental Panel on Climate Change called for an immediate 20 per cent reduction in the emission of greenhouse gases, but politicians lagged behind and a World Climate Conference in Geneva in November 1990 made no recommendations for action.

Globally, the United Nations had tried to grapple with the problem through its World Commission on Environment and Development resulting in the 'Brundtland Report', *Our Common Future* published in 1987. This had acknowledged that the security, well-being and very survival of the planet depended on concerted international action. It tried to bring together the problem of environmental limits and the needs of the poor in a development programme that was ecologically sustainable, but it failed to penetrate the self-interest of the richer nations and the whole problem has rolled on to 'Earth Summit', the UN conference on Environment and Development in Brazil in 1992. Few Greens hold out much hope for it and argue that effective action will not be taken until we embrace a green perspective on our relationship with the natural world.

Green Politics

The Green Party offers not a panacea, but a foundation
for a new way of life.
(Manifesto of the British Green Party, 1987)

Members of the green movement have claimed it to be 'the most radical and important political and cultural force since the birth of socialism' (Porritt and Winner, 1988, p. 9). Like the socialist and feminist movements, the green movement is not new; it has challenged urbanised and industrialised society for more than a hundred years (Paelke, 1989; Pepper, 1984). What is new is the assertion that there is a distinctive green politics as the basis for an alternative to the 'old order' (Dobson, 1990).

Although the first Green Party (originally called the Ecology Party) was formed in Britain in 1973 and Greens were first elected to (local) government in France, green politics came to international notice on 6 March 1983 when the German Green Party (Die Grünen) broke through the 5 per cent barrier to take twenty-eight seats in the West German Federal Parliament (the Bundestag) and make Petra Kelly an international name. By making such a substantial entrance into parliamentary politics, Die Grünen set the political trend for other Green Parties by aligning themselves firmly with the feminist and peace movements and placing themselves on the left of centre with a firm commitment to global social justice and the need to redress the balance between North and South. The German Greens were the first political party to advocate positive action for women and aimed to have 50 per cent representation at all levels in the Party. They demanded that women should no longer be condemned to 'passive femininity', watching silently as men disregarded their interests. Die Grünen argued that women must play an equal role in the economic and political arena if the life of the next generation was to be safeguarded. In 1984 the Party was led by an all-women group.

It seemed as if the future of the green movement was assured, and there was a tremendous spirit of optimism in other Green Parties as the German Greens seemed to go from strength to strength, providing the focus of a growing European Green political movement. Petra Kelly felt on reflection that too much faith had been placed in Die Grünen, and that she often felt she wanted to tell people to be 'a little bit more sober' (*Living Marxism*, no. 4, 1989). She was right – having made substantial gains in the elections of January 1987, the German Greens were eclipsed in the first elections after the unification of East and West Germany in December 1990, when their vote fell just below the vital 5 per cent threshold and they lost all their seats. This was largely the result of a political miscalculation. Die Grünen had argued against unification, proposing instead that the two Germanys should be part of a federal Europe. This went against the public mood and, together with uncertainty about the Green Party's relationship to the remnants of the East German Communist Party, produced their electoral defeat.

All was not lost, as in the state elections in Hesse in January 1991 the Greens pulled back up to 8 per cent, and in April they made substantial gains in the conservative state of Rhineland-Palatinate. It does seem, however, that in electoral terms the green movement is condemned for the present to remain a minority party. The problem for Green Parties is that while there is widespread public concern about environmental issues, it is very difficult to convert it to a commitment to green politics, particularly against the adverse electoral systems in Britain and North America. In Britain 14.9 per cent of the electorate voted Green in the 1989 Euro-election but reverted to their traditional parties in bread-and-butter national and local elections. By 1991 the Green Party was barely registering in the polls. After implementing some of the world's most progressive environmental legislation in Oregon and elsewhere, Americans proved unwilling to commit themselves to further action in November 1990, when a referendum to impose strict environmental laws in California was defeated by a majority of two to one and New York voters refused to sanction the borrowing of $2 billion for environmental purposes. If, however, Green Parties are tempted to advocate less ambitious policies, these can easily be stolen by traditional political parties such as the SPD in Germany.

For many greens, green politics are revolutionary or they are nothing.

A Crusade for the Planet?

Greens believe that reformist efforts merely forestall
the impending collapse of the industrial economies, a
collapse which may need to occur before the real work of
construction can begin.
(Brian Tokar, 1987, p. 138)

Fundamentalist greens are on a moral crusade for the future of the planet. They have set themselves against the institutions and power structures of modern society on behalf of people who are not yet born and species who have no vote. That moral crusade is both a political programme and a way of life. It launches a fundamental challenge to the large, centralised structures of modern industrial societies and asks whether they can continue on their present expansionary path. Greens question the morality of ever-increasing human consumption at the expense of other species and future generations, and argue that the quality of life is more important than the quantity of material goods.

When the German Green Party was founded in 1980 it set out to launch a fundamental challenge to the male, militaristic, industrial, capitalist and white North in the name of women, peace, sustainable production, social justice and the rights of the oppressed people of the South. Such a radical position was achieved only with some difficulty, as the Greens had emerged haphazardly through a variety of routes: local 'citizens' initiatives' environmental groups, people of various political complexions – Romantic conservatives, Christian Democrats, Social Democrats, democratic socialists, revolutionaries from the 1960s such as Rudi Dutschke and Daniel Cohn-Bendit; representatives of alternative movements, peace activists, feminists and remnants of the countercultural groups of the 1960s; anthroposophist followers of the German educationalist Rudolf Steiner and other spiritually orientated movements (Hülsberg, 1988). Such a ragbag of groups did not hold together for long, and the new party emerged as a centre-left grouping that based itself around four main political principles – ecology, non-violence, decentralisation and social justice – and embraced new forms of thinking associated with feminism and spiritual awareness.

Die Grünen was to be an anti-party party that would not be compromised by the 'long march through the institutions' of parliamentary politics. This was not to be. In trying to combine a fundamentalist green politics with the parliamentary political process, it fell into warring factions. The radical green demands for a new politics and a new economics, a new relationship between North and South, and between men and women, could not be contained within the parliamentary process of piecemeal reforms and the need to respond to the immediate political and economic interests of German industry, state and people. While the Greens made a huge impact on public opinion when they were first elected, they needed to engage with the governmental process if they were to have any practical influence. Given their size, this meant coalition with the social democrat SPD, and once that decision was taken, a split between the 'Realos' (Realists) and the 'Fundis' (Fundamentalists) became inevitable. The problems of coalition politics are not limited to Germany. In October 1990 nearly two years of Green coalition with Labor in Tasmania broke down over the export of woodchips to Japan.

Problems in social democratic/green coalitions arise not in the minutiae of social policy but in broader questions of principle. In Germany these included the role of the market economy, law and order and the right to protest, defence and membership of NATO and nuclear power. Even so, the divisions within Die Grünen are complex, with deep greens and 'Left' greens in the Fundi camp and 'socialist' greens and lighter greens in the coalition camp. Another divide was between those who wanted to stick by the principles of grass-roots democracy and those who wanted to build a party on traditional lines. Rudolph Bahro, one of the leading members of Die Grünen in its early days, was quite certain that Greens should not compromise with the existing social order, 'the death machine':

> Every rejected proposal of ours which contains the WHOLE
> message is worth a hundred times more than an accepted
> one which just sets about correcting the symptom
> without intervening in the suicidal logic of the whole
> process. (1986, p. 160)

Bahro's position has an echo in the North American green movement, where eco-anarchists like Murray Bookchin are adamant that there should be no participation in the 'filthy reality' of traditional political systems, although in California there is a strong move to form a Green Party.

It is hardly surprising that Green Parties split when they try to work with social democratic parties, as the socialist movement itself is also split along Realo and Fundi lines. With Bahro I would argue that the green movement, like the socialist movement, is revolutionary or it is nothing. At the same time I do not agree that 'correcting the symptoms' of ecological crisis or inequality is a waste of time. If we can alleviate a little suffering along our path, let us do so. The choice we are asked to make between reformism and revolution is a disempowering one. It is an unnecessary and divisive boundary. There is room for some people to 'tinker' with the system while others concentrate on ways to create more fundamental changes. What is important is that we all share and work towards the same vision. The more important boundary is between those revolutionaries and reformers who are still fired by a radical vision and those who are seduced by the trappings of dogma, organisation or power. Revolutionaries and reformers should be in partnership, not in opposition; the poor and the environment have enough enemies as it is, without us dividing against ourselves.

The disempowerment of such divisions was clearly shown in the British Labour Party. As international capitalism spread its tentacles around the world and workers were stripped of their jobs and traditional protection; as the homeless huddled in cardboard boxes; as racism and anti-Semitism erupted on to the streets; as the old, young, sick and women sank into poverty; the British Labour Party became excessively preoccupied with a small group of left-wing 'entryists' and the machinations of politics in a medium-sized Northern city – much like a dog which, when faced with an overwhelming opponent, suddenly finds itself intensely concerned to eliminate a flea in the region of its tail. In contrast, the Conservative Party shrugged off accusations that it had been infiltrated by the National Front and was not diverted from its aim of opening up the British economy to international capitalism.

Despite their political and electoral difficulties, Die Grünen did begin to create a vision of a feminist, green and socialist politics based on the four main political principles of ecology, social justice, non-violence and decentralisation, together with their commitment to feminism.

Ecology

There is no such thing as a free lunch. Because the global ecosystem is a connected whole, in which nothing can be gained or lost ... anything extracted from it by human effort must be replaced. Payment of this price cannot be avoided, it can only be delayed.
(Barry Commoner, 1971, pp. 45–6)

Unlimited growth is impossible in a limited system.
(Programme of the German Green Party [PGGP] 1983, p. 7)

This is the fundamental principle that unites the whole green movement. Human activity on the planet has reached unsustainable levels; there is an ecological 'limit to growth' in terms of available resources, the number of people the Earth can carry and the amount of waste it can absorb. Central to the ecological view is the replacement of the human-centredness of traditional scientific and economic thinking with a perspective that reflects our connectedness with the planet. The Earth is not just a larder and dustbin for human beings, it has its own needs and dynamic which we ignore at our peril. The first political priority must be to stabilise the ecosystem, to introduce what Herman Daly has called a 'steady-state economy' (1973). Human society should live in a way that is sustainable for future generations and other species. We must leave the world the same as, or preferably better than, when we came into it. The ecological principle implies 'all-round rejection of an economy based on exploitation and the uncontrolled pillage of natural wealth and raw materials' (PGGP, 1983, p. 7).

Greens argue that all agriculture and manufacturing should be carried out in a resource-efficient way. There must be minimal waste, and all materials should be recycled wherever possible so as not to deplete the 'irreplaceable' capital of nature

(Schumacher, 1973, p. 11). We should follow the 'soft' energy path of renewable resources – sun, wind, wave or plant and animal matter. Communities should attempt to meet their needs locally and aim as far as possible for self-reliance, reflecting the principle of decentralisation. As people will respect the Earth more the closer they are in touch with it, agricultural and industrial production should be carried out in communities of 'humanly surveyable size'. The present system of ever-increasing growth in production and consumption should be replaced with a 'basic needs' economy orientated to the necessities of human life, in which people would become increasingly aware of their relationship to nature and each other. Science and technology must no longer control us; rather:

> Wisdom demands a new orientation of science and
> technology towards the organic, the gentle, the
> non-violent, the elegant and the beautiful. (Schumacher,
> 1973, p. 29)

There are several problems in the ecological principle as the basis of a feminist green socialism. Greens want to break down the boundary we have constructed between ourselves and the natural world, but how is our new relationship with nature to be realised? What political form will it take? How do we determine the balance between the 'needs' of the planet and the 'needs' of humanity? These questions are most marked for 'deeper' greens, and I will return to them in my discussion of deep ecology. Ecofeminists have argued that men and women differ in their relationship to nature, and I will discuss this more fully in the next chapter. From a socialist perspective there are the immediate political questions of how the existing economic system is going to be confronted in the interests of global equality and the needs of future generations. This reflects a tendency in green thinking to place the blame for our ecological plight upon the scientific and industrial revolutions while being more reticent about the equally destructive role of capitalism and the emphasis on individual self-interest in liberal philosophy.

Non-Violence

When we are facing a nuclear and/or ecological
holocaust, when not only the forests but also the children
die, when all over the world we are turning into nuclear
victims, whether it be through the fallout of French or
Soviet or American nuclear tests or through living too
near a nuclear power plant, then we must . . . go to the
root, be radical and subversive and gentle . . . the soft
path towards a soft politics.
(Petra Kelly, *Green Line*, 1986/7)

One of the principal triggers of the green movement in Germany was Germany's status as military hostage in the Cold War. As in Italy and Britain, opposition increased dramatically with the announcement of the deployment of cruise missiles in 1979. Many of the new Greens had been members of the peace movement and/or the women's movement. However, the non-violent principle was much more fundamental than opposition to a particularly horrific weapon system:

> Non-violence should prevail between all human beings
> without exception, within social groups and within society
> as a whole, between population groups and between
> nations. (PGGP, 1983, p. 7)

Ends can never justify means; the way we act must always reflect our ultimate goals, and 'humane goals cannot be achieved by inhumane means'. Non-violence is justified on both ecological and moral grounds. War – particularly nuclear, chemical or biological war – threatens the survival of other species and the planet as well as ourselves. Morally, we do not have the right to destroy the physical environment to settle our own petty squabbles. We have to break out of the military bloc mentality and attempt to establish an 'active peace' which is more than the absence of war (Kelly, 1988).

Non-violence is also a principle of political action in green movement organisations such as Greenpeace. However, this principle is less certain for other parts of the green movement, particularly those who take a militantly pro-animal or pro-nature line such as some supporters of Animal Liberation or organisations such as Earth First!, whose direct action has on occasion come perilously close to endangering human life (Dobson, 1990).

The principle of non-violence would seem at first sight to present no problem for a feminist green socialism, but it does raise questions about support for armed liberation struggles. Do members of a dominant class, race or culture have any right to tell those who are fighting for political rights, social justice or cultural identity to lay down their arms? If greens are saying, as some do, that non-violence is a more effective form of struggle in the long run, that may be acceptable. If they are saying that violence in all situations is morally wrong, the issue of how people can resist oppression must be addressed.

Decentralisation

Think globally, act locally.
(Green slogan attributed to René Dubos)

We are looking for a common power, a power to be used
by all and shared by all.
(Petra Kelly, *Green Line*, no. 70, 1989, p. 14)

Green politics is opposed to what it sees as the centralisation and giantism of modern industrial societies. Against these it advocates the principles of anti-hierarchy and decentralisation, with greens drawing strongly on the ideals and methods of organisation of the women's movement and countercultural groups. The political must be personal; the way decisions are made is as important as the outcome.

The principle of decentralisation also drew on Fritz Schumacher's claim that 'small is beautiful'. Schumacher argued that modern industrial society had become so large and complex that individual people no longer mattered. Life was characterised by a lack of autonomy and a lack of opportunity to participate effectively. Political and economic organisations needed to be brought back to a point at which people could exercise direct control. Schumacher was particularly concerned about the use of technology and stressed the importance of designing technologies that were appropriate to the needs of small-scale communities, thereby restoring control over processes of production to the local level. Die Grünen wanted the 'grass-roots-democratic' principle to be applied throughout all political and economic systems. All decisions should be taken at the most local level appropriate. 'Basic democracy' would be decentralised and direct, with 'replaceability at any time so as to make organisation and policy transparent to everyone and to counter the dissociation of individuals from their base' (PGGP, p. 7).

When the principle of decentralisation is combined with the principles of autonomy and self-reliance, there is some confusion about what the appropriate size of such a community would be. The British Green Party suggests that in the first instance the whole of Britain would be the 'effective unit', with the long-term aim that each town or village would 'contain all the facilities for work, social and cultural activities required by the community' and 'be surrounded by an agricultural hinterland that feeds it'. The German Greens talk of 'surveyable and decentralised basic units at the local, community, and district levels'.

The wider literature is no less confusing. Bahro sets a limit of about 3,000 people, while Schumacher talks of a city with a maximum of 500,000 and advocates something akin to a local council to run it. Bookchin praises the commune movement of the 1960s but, like the earlier anarchist Peter Kropotkin, also advocates returning to something of the size of a pre-industrial city (Bookchin, 1989; Kropotkin, 1955). In America the idea of a bio-region has been put forward; this would be a geographic region large and diverse enough to meet all the needs of the human community that lives in it. Kirkpatrick Sale has suggested that a typical bio-region would contain between 5,000 and 10,000 people (Dobson, 1990).

The image that runs through green politics is of the self-reliant community of co-operatives or self-employed craftsmen [sic], conducting its business in face-to-face community meetings. Writers call up the examples of the Athenian or medieval city-state, the early New England Town Meeting, the Anarchist collectives of the Spanish Civil War or the clan systems of native Americans and other indigenous peoples (Tokar, 1987; Bookchin, 1989). In eco-anarchist circles the emphasis is on municipalities linked together in a loose confederation. Such an image does not equate with the reality of politics in modern industrial societies. In 1988 the British Green Party launched a new Magna Carta for Britain, arguing for decentralisation to the regions despite the fact that it has itself been virtually split for some time over the need to stand by its decentralised grass-roots-democratic organisation as against setting up a centralised structure that mirrors the traditional political machines (Kemp and Wall, 1990; Parkin, 1989). In March 1991 Jonathon Porritt threatened to leave the Green Party if it did not stop 'living in a world of fantasy' with its 'wholly irrational abhorrence of political leadership' (*Guardian*, 22 March 1991). In September 1991 the 'realos' of the British Green Party got their way as the Green 2000 group achieved its aim of putting the party on a more traditional footing with two spokespeople and a more centralised structure. Similarly in April 1991 the German Green Party shed its principle of the rotation of posts. This and other factors led Jutta Ditfurth to form a two hundred strong breakaway faction, the Ecological Left/Alternative List in May 1991.

The decentralised and non-hierarchical approach to political organisation in the green movement reflects feminist as well as anarchist principles. While at first sight it would appear that feminists would have no quarrel with this approach, it has not proved successful in practice, as I shall discuss below. Further, it is not always clear in green writings to what extent local self-reliant communities will address the question of the boundaries that men have constructed around women in terms of production, reproduction or sexuality. There is, in fact, a great deal of coyness about reproduction and sexuality. Most discussions of green communities concentrate on work (craft, small-scale production and agriculture).

There is some pessimistic evidence from the history of alternative communities in the past. As Kropotkin warned in 1895:

> In most communities . . . the women and girls remained
> in the new society as they were in the old – slaves of the
> community. Arrangements to reduce as much as possible
> the incredible amount of work which women uselessly
> [sic] spend in the rearing of children, as well as in the
> household work, are, in my opinion, as essential to the
> success of the community as the proper arrangements
> of the fields, the greenhouses and the agricultural
> machinery. (quoted in Todd, 1986, p. 19)

This is echoed by Petra Kelly's concern: 'we don't want an ecological society where men build windmills and women silently listen, bake bread and weave rugs' (1984, p. 107).

From a socialist perspective there is also a large question mark over how local self-reliant communities will ensure a redistribution of resources across community boundaries and what patterns of social ownership will prevail. This is a crucial issue, given the way that extreme right-wing movements and racists have embraced green ideas. In Britain the National Front went 'green' in 1984, while Patrick Harrington, who gained some notoriety as a member of the National Front as a student, has now left it to form a 'Third Way' group, arguing for 'decentralisation, nationalism and separatism for cultural reasons' (*Guardian*, 27 April 1991). This is particularly worrying in the light of Anna Bramwell's reappraisal of ecology and Nazism and her claim that the peasant land reforms of the Third Reich are an appropriate model for a green society (1989, p. 242). Bramwell argues that there is a tension in green politics between 'those who want the egalitarian sharing of resources, on an international basis, using the tools, techniques and rhetoric of traditional economic socialism; and those who, in accordance with what is for many the green image, seek a local, ethnic or tribal autarkic protectionism' (ibid., p. 224). It would be a tragedy if green decentralism broke down the boundary between human society and nature, only to see the continuation of barriers of race and culture within the human community.

Social Justice

The ecological, economic and social crisis can be
countered only by the self-determination of those
affected. Since we stand for self-determination and the
free development of each human being, and since we
want people to shape their lives creatively together in
solidarity, in harmony with their natural environment,
their own wishes and needs, and free from external
threat – we take a radical stand for human rights and
far-reaching democratic rights both at home and abroad.
(Programme of the German Green Party, 1983, p. 8)

A politics of ecology that does not embrace social justice
is meaningless.
(Penny Kemp and Derek Wall, 1990, p. 87)

Although for Die Grünen ecological sustainability could not be achieved without social justice on a global scale, it is unclear whether these are to be framed in terms of political rights or social rights. They see the divisions between rich and poor, destruction of the living environment, impoverishment through the commercialisation of life, leisure and nature as being challenged by a 'radical stand' for 'human' and democratic rights for all the world's peoples. Die Grünen wish to place power in the hands of the people to enable them to build a stable social system with an integrated economy so that state and capitalistic economic power could no longer threaten society and the environment: 'exploitative compulsions of growth arise from both the competitive economy and the concentration of economic power in state and private-capitalist monopolies' (PGGP, 1983, p. 8). The social principle seeks to achieve 'self-determination and the free development of each human being' regardless of race, ethnicity, gender or sexuality.

The problem for green politics lies in the absence of an economic programme that can achieve both sustainability and social equality, particularly given its opposition to the industrial system. Even the German Greens have been criticised for being a party of 'workers by brain' with little contact with the needs of 'workers by hand' (Kagarlitsky, 1990, p. 144). Even so, Die Grünen took a far more radical approach to social justice than many greens who seek to distance themselves from the socialist challenge to capitalist society, seeing it as another attempt to rearrange the deckchairs on the *Titanic* (Parkin, 1989). For most greens the priority is to get rid of industrial society (socialist and capitalist) rather than argue about who owns and controls its benefits. The socialist concern with class struggle is replaced by the idea of a rupture of our 'connectedness' to the planet and to each other through the 'dog eat dog' mentality of the politics of greed (Crosbie, 1988). Change will take place through the development of new values and ideas rather than shifts in the ownership and control of finance and industry.

These new values have been developed in Britain and elsewhere in the form of a 'new economics' that aims to meet basic needs (as opposed to the artificially created demands of consumer society), to break down the relationship between work and income (with the proposition in Britain of a Guaranteed Basic Income Scheme) and the need to be self-reliant as far as possible (Ekins, 1986). Less clear is the relationship between these aims and the present structures of economic inequality, and how the transition to a green economy will be achieved.

The commitment to social justice in green politics hovers uncomfortably between a liberal and a socialist perspective: the rights and responsibilities of individuals as against the need to create an egalitarian community through collective action. It has not clearly transcended the boundaries of the possessive individualism that underpins the market economy, with its emphasis on self-interest and private ownership. This is reflected in the often ambiguous use of the term 'self-reliance' in green writings. It is unclear whether this is supposed to apply to the individual, the household or the community (however that is defined).

Feminism and Green Politics

Feminism is ecology and ecology is feminism.
(Petra Kelly, 1984)

Ecology claims feminism as a guiding star.
(Andrew Dobson, 1990, p. 28)

According to Petra Kelly, Greens are fighting a system where 'men are are at the centre of a patriarchal world, North, South, East and West' (Kelly, 1988, p. 111). This is a recurrent theme in green politics and writing, and it could be argued that feminism is perhaps *the* central thread of green political thought. Die Grünen's commitment to ending 'the oppression, exploitation, injustice and discrimination that women have suffered for many thousands of years' reflects the Party's origins in the women's movement and local citizens' initiatives, the majority of whose members were women.

Die Grünen set out to establish firmly the political relationship between the green and feminist movements by arguing for a society 'built on complete equality of the sexes in the context of an overall ecological policy' (PGGP, 1983, p. 40). Their policy for women demanded that housework should be recognised as full-time work, with the same rights as other jobs, and men and women should share domestic work and childcare equally. Rape and violence in marriage and sexual discrimination at work would be illegal. Abortion would be freely available, although 'it should be made unnecessary' through sex education, social assistance to mothers and new methods of birth control. Pregnancy leave should be available to either parent, with extensive support for antenatal and postnatal care. Women's sexuality and that of all other groups should be freely expressed. Women's refuges and legal and financial support should be available for women who are beaten or maltreated by men. Women doctors should be available at all times, and cases involving violence and discrimination against women should be dealt with only by women legal officers.

Within its own structures Die Grünen's policy of positive action for women was fairly successful in the early days, with the 'Feminat' of six women heading the national parliamentary group in 1984 and women heading all but one of the Green electoral lists for the Bundestag in 1987 when twenty-five women and nineteen men were elected. However, this did not mean that the Party embraced feminism or feminist issues in practice:

> Inside our parliamentary group women have to fight very hard, even more than before we entered the Bundestag, to get our views collectively known. The men now tend to consider abortion and other social issues less political and therefore less important than others. We women sometimes have to argue very aggressively to make sure that the questions are treated as part of the larger question. (Petra Kelly quoted in Spretnak and Capra, 1985, p. 48)

Die Grünen have also found it very difficult to sustain their aim of having 50 per cent representation of women at all levels. In a rather depressing early study of green politics in Germany, Charlene Spretnak and Fritjof Capra found that the pro-women policy was purely mechanistic, without any deeper analysis on the part of men of the problems women faced in actually taking public office (1985, p. 47). Activism is possible only for women who are relatively 'free' of domestic burdens, economically secure (or without dependants) and mobile. In an interview in 1986, Petra Kelly described the cost to her health imposed by a 'breathtaking schedule of conferences, lectures, committee meetings and international tours . . . pamphleteering, letter writing and campaigning' (*Green Line*, no. 48, 1986/7).

Even where structures are rigorously non-hierarchical, as in the North American Green 'committees of correspondence' (correspondence here means a meeting of equals, not letters!), women still feel excluded as men 'fill the space' in the absence of strong chairing (Gahrton, 1990). It seems that green politics has not yet managed to overcome the 'tyranny of structurelessness' (Freeman, 1970).

Women's experience is also being marginalised in the histories of Die Grünen. Werner Hülsberg, in his history of the German Greens, acknowledges that the 'Greens are very strong on this question' (1988, p. 132), but the history, policies and voices he records are overwhelmingly male. From his book it is possible to get only the most sketchy idea of women's role as voters or members of the German Green Party, and only then by combing very carefully: there is nothing in the index, and most of the information is given on one page (p. 132) of 220 pages of text. Even then, he reports the existence of the period of women's leadership of the German Party only in the context of political support for issues around sexual oppression. What is even more alarming is that he concludes with a strong argument for an eco-socialism that is bereft of feminism. Sara Parkin's sketch of Die Grünen also saw women as a 'special interest group' rather than as a fundamental core of the green critique of traditional society (1989). Additional evidence that women's contribution to green politics was being marginalised came in the Green Book Fortnight in Britain in 1991, which included only one book by a woman author among those selected for promotion.

Despite the fact that women tend to be more concerned about environmental issues than men, as the 1991 Social Attitudes Survey shows, and have a higher representation in Green Parties than in traditional parties, this does not necessarily mean that their interests are of central concern to the green movement. The British Green Party's *Manifesto for a Sustainable Society* (MFSS), as its title suggests, is mainly preoccupied with the ecological issue and refers to women only indirectly in the section on population, roughly halfway through the document, with its aim:

> To encourage smaller numbers of children per couple while re-establishing mutually responsible local communities, free of sexually-stereotyped roles, to provide a supportive and satisfying way of life. (MFSS, 1987, p. 405)

A number of male writers welcome women's liberation where 'there is a happy correlation between women's liberation and population control' (Irvine and Pontin, 1988, p. 23; Icke, 1990: Paehlke, 1989). It is clear that equal opportunities are introduced as a mechanism of population control, and there is an implied threat of (male?) intervention if this policy does not 'work':

> Educational and employment opportunities for women lead to smaller families, without further intervention. (Paehlke, 1989, p. 266)

Schumacher, from a Buddhist perspective, argues that a mother's place is in the home:

> Women on the whole do not need an 'outside' job . . . to let mothers of young children work in factories while the

children run wild would be uneconomic in the eyes of a Buddhist economist. (1973, pp. 51–2)

Even where green thinkers claim that a commitment to feminism is at the centre of their politics, this often slides into a discussion of *feminine* values.

In Jonathon Porritt's *Seeing Green*, women appear in any substance only by the fourteenth chapter, where he takes up Adrienne Rich's definition of patriarchy as a system of power in which the identities and actions of women are determined by men but goes on to argue that a patriarchal world-view oppresses men as well as women:

> Patriarchy means nothing less than compulsory masculinity. Positive moral values *are* conferred on masculine qualities, while feminine qualities *are* consistently denigrated and suppressed. (Porritt, 1984, pp. 201–2; original emphasis)

He goes on to declare the need to reclaim the 'feminine principle', the 'soft/yin' qualities of co-operation, empathy, holistic thinking, emotion and intuition. The problem is not male domination of women, but the lack of 'balance' in men being too tough and hard (competitive, assertive, rational, analytical, materialist and intellectual) and women too gentle and soft. The solution is a change of values so that we all become 'balanced' in a 'cultural transformation' whereby men recover the 'feminine' side of themselves and women become more assertive.

Women are even denied exclusive ownership of the 'feminine principle'. David Icke, until recently a leading member of the British Green Party, although acknowledging that 'men and male values are killing the earth', goes on to give men an equal role in liberating it:

> The most important aspects of our emotions, in terms of environmental destruction and much else, are what

> greens call *feminine values*. This can be misleading
> because men and women have these values and
> emotions. (Icke, 1990, p. 203)

A similar view is taken by other male writers (Rivers, 1988; Dauncey, 1988). Dorothy and Walter Schwarz similarly argue that 'these values do not belong exclusively to women, but in our society women are traditionally more adept at expressing them'; they then go on to express exasperation that women have 'allowed themselves to become the weaker sex' (1987, p. 190).

Although green politics are strongly identified with women, it is largely at the level of rhetoric rather than the reality of women's lives. In emphasising women's *feminine* qualities, feminist concerns with the imbalance of power between men and women are generally ignored. The feminine principle is brought into the green movement not for the liberation of women but as a source of purification for human society: 'the present crisis of industrial society and the world is a crisis of masculine values' (Robertson, 1983, p. 23).

The relevance of women for green politics lies not in their disadvantage at the hands of men but in their moral superiority in a world debased by men. Women can show men the way to a 'new moral world'. Men may be the problem, but women are the solution. Male domination is seen not as a problem for women, but as a problem that all human society shares. Men, too, are disadvantaged because they have 'lost' the feminine side of their nature.

Women need to look very carefully at what lies behind that rhetoric. The danger is that the failure of green politics to address the real, material problems of the imbalance of power between men and women will result in the reproduction of patriarchy within the green movement, and there is evidence that this has already happened.

Green Spirituality

My own working definition of spirituality is that it is the aspect of human existence that explores the subtle forces

of energy in and around us and reveals to us profound
interconnectedness.
Charlene Spretnak, (1985, p. 240)

Perhaps the most fundamental green challenge to the values
of Western society lies in their introduction of a non-Judaeo-
Christian spiritual dimension to political thinking. It may cause a
certain bemusement among political commentators when Green
Party members make space for attunement and meditation as part
of their deliberations. The difficulty of 'fitting' spirituality into a
political programme would sometimes lead us to underestimate
its importance in green thinking (Dobson, 1990). For greens,
human spiritual development will play a central role in the
necessary transformation of social values that will enable a new
ethics for the environment to be built. Greens argue that our
present values are corrupted in modern consumerist societies
by being limited to generating and meeting material needs. The
Western scientific rationalism that underpins industrial society
has denied the spiritual needs of human beings and produced
a 'deep hunger in modern experience' (Spretnak and Capra,
1985, p. 255). Greens argue that material values cannot develop
the whole human being, and the loss of spiritual values is both
cause and consequence of the drive to materialism.

Spirituality is essential to green politics because it emphasises
the whole, the oneness and connectedness of human beings
with nature and with each other (Porritt, 1984; Bahro, 1986;
Spretnak, 1985; Dobson, 1990). Greens argue that we have
lost the reverence and wonder in our relationship with nature
which were present in traditional communities such as that of
the native Americans. The spiritual needs of humanity are
often expressed as the need for balance, and this is best represented in Eastern religions like Taoism and Buddhism rather
than the human-orientated Western religions like Christianity
(Schumacher, 1973; Capra, 1983). Despite the Taoist emphasis on the feminine principle, neither Taoism nor Buddhism

offers much comfort to women as the spiritual basis of green thinking.

For example Buddhism, favoured by Schumacher as the basis for a green spirituality, is quite explicit about the inferiority of women. It is no wonder that Schumacher wanted women returned to the home if we listen to the teachings of Lord Buddha:

> Women are soon angered; women are full of passion; women are envious; women are stupid. That is the reason, . . . that is the cause, why women have no place in public assemblies, do not carry on business and do not earn their living by any profession. (quoted in Truong, 1990, p. 134)

According to Buddhist teachings, women are held to be the source of sexuality and passion and therefore unable to reach nirvana unless reincarnated as a man. The fact that a particular form of spirituality has a benign attitude towards the natural world can lead to no assumption of a benign attitude towards women.

Later attempts to create a green spirituality have focused on more mystical 'ancient' earth-based religions. As a result, green spirituality has been – perhaps wrongly – dismissed for its association with the mysticism of the New Age movement. However, given the seemingly sudden switch made by David Icke from parliamentary candidate and spokesperson for the British Green Party to mystic and seer, this confusion is hardly surprising (Icke, 1991). Certainly there is an overlap between the two movements. New Agers argue that the human race has not yet achieved its full potential and the next stage will be one of heightened consciousness. Change will come through personal transformation as individuals expand their consciousness through various mystical means. On the evidence of Marilyn Ferguson's *The Aquarian Conspiracy* (1981), the typical New Age person is a professional of the 1960s generation living in California.

The problem in New Age thinking is the relationship between personal transformation and wider communal change. Marilyn Ferguson talks of building a great interconnectedness through travel, new technologies of communication and thousands of international conferences. She talks of public responses to human need as people unite against the hunger and misery of others worldwide. In the ten years since Ferguson wrote her book, things have deteriorated rather than improved. Certainly people are attending conferences around the globe, but it is doubtful how many achieve any meaningful help for those in need. We will never know the exact number of those meaningless jamborees depicted by David Lodge in his novel *Small World*. New communications technologies have brought quicker missiles rather than readier international understanding.

New Agers have also been accused of a racist misappropriation of the mysticism of traditional cultures such as that of native Americans:

> Indigenous people and indigenous cultures have become
> commodified in the New Age Movement. What is
> happening is that our culture is taken out of context
> and certain parts of it are sold or just extracted. It's like
> mining. And this is what is happening to us. Certain
> things are taken out and certain people practicing those
> things in their own ways, and to me, that's appropriation
> of our culture. It's the same as expropriating our wild
> rice or our land. And it is one of the last things we have.
> It is our culture. (LaDuke, 1990, p. 32)

LaDuke goes on to argue that those who want to challenge Western society should not seek a way out through taking the culture of others but find their own path, through their own culture. New Age is certainly big business. In America the market for New Age books was worth $100 million in 1990, with around a hundred New Age magazines as well as radio stations (*Independent on Sunday*, 14 October 1990).

While I would not want to argue against the development of a spiritual dimension to our lives and a displacement of the emphasis on materialism, it is important to listen to what Winona LaDuke is saying. If green spirituality goes too far along the New Age path, it risks diverting us into an inappropriate self-obsession. While this may help us individually to develop a wider spiritual awareness and 'bring together' parts of ourselves that have become divided in modern society, it will not necessarily lead to any wider social transformation. That must be done by transforming the materialism of our culture, not running away from it. In many ways New Ageism can be seen as just another manifestation of the 'me' generation: a movement for the powerful, not the powerless. It is a world where individuals change themselves and their circumstances by acts of 'pure decision' and follow Joseph Campbell's injunction to find their 'bliss'. Will the rich Californian following her/his bliss listen to the needs of poorer members of the community?

The emphasis in New Age thinking, in common with much green thinking, is on autonomy and self-help. Marilyn Ferguson cites approvingly the example of one of the leaders of the 'Gray Panthers' who urged fellow senior citizens not to put their efforts into getting services more cheaply but to become more 'self-actualizing' by going to college, starting up an enterprise or a collective housing scheme. However, such an individual solution will not benefit the weak and powerless. People's capacity for autonomy is dependent on their social situation. The well-educated products of the dominant race and class have always been able to 'drop out', knowing that if things go badly they can always drop back in. It is no good breaking down the boundaries within ourselves, between mind, body and spirit, or even reconnecting ourselves with nature, if we do not mend the divisions in human society. In fact the danger of New Ageism is that we redraw the boundary tightly around ourselves. Connectedness within ourselves or with the planet may be achieved by an individual quest, but connectedness within the human community has to be carefully, lovingly and collectively constructed.

Going Backward to Move Forward?

What is needed is to discover both the subjective and objective modes of knowing, creating newer and richer perceptions of knowledge that are more complex, creative. In weaving together these new knowledges, we will find new words, invent new meanings, envision new patterns, regenerate new cultural and 'people's spaces', creating a new world order.
(Corinne Kumar D'Souza, 1989, p. 35)

Ecology as science, and as spirituality has helped us to begin to dismantle the boundaries that constrain our relationship with the natural world. The green movement has articulated clearly many of the problems of our age, but it has not given us the political solutions to them. It is still not clear whom the green movement really blames for our predicament: science, technology, industry, capitalism, religion, men, human nature? We are told that modern industrial societies are not sustainable, but where do we turn for an alternative? If we have taken the wrong path, were we once on the right path? Many greens argue that we were, and look to those who do not bear the guilt of our modern folly to guide us back: women, early human societies and their contemporary representatives, and nature itself. Each of these raises fundamental questions. Do men and women differ in their relationship to the natural world? If so, how and why? What would constitute an appropriate ecological balance between humanity and the natural world? Can 'nature' guide us to that balance? In answering these questions, can we draw ecological, social and spiritual inspiration from earlier human societies?

The boundaries between present and past, humanity and

nature, the material and the spiritual, have been profoundly challenged by ecofeminists and deep ecologists. Both take us beneath and beyond questions of electoral politics and environmental policy to a more fundamental questioning of human existence.

CHAPTER 2

Women and Nature: the Challenge of Ecofeminism

Women strongly affirm the celebration of life and a
new spirituality of the earth which praises the ever new
wonder of creation, the beauty and splendour of nature
in its myriad forms ... This is an integral vision of the
sacredness of life which sees all living things bound up
together in one single interdependent web without any
boundaries.
(Ursula King, 1989, p. 219)

The special message of ecofeminism is that when
women suffer through both social domination and the
domination of nature, most of life on this planet suffers
and is threatened as well.
(Ynestra King, 1989, p. 25)

Ecofeminism emerged in the late 1970s, although it was first
'named' in France in 1974 by Françoise d'Eaubonne. This is
perhaps apt, as it was Simone de Beauvoir who, in 1949, first
pointed to the way in which men treated both women and nature
as the Other, to be both dominated and feared:

> Man seeks in woman the Other as Nature and as his
> fellow being. But we know what ambivalent feelings
> Nature inspires in man. He exploits her but she crushes
> him, he is born of her and he dies in her; she is the
> source of his being and the realm that he subjugates to
> his will. (1968, p. 144)

While ecofeminists share with de Beauvoir her analysis of

women's affinity with the natural world and their common exploitation at the hands of men, they do not, like her, seek to 'free' women from nature. Rather, they want to celebrate that relationship and use it to break down the false boundary between nature and culture that men have created. In bringing together ecology and feminism, ecofeminists see women and nature as subject to the destructive technologies of modern patriarchal society: war and militarism, capitalism and industrialism, genetic and reproductive engineering. They seek to undermine Earth-destroying male culture by expressing the nurturing and caring values associated with women as the basis of an alternative culture, more peace-loving, less hierarchical and able to address issues in a wider social, personal and ecological context.

Irene Diamond and Gloria Orenstein see the emerging ecofeminist movement as a major catalyst of ethical, political, social and creative change (1990, p. ix). Together with deep ecology, ecofeminism is arguably the most dynamic area of theoretical and philosophical development within the green movement. As a newly emerging movement ecofeminist thought is many-stranded; this is hardly surprising for the aim of ecofeminism is to 'reweave' the world, as the title of their book claims. Within the interweaving of ecofeminist ideas there is a tension between those who see the relationship between women and nature as *socially* created and therefore capable of being socially resolved, and those who see it as a deeper relationship of biological and spiritual *affinity* that transcends particular societies and eras. For Petra Kelly:

> Women are the 'ombudsmen' [*sic*] of future generations
> ... because only she, I feel, can go back to her womb,
> her roots, her natural rhythms, her inner search
> for harmony and peace, while men, most of them
> anyway, are continually bound in their power struggle,
> the exploitation of nature, and military ego trips.
> (1984, p. 104)

Despite the tension between 'social' and 'affinity' explanations of women's relationship to nature, it is not easy to slot ecofeminists into particular 'camps', and to do so would be to introduce new and artificial boundaries within women's thinking. For instance, Caroline Merchant from a socialist ecofeminist perspective and Adrienne Rich from a radical feminist perspective both see the biological and the social as entwined in women's lives. They argue that it is male thinking that has tried to 'separate off' the one from the other. Charlene Spretnak argues that women can achieve eco-spirituality through a celebration of their bodies, while at the same time denying that it is enough just to be female. Starhawk argues for a return to the 'old religion' of Witchcraft, but holds that this cannot be separated from political struggle: 'whatever we do, our spirituality should be grounded in action' (1990, p. 85).

In uniting ecology with feminism, however, there is a danger that the balance of the partnership may tip towards saving the planet at the expense of the politics of women's liberation, and I will argue that some ecofeminist thinking drifts in this direction. Overstressing spiritual identification or women's physiological affinity with nature can obscure the material oppression and exploitation of women and ignore the inequalities between them. On the other hand, Janet Biehl errs in the opposite direction. She opposes affinity ecofeminism, as she does not 'consider it promising to work in a particularistic vein, advancing women as in any way the special custodians of nonhuman nature'. Following the eco-anarchic perspective of Murray Bookchin's 'social ecology', she goes on to subsume even feminist claims under 'the *general* interest of human beings as a *whole*' (1991; original emphasis). Biehl argues that 'neither nonhuman nature nor humanity will cease to be subject to domination until every human being is free of domination. In this respect women are objects of domination but not sole or *primary* objects of domination' (ibid.; emphasis added). Effectively, Janet Biehl is denying both social and affinity ecofeminism.

While social (or socialist) ecofeminism shares at least the same social parameters as traditional political perspectives, affinity ecofeminism offers a fundamental challenge to them by moving beyond society and culture to a more essentialist view of women's spiritual and biological affinity with nature. Affinity ecofeminism has developed most fully in North America and overlaps with both New Age thinking and the radical cultural feminism associated with Mary Daly and Susan Griffin. As with New Age thinkers, a good deal of ecofeminist inspiration comes from the spirituality of native American culture and thereby suffers from the same dangers of indulging in cultural grave-robbing. The primary aim of affinity ecofeminism is to develop a new Earth-based consciousness that will call a halt to the destructive practices that threaten the planet. It is a movement that seeks to break the boundaries of both our existence and our knowledge by transcending modern male-dominated society and culture. Affinity ecofeminists express their identity with nature in many forms: songs, performance art, retelling of myths, drawings, poems, prose and rituals, and in many different types of activity from witchcraft covens and healing communities to organic food coops, direct environmental action and peace camps (Starhawk, 1990).

Despite their differences, both social and affinity ecofeminists share a core of common ideas, including the concerns of feminism: violence against women, women's health, the impact of genetic and reproductive technologies, the sexual division of labour and the struggle of women in the South. Most fundamentally, ecofeminists see the primary role of patriarchy in creating the modern scientific, industrial and military systems that are threatening the planet. They argue that men's attempt to 'master' nature is in danger of losing us the Earth.

Mastering Nature and Losing the Earth

The brutalization and oppression of women is connected with the hatred of nature and with other forms of domination, and with ecological catastrophe.

It is significant that feminism and ecology as social
movements have emerged now as nature's revolt against
domination plays itself out in human history and
non-human nature at the same time.
(Ynestra King, 1983, pp. 124–5)

Ecofeminists, like most greens, trace the destruction of the
natural world to the hierarchical dualisms of Western society:
culture/nature, men/women, mind/body, science/folk knowledge, reason/feelings, materialism/spirituality. They argue that
these dualisms have resulted in a one-dimensional public world
devised by men in their image embodying culture, mind, science, reason and materialism, eclipsing and suppressing women
in a private world associated negatively with nature, body,
folk knowledge, emotion and spirituality. This division has
allowed the unrestrained development of science and technology,
industry and militarism. Male-dominated societies also exhibit
destructive attitudes: aggression, competitiveness, single-path
reasoning (following only one line of thinking, as in military
logic, economic calculation, or the scientific method). This has
created huge unfeeling bureaucracies, atomised self-seeking and
self-interested individuals and the amoral marketplace. In turn it
has eclipsed women's values of nurturing, caring and the need
to sustain future generations.

Two early ecofeminist books traced the dominance of men
over women and nature: Susan Griffin's *Women and Nature*
in 1978 and Carolyn Merchant's *The Death of Nature* in 1980.
The first was a poetic expression of these divisions; the second
a historical exposition of how they occurred. Merchant lays
the blame for the exploitation of women and nature at the
feet of male-dominated religions and male-dominated science.
She shows how the scientific revolution of the sixteenth and
seventeenth centuries overthrew the previous organic view of
nature that restrained exploitation. This led to the 'death
of nature' in that the view of nature changed: from a living

organism, 'Mother Earth', to a lifeless machine which could be manipulated and exploited. Before the scientific revolution the 'female principle' was uppermost in the interaction between humanity and nature, which:

> emphasized the interdependence among the parts of the human body, subordination of the individual to communal purposes in the family, community, and state, and vital life permeating the cosmos to the lowliest stone. (Merchant, 1980, p. 1)

According to Merchant, the female principle was overthrown when the Judaeo-Christian God-given right to the domination of nature was embodied in the development of modern science. One of the main exponents of the new methods was Francis Bacon who, as Carolyn Merchant notes, was Attorney General to James I during a wave of witchcraft trials. Bacon's language is rife with the imagery of torture, and even makes reference to the persecutions:

> For you have but to follow and, as it were, hound nature in her wanderings, and you will be able when you like to lead and drive her afterward to the same place again ... Neither ought a man to make scruple of entering and penetrating into these holes and corners, when the inquisition of truth is his whole object – as your majesty has shown in your own example. (quoted in Merchant, 1980, p. 168)

The Earth was no longer alive and sacred, she was a passive object to be raped and pillaged. Mechanistic science saw the natural world as a series of machines in motion. The life history of natural structures was less important than the immediate benefits they could offer to 'Man' and the unchanging 'laws' of nature they could reveal.

In Merchant's work we are offered two 'moments' in the

oppression of women and nature: the development of Judaism and the scientific revolution. The first occurred sometime in the second millennium BC; the second in the middle of the second millennium AD. Both represent the domination of men over women. Some feminists have traced the development of patriarchy to a much earlier period. Riane Eisler (1987) claims that a Neolithic 'gylanic' Goddess-worshipping woman-orientated society existed in Old Europe (South-Eastern Europe from present-day Yugoslavia to Crete). These early 'partnership' societies were overrun sometime after 4500 BC by 'Kurgans', Indo-European patriarchal nomads from the steppes of Russia, who instituted 'dominator' societies in place of the benign egalitarianism of the gylanic communities. Such a huge span of historical explanation of male domination leaves us with some difficulty in determining the most appropriate way to move forward. Have we got an age-old, almost universal, battle between men and women? Where, for instance, did the patriarchal Kurgans come from? When was their patriarchy born?

Did the emergence of Judaeo-Christianity signal the beginning of dominance of men over women (Sky-God over Earth-Goddess) or the attachment of a dominance over nature to a dominance over women that already existed? Were the philosophical and scientific revolutions of the Enlightenment a continuation of a domination of women and nature that already existed, or did they mark a distinctive break with traditional Earth-orientated organic thinking?

Janet Biehl presents a different view of human history. She finds in Old Europe and Minoan Crete evidence of hierarchy and human sacrifice. She sees the Hebrew religion as a force for liberation in that it threw God out of the Earth into the Sky, thereby rescuing the human race from animistic fatalism and creating the basis for the beginnings of human history. While accepting the destructive nature of modern society, Biehl wants to hold on to the principles of individual rights and democracy that grew out of early European society and the Enlightenment, declaring that 'human freedom is too important to be erased by appealing to the need for ecological stability' (1991, p. 97). Biehl is right – we cannot jettison all that the Enlightenment achieved; feminism itself has been framed within its ideals. Nor do ecologists suggest that we jettison all science or all technology. As Riane Eisler argues, it is not technology itself that is the problem, rather how it is used:

> The problem is not now, nor has it ever been simply that of technology. The same technological base can produce very different types of tools: tools to kill and oppress other humans or tools to free our hands and minds from dehumanising drudgery. The problem is that in dominator societies, where 'masculinity' is identified with conquest and domination, every new technological breakthrough is basically seen as a tool for more effective domination and oppression. (1990, p. 32)

Ecofeminists and greens praise some developments in modern science such as the 'new physics', cybernetics and systems theory (Lovelock, 1979; Capra, 1983) as well as earlier theories such as entropy, the second law of thermodynamics (Henderson, 1978; Rifkin, 1980). Starhawk sees science as coming full circle back to meet the old ideas:

> Scientists have conferences on the Gaia hypothesis without acknowledging that this is exactly what people in tribal cultures, what Witches, shamans and psychics have been saying for thousands of years. (1990, p. 74)

Irene Diamond and Gloria Orenstein also see ecofeminism as 'a new term for an ancient wisdom' (1990, p. xv). The task for ecofeminists is to envision another world, a whole world that 'heals' the one-sided destructive world that male domination has created. The beginnings of the search lie in women's knowledge and experience, which men have repressed.

Seeing Things Differently

Feel your natural tendencies toward multi-layered
perceptions, empathy, compassion, unity and harmony.
Feel your wholeness. Feel our oneness. Feel the
elemental source of our power. Discard the patriarchal
patterns of alienation, fear, enmity, aggression, and
destruction. It is not necessary to force them away; by
merely focusing awareness on the negative, masculinist
thoughts as they begin to arise and then opting not to
feed them any more psychic energy, their power becomes
diminished and they fade ... The authentic female mind
is our salvation.
(Charlene Spretnak, 1982, p. 573)

It is the strength of the feminine which can guide
us towards a consciousness which, though aware
of polarities, is concerned with their interplay and
connectedness rather than their conflict and separation.
(Stephanie Leland, 1983, p. 71)

Ecofeminism sees the route to 'oneness' in women's ability to
overcome the false divisions that male reasoning has set up.
Women's distinctive form of reasoning is seen as holistic and
intuitive rather than linear and cerebral (Henderson, 1988;
Swimme, 1990). Male thinking is seen as dominated by scientific
rationalism, which isolates particular issues and problems and
tries to break down information into ever smaller units of
verifiable knowledge. Intuitive thinking, on the other hand,
is a direct non-intellectual experience of reality that expands,
rather than concentrates, awareness. It brings many sources
of information together and operates on the basis of feelings
rather than demonstrable truths; we are enjoined to 'think
feelingly' (Plant, 1990). It is a form of thinking that could more
correctly be described as wisdom: 'the ability ... to think and act
utilizing knowledge, experience, understanding, common sense,
and insight' (*Collins English Dictionary*).

Wisdom is a much more profound awareness than knowing: 'to be or feel certain of the truth or accuracy of (a fact, etc.)' (ibid.). The benefit of masculinist single-path thinking is that it can, within its own terms, get results (find a new vaccine, win a battle, negotiate a new contract). Placing knowledge within a wider context makes things less clear-cut and slows down decision-making. Single-path thinking creates the expert: the economist, the military strategist, the political analyst, the medical specialist. Reintegrating knowledge into wisdom brings it back to the people. Wisdom and knowledge are not two distinct orders of thought; the difference is that the latter is more restricted than the former. Patriarchal forms of reasoning place boundaries around knowledge that both limit its parameters and exclude women and other oppressed groups from 'knowing'. Women not only have to look at things differently, they have to find a new basis for their knowledge outside patriarchal control. Spiritual ecofeminists maintain that we can find this by reclaiming older forms of wisdom which patriarchy has sought to obliterate.

Earth-based Consciousness

When we understand that the Earth itself embodies
Spirit and that the cosmos is alive, then we also
understand that everything is connected.
(Starhawk, 1990, p. 73)

What was cosmologically wholesome and healing was
the discovery of the Divine as immanent and around
us. What was intriguing was the sacred link between
the Goddess in her many guises and totemic animals
and plants, sacred groves, and womblike caves, in the
moon-rhythm blood of the menses, the ecstatic dance –
the experience of *knowing* Gaia, her voluptuous contours
and fertile planes, her flowing waters that give life, her
animal teachers.
(Charlene Spretnak, 1990, p. 5)

Ecofeminists searching for an Earth-based consciousness embrace a mixture of mysticism and spirituality. Mysticism implies the existence of an otherworldly reality that surpasses human understanding; that must be embraced in 'love and surrender' (Ursula King, 1989, p. 99). Spirituality describes a more generalised change of consciousness that may or may not be related to a mystical experience.

Many ecofeminists seek to recover the lost mystical world of older Earth-based religions of Paganism, Witchcraft and Goddess-worship:

> In ancient times the world itself was one. The beating
> of the drums was the heartbeat of the Earth – in all
> its mystery, enchantment, wonder, and terror. Our feet
> danced in sacred groves, honoring the spirits of nature.
> What was later broken asunder into prayer and music,
> ritual and dance, play and work, was originally one.
> (Eisler, 1990, p. 33)

Feminists have found in old myths and legends, and in archaeological discoveries, evidence of a period in early human history when female images suffused human spirituality (Stone, 1979). They have seen women's fertility and sexuality as embodied in the image of the Goddess that can be traced through from the plethora of so-called Venus figurines of 25000–15000 BC to the shrines of the Mother Goddess in Jericho in 7000 BC; from the ceremonial burials of women from 12000–9000 BC to the destruction of the last temple to the Goddess by Christians in AD 500 (Miles, 1988, pp. 19–20). Even if there is no 'real' Goddess to be rediscovered, it is argued that women need to create one in order to have a female mystic power equivalent to the Sky-Gods that have served men so well for so long (Mary Daly, 1986). Social ecofeminists have condemned this search as diversionary, as it makes the false assumption that 'merely changing our myths from "bad" ones to "good" ones will change our social realities' (Biehl, 1989, p. 18). For many ecofeminists, however, spirituality is a source of inspiration for women in their struggle to change social realities.

Starhawk sees three threads to ecofeminist spirituality: immanence, interconnection and community. The idea of immanence sees the Earth as a living thing: 'what that means is that spirit, sacred, Goddess, God – whatever you want to call it – is not found outside the world somewhere – it's in the world: it *is* the world, and it is us' (1990, p. 73). This aliveness and the pervasiveness of the Spirit mean that we are all part of that life, we are all inter-connected. In being alive and inter-connected, we are all part of the same living community. The goal of an Earth-based spirituality is to make that community 'a place where we can be empowered and in which we can be connected to the Earth and take action together to heal the Earth' (ibid., p. 74). Recognising immanence, interconnection and community is inevitably egalitarian, because 'each of us is the Goddess, is God, we have an inalienable right to be here and be alive' (ibid., p. 76).

At the same time, awareness of our oneness with the life of the planet diminishes our own egoism and fear of death:

> We come from the Earth and to the Earth we shall also return. Life feeds on life. We live because others die, and we will die so that others may live. The divinity that shapes our ends is life, death and change . . . (Christ, 1990, p. 65)

Like other spiritual feminists, ecofeminists argue that attitude to death is one of the most profound differences between patriarchal and feminist values. They see men as driven by fear of their own personal mortality, whereas women have always had to accept the possibility of their own death in creating new life. The futile irony of the patriarchal drive to achieve immortality is that it has reached its pinnacle in life-threatening technological systems. The supremacy of the male ego over the needs of women and the planet has been achieved by a science, a religion and a philosophy that have separated the human race from its natural and spiritual context.

Ecofeminists argue that women and tribal peoples have kept these channels open and are therefore best placed to regain the 'other world'. In 'reclaiming those values associated with pre-patriarchal and contemporary tribal cultures' we will be 'led to understand the many ways in which we can walk the fine line between using the Earth as a natural resource and respecting the Earth's own needs, cycles, energies and ecosystems' (Diamond and Orenstein, 1990, pp. xii–xiii). If we are to reclaim the values of an Earth-based consciousness, where do we reclaim them from? Do they lie dormant within us? Do we reconstruct them in political action? Or do we look to a mystical source for the 'message'? If the last, where does that leave traditional political action?

Mysticism and Messages: Politics and the 'Other World'

The subtle suprarational reaches of mind can reveal
the true nature of being: All is One . . . The experience
of union with the One has been called cosmic
consciousness, God consciousness, knowing the One
Mind, etc. . . .

In truth there is nothing 'mystical' or 'otherworldly'
about spirituality. The life of the spirit, or soul, refers
merely to functions of the mind. Hence spirituality is an
intrinsic dimension of human consciousness and is not
separate from the body.
(Charlene Spretnak, 1982, p. xv)

The fact that these two completely different views of the relationship between mysticism and spirituality appear on the same page illustrates some of the difficulties in the ecofeminist approach to the development of an Earth-based consciousness. Are women supposed to be looking 'in faith' for a Truth to be revealed, or are they themselves to be the source of a new way of 'knowing' about humanity in relationship to nature? The answer to this question has important implications for the relationship between ecofeminist spirituality and political action. If we take a 'mystical turn', we will be looking for a message from some source external to ourselves, an eternal Truth. If we do not take a mystical turn, it will be a Truth that we tell to ourselves. While both mystical and non-mystical spirituality may propel us into political action in defence of the environment, as Starhawk enjoins, there is a profound difference between them in the way they relate to political organisation.

If the mystical is seen as 'real' rather than as a metaphor for an affinity with nature, the active agent of change moves beyond society and traditional forms of political organisation. The political dynamic is between each individual and the mystical source. This might prove both hierarchical and divisive as between those who are 'aware' or have 'awakened' to the 'message' and those who have not: a separation of the apostles from the infidels, with the latter seen as part of the problem rather than as a political route to the solution.

There is a clear example of this process at work in a contribution to a recent ecofeminist anthology. The writer starts with the myth of the 'First Mother and her Rainbow Children'. The myth starts with a Great Egg which carried inside it the promise of all life. Out of this flowed the River of Life. Finally the Creator, 'The Voice Which Must Be Obeyed', created the First Mother from the Earth. The First Mother produced Rainbow Children who followed the Dream of harmony and love, responsibility and commitment, honour and respect. Native Americans are one of the few peoples who are still guarding that Dream. The writer urges that our task is to learn the Dream and take up our responsibilities to sustain the planet (Cameron, 1989, pp. 54–66).

Anne Cameron is deeply committed to direct action in response to the Dream, and has little time for 'apologistic and spineless parrots' who try to change the system from within.

Given the urgency of her commitment, we can understand her exasperation when a 'soft-voiced woman with the vocabulary of a middle class lady' phoned her one tea time because 'she wanted to get involved in some environmental issues' (1989, pp. 64–5). Cameron recounts that she

> told this woman to stop wasting her time and mine. To stop dithering and get involved. Write letters to editors and take it up with people you know. Find out which organizations are moving to defend our homeland, and lend your support, give your energy and contribute money. (ibid., p. 65)

We can all sympathise with Cameron's frustration, but her anger is directed not only at this woman's political naivety but also at her failure to get 'the message'. Cameron argues that there is no need to talk any more because 'The Voice Which Must Be Obeyed gave us all the intelligence we need. We are the ones who have chosen not to use our innate ability to reason' (1989, p. 65). She goes on to claim that the woman on the phone did not need to 'spend forever wondering about what she might decide to do ... all she has to do is start DOING. Anything else is bullshit' (ibid., pp. 65–6). Cameron claims that 'the meek and mealy-mouthed are helping the patriarchy as it spreads like a mad sickness, infecting the Earth and threatening us all with extinction' (ibid., p. 65). People like the woman on the phone are 'black holes who suck energy' (p. 66). She sees the 'meek' as enemies of the 'Homeland'. She seeks to protect not only the Earth but her own private space on it:

> I live here. This small piece of land nourishes me physically and spiritually ... I am very jealously protective of this place and it matters very much to me who comes here or who doesn't. I don't want ineffectual and crappy energy turned loose here, I don't want energy draining black holes coming here ... (1989, p. 65)

There are unfortunate resonances in Cameron's language and tone. Obedience to the 'Voice' and action without 'time-wasting' discussion are praised in defence of the 'Homeland'. Undesirables are to be kept away. Dismissal of those with 'meek . . . ineffectual . . . crappy energy' gives the – perhaps unintended – message that the eco-sisterhood is now closed. Gone is the idea of spreading the word through organisation and contact, bringing in the – as yet – unconvinced people. Gone is an appreciation of the need to educate politically and build strength through collectivity.

Those outside the 'Dream' are not seen as untapped political supporters, they are seen as part of the problem. Because women like the one on the phone have not heard the 'Voice' or been in on the earlier political debate, they are seen as sustaining the enemy, helping patriarchy to infect us with its 'sickness'. Such anger and rejection cannot help us to build a tolerant and peaceful world. We must be certain that ecofeminism does not form itself into an irrational 'other world' that divides, rather than unites women. The woman on the phone is at the beginning of a process of political change and needs guidance and support. She is lacking political consciousness, not morally and spiritually culpable for the triumph of patriarchy.

Despite the political dangers of mysticism, there is still an empowering force in spirituality that has not been appreciated by Western political activists, particularly socialists, who have been trapped in a politics limited to material demands. Developing an Earth-based spiritual consciousness is an important way of strengthening women's spirit – 'believing in your own strength', as Petra Kelly has put it (in Plant, 1989, p. ix). But women's spiritual and emotional identification with the natural world should not replace political action or lead us to depend on some 'otherworldly' or 'inner-worldly' source of Truth. Once we leave the realm of political dialogue in seach of the 'other world', we release a force that is easily manipulated and corrupted. It is difficult to keep spiritual ideas and feelings from developing into religious structures, and history is littered with horrific destruction and cruelty in the name of faith.

Whose Spirituality?

The household life is full of hindrance, a path for the
dust of passion. How difficult it is for the man who
dwells at home to live the higher life in all its fullness,
purity and perfection. Free as the air is the life of him
who has renounced all worldly things.
(The Lord Buddha, quoted in Truong, 1990, p. 136)

In rescuing mysticism and ritual from men, women must be aware that men can wrench it straight back again. The Enlightenment that produced destructive mechanistic science also rescued human society, and women in particular, from the limitations of patriarchal spiritual authority. In bringing the search for spirituality back to our political life, we need to be very careful that we do not release a power that will reimpose those constraints.

'Otherworldliness' has a strong tendency towards hierarchy and authoritarianism, as people (usually men) take on the role of visionaries and interpreters of the faith. Spirituality has a dis-spiriting tendency to coagulate into cults around (male) gurus or hierarchical religious organisations. The spiritual life requires very committed ways of living that can be achieved only by withdrawing from the 'material' world. The development of deep spirituality is immensely time-consuming. Meditation, chanting or prayer must take up most of the day if a state of perfection is to be reached. Very few women have the social freedom to follow a cumulative form of spiritual development. We must be very careful that we do not create a spiritual 'public world' which, like the material 'public world', ignores women's very real commitments.

There is no *earthly* reason why a mystical relationship to the

Goddess should be sexually egalitarian unless women can defeat patriarchy in its material form. Unless we do, even if we adopt an Earth-based spirituality, you can bet your last bowl of muesli it will be led by a man. Women have launched spiritual movements in the past, only to find them taken over by men (Ritchie, 1991). Even the voices of native American spirituality, from whom many ecofeminists draw their inspiration, are overwhelmingly male. Without a specific commitment to liberating women as *women*, rather than as spiritual guardians of the Earth, women may once more find men 'free as the air', while they themselves remain 'full of hindrance' in the household life.

Men as well as women can also search for atavistic sources of strength. Men are reaching out to the cult of the warrior, even as women reach out to the cult of the Goddess. The American men's movement around Robert Bly has been exploring the ways that rituals such as war-dances and chants can help male self-affirmation (1991). Such a process may support ecofeminism if it helps men to control and direct their masculinity more constructively, but on the evidence of one report of a Bly-led weekend in England, it seemed more to help men celebrate their masculinity at the expense of the 'feminine'. In particular it helped one man to overcome his 'inability to feel strongly, his overattachment to his mother and his fear that he felt more female than male'. It made him

> more erect, self-affirming, relaxed, engaged and amused
> . . . some kind of different model was there to witness,
> men more comfortable with their manhood and enjoying
> it . . . perhaps all we were getting was permission to be
> what we could always have been, but something we had
> forgotten until we saw it. (*Guardian*, 9–10 March 1991)

Moving to a spiritual or mystical level in no way diminishes the political problem of gender relations – nor, for that matter, other relations of inequality. If ecofeminists are to claim that women have a distinctive spiritual affinity with the Earth upon which male authority cannot intrude, this can only be based on 'women's biological particularity' (Diamond and Orenstein, 1990, p. xi), her ability to 'know from the inside out what it is like to weave the Earth into a new human being' (Swimme, 1990, p. 21); to realise her spirituality through her body (Spretnak, 1990). Andrée Collard sees women's affinity with nature as drawn from their common experience as life-givers and nurturers, bearing and sustaining new life. Women's task is to 're-member and re-claim our biophilic power', to claim the future in the name of the mothers from the 'nowhere of the fathers' (1988, p. 168).

Mothering Nature

Nothing links the human animal and nature so
profoundly as woman's reproductive system which
enables her to share the experience of bringing forth and
nourishing life with the rest of the living world.
(Andrée Collard, 1988, p. 102)

Birth is an event of incredible human significance. It
has profound spiritual, psychological and emotional
importance ... And all of us have entered life through
the body of a woman ... It is the first act of magic
– and physical testament to the continuity of human
and all life.
(Arisika Razak, 1990, p. 168)

Razak argues that we must rescue the 'womanist' symbolism of birth from the male symbolism of rape in our relationship to the natural world. She sees both men and women as able to learn from birth as the 'nucleus of a model for positive human action'. Collard takes a more essentialist approach, seeing all women as united in a common mother-identity, even if they are not mothers:

Whether or not she personally experiences biological mothering it is in this that woman is most truly a child of nature and in this natural integrity lies the wellspring of her strength. (1988, p. 102)

In seeing motherhood as the foundation of women's relationship with nature, Collard conflicts with those feminists who have seen motherhood as something that limits and constrains women (de Beauvoir, 1968; Firestone, 1979). The earliest feminist demands were for collective childcare and the right of women to take their place in the public world (Coote and Campbell, 1982). They rejected the biological assumptions that accompanied the institution of motherhood – that women's ability to bear children should determine their social role – and argued that 'women are no more innately gifted for intensive childcare than men' (Barrett and McIntosh, 1982, p. 145). The danger in reasserting the 'naturalness' of women's mothering role is that far from being an agent for change in society, it could become a reaffirmation of women's present position, as in the following criticism of radical feminism from a Catholic perspective:

Radical feminists stipulate that the liberation of women depends not on their liberation from sex-*roles* but from being a woman, i.e. the reproductive role . . . a sort of rebellion against nature and not against patriarchal institutions. (McMillan, 1982, p. 108; original emphasis

Adrienne Rich has argued (1986) that we must separate women's mothering role from the male-dominated institution of motherhood. However, that is very difficult to achieve, as for most of human history women have borne their children in male-dominated societies. Bearing children was not a joyful unity with nature but a burden imposed by biology and men. 'Motherhood' also covers a number of stages in a child's biological and social development: conception and birthing; early nurturing; childhood. Which of these creates a woman's affinity with nature? Is it in the physiological process of birthing or the emotional connection between mother and child, mother love?

So What's Natural about Being a Mother?

If children benefit from the suffering and sacrifice of
women, that is only an incidental fact, not the cause.
Sacrifice and suffering are the definition of womanliness
in our culture.
(Susan Griffin, 1978, p. 75)

The fact that women carry and give birth to the future generations of human society is immensely important, both biologically and socially. Reproduction is a battleground over which men and women have long struggled for control. Women's 'right to choose' and men's desire to control extends to procreation, contraception, abortion, birthing and childcare. Procreation is perhaps one of the most fundamental forms of control as men attempt to establish their 'legitimate' claims over children through patriarchal family structures and heterosexuality as a sexual norm. The recent furore over 'virgin births' represents a moral panic on the part of men that women will dispense with their 'services' altogether. However, the issue of technological intervention in procreation is not simple. It is both a means of controlling women's reproductive powers and a way of meeting the needs of women who are 'naturally' unable to engage success-fully in, or do not wish to engage in, the heterosexual process of procreation. Feminists are, in any event, deeply suspicious of the motivations that lie behind the new genetic engineering and reproductive technologies (Corea, 1988).

Claims for 'natural' childbirth are equally problematic. The natural childbirth movement is an understandable revulsion against male-dominated birth technologies, although men are well represented among those advocating alternative methods of birthing (Odent, 1984). Natural childbirth seeks to return the birthing process to female control, ending more than three centuries in which women have been tormented by changing medical male 'fashions' governing childbirth and childcare (Ehrenreich and English, 1979; Hardyment, 1983). However, returning reproduction to female control does not necessarily return us to a 'natural' state. Those arguing for 'natural' childbirth, like those advocating 'natural' ecofeminism, tend to be products of the well-heeled North. The pleasurable image of childbearing that lies behind the assertion that women identify with nature as mothers rests, paradoxically, on the high level of economic and social development that has proved to be so ecologically destructive. Successful 'natural' birth requires healthy women, clean surroundings, good antenatal care and accessible medical aid in an emergency. It requires readily available contraception so that two hundred thousand women do not have to die each year in botched abortions (Jacobson, 1990). Motherhood may be a 'fact' of nature, but it is not always welcome to the woman concerned.

Childbirth is a process in which 'nature tends to be wasteful of life' (Ann Dally, 1982, p. 40). Until very recent times, motherhood was always threatened by the death of either mother or child or both. In the clan societies that greens think of as being closer to nature, childbirth was often a traumatic process. Among the Mbum Kpau of South-Western Chad, childbirth was considered painful and dangerous, with high mortality for both mothers and children (O'Laughlin, 1974). There was also the painful issue of population control, as Lorna Marshall noted among the !Kung people of the Kalahari desert of Southern Africa:

> A woman goes into the veld to give birth either alone
> or with her own mother. If she decides not to keep
> the baby, it probably never breathes. I did not have the
> fortitude to learn more. It is my impression that the
> !Kung do not feel that they commit a crime or sin when

> they practise infanticide but it is very disturbing to them
> none the less. (1967, p. 18)

Women's 'natural' ability/willingness to nurture children is virtually inseparable from social circumstances. The impact of social pressures on childcare ranges from the abandoned children in the streets of Latin America to the infanticide, particularly of girl babies, in India and China. In the absence of adequate contraception or welfare support, infanticide and abandonment become commonplace, particularly in urban areas. Ann Dally reports that even in the 1890s it was not possible to walk in certain streets in London without finding the bodies of abandoned babies. Even Jean-Jacques Rousseau, one of the philosophers most responsible for creating the idea of childhood, abandoned his five illegitimate children to a foundling hospital (Hardyment, 1983, p. 18). Thomas Coram set up his Foundling Hospital in the mid eighteenth century in response to the number of children left upon 'dunghills' and:

> to prevent the frequent murders of poor miserable
> children at their birth and to suppress the inhuman
> custom of exposing new-born infants to perish in the
> streets, and to take in children dropped in churchyards
> or on the streets, or left at night at the doors of church
> wardens or Overseers of the Poor. (quoted in Ann Dally,
> 1982, p. 64)

While poor women disposed of their children, prosperous women avoided nurturing by employing wet nurses until children became 'fashionable' in the eighteenth century (Ariès, 1962).

The Social Creation of Motherhood

Neither a woman nor a man is born a mother; people
become mothers in particular historical and social
circumstances.
(Sara Ruddick, 1990, p. 520)

The biological facts of motherhood do not produce
a universal and immutable mother–child relationship
or unit.
(Henrietta Moore, 1988, p. 26)

From an extensive survey of anthropological studies, Henrietta
Moore concludes that the idea of the universal mother–child
bond was an invention of male anthropologists. Ann Dally also
concludes that 'the total and exclusive exposure of mothers to
their young children has never existed on a wide scale in any
. . . society since civilisation began, and does not exist in many
societies today' (Dally, 1982, pp. 276–7). She argues that the
modern idea of motherhood is a trap for women:

> The discovery that children need the continuous and
> exclusive presence of their mothers and that anything
> which separates mother and child is destructive
> and psychologically damaging to the child . . .
> has been a most convenient philosophy in a world
> which is dangerous and unsuitable for children on
> their own and in which the cheapest form of social
> existence is to make no provision for them – spend
> no money on the everyday lives of mothers and
> children. By insisting the only psychological essential
> is to keep mother and child together, the individual
> needs of both can be conveniently ignored. (1982,
> pp. 9–10)

Dally contends that the myth of motherhood has been sustained
by the development of theories like psychoanalysis, which led
'experts' to advise mothers to act in such a way that babies
become conditioned to exclusive maternal attachment. Having
achieved this, academics and researchers then found that babies
experienced distress when they were suddenly separated from
their mothers. It is notable that it is a man who has been

most influential in arguing for the importance of exclusive caring (Bowlby, 1953), and his work emerged at a suspiciously opportune time – when women were being cajoled back into the domestic roles they had forsaken during the Second World War. Politicians have enthusiastically taken up the idea of 'bad' mothers who leave their children or do not give them adequate love as an explanation for many of the problems of modern society. As a result, women have been held responsible for many of the ills of new generations. We must be careful that the demands of affinity ecofeminism do not compound women's burdens by adding responsibility for the survival of the planet to their responsibility for the survival of the human race.

The idea of motherhood exists within a framework of patriarchy and heterosexuality (Rich, 1986; Ann Ferguson, 1989) that is deeply suffused by differences of race and class. As bell hooks and Sheila Rowbotham have pointed out, poor women, many of whom are Black or from minority ethnic communities, have never had the chance to become 'isolated' mothers. They have always had to fit their mothering around the need to earn a living (hooks, 1989; Spelman, 1990; Rowbotham, 1989). Isolation has also not been a problem for better-off women, who have sought freedom from child-rearing at the expense of other women: servants, nannies, childminders. Motherhood is also no guarantee of benign attitudes, as shown by the many examples of mothers who have supported military adventures or supported reactionary or fascist regimes (Koonz, 1986; Ruddick, 1990). The complexities around the social construction of motherhood has led Sheila Rowbotham to conclude:

> 'Motherhood' has clearly been a repository of
> conservative iconography in our culture. Women's
> liberation has indicated that mothering can be the source
> of a profoundly radical social inspiration. From the

contradictory experience of the 'mother knot' the desire
for a more humane society can arise. (Rowbotham,
1989, p. 119)

Linking the Biological and the Social

Women's values, centred around life-giving, must be
revalued, elevated from their once-subordinate role.
What women know from experience needs recognition
and respect. We have generations of experience in
conciliation, dealing with interpersonal conflicts daily in
domestic life. We know how to feel for others because
we have been socialised that way.
(Judith Plant, 1990, p. 15)

The 'natural' function of motherhood is so overlaid by problems
of fertility, poverty and socially constructed images of 'motherhood' that it is hard to see on what basis women can have
a 'natural' affinity with the natural world. It would be hardly
surprising, therefore, if ecofeminists, as both feminists and
ecologists, did not experience a 'love–hate' relationship with
motherhood (Ann Ferguson, 1989). For women, despite the
social overlaying of their reproductive and nurturing work, there
remains the biological imperative to maintain the future of the
human species and the pleasurable experiences of nurture and
care. From an ecological perspective there is a potential conflict
between the needs of the human race to sustain itself and the
needs of the planet. A strong emphasis on motherhood and nurturing could lead to increased population pressure. Ecofeminists
are therefore asking women to restrain their biological capacity
for giving life while at the same time celebrating it.

Far from the argument that Andrée Collard has made for the
natural role of mothering and its relationship to care for the
natural world, Ann Dally argues that it works the other way
round. A good experience of mothering depends on a supportive
social and physical environment:

Among the most supportive influences that can surround
a mother and aid her in her efforts to bring up healthy
children are a safe country-side with plenty of space
to move about, a number of other caring supportive
adults to take an interest in the child and free access to
children of a similar age. (1982, p. 287)

Maintaining a supportive environment for women and children
is undeniably a social question, but the more important question
is: Why is human society so unsupportive of the needs of future
generations? Mothering is not an essential part of the 'nature'
of women, but it *is* an essential task in the creation of a human
community. Mothering has become so identified with women
that men have been almost totally excluded (or have excluded
themselves) from the experience of care, nurturing and love. As
a result: 'it is now unlikely that a child can make friends with a
man outside [its] own family. Even if it does, the relationship is
likely to be regarded with suspicion' (Dally, 1982, p. 303). This
situation fills Arisika Razak with alarm:

The last time I looked men had tear ducts. They have
arms for holding babies. They cared about their children
and they cried at births. In a society that wishes us to see
men as devoid of feelings, let us hold an image of men
as nurturers ... Let the shared experience of childbirth
reclaim the human soul. (1990, p. 172)

Men's and women's biology does not create in them particular
predispositions. Not all women are mothers or peacemakers; not
all men are monsters or warmongers Segal, 1990). Women have
not sought to avoid male-dominated culture, they have been
prevented from taking part in it. Where women have taken part
in scientific and technical developments, their contribution has
been 'hidden from history' (Alic, 1986). Women soldiers are
challenging their exclusion from frontline fighting, and where

they have the opportunity to fight they have done so, as in liberation struggles (Randall, 1981). Rather than directing our attention towards women's biological affinity with the planet, we need to look at the reasons for men's lack of affinity. We need to ask: What is the effect on men of *not* being mothers? Why have men marginalised women and the experience of nurturing and caring they have accumulated? More importantly: What is the result of this separation? I will look at this question more deeply in a later chapter.

One of the main dangers in a predominance of affinity ecofeminism over social ecofeminism is that ecofeminism risks losing its feminist dynamic to become a celebration of the ecofeminine, the 'female' or 'feminine' principle.

Ecofeminine or Ecofeminist?

Ecofeminism's attachment to its own metaphors leaves the movement itself without any clear understanding of women's and men's actual relationship to nonhuman nature, let alone of men and women's actual relationship to each other.
(Janet Biehl, 1991, p. 26)

In its emphasis on overcoming the dualities that men have created, it is not clear whether ecofeminism is seeking to replace the masculine domination of society with a feminist world or to supply the missing half of the duality, the 'feminine principle' to balance the overdominant masculine principle. While the former position could quite appropriately be described as ecofeminist, the latter position should more appropriately be described as ecofeminine. The feminine principle attributes certain ways of thinking to women that, in practice, reflect their powerlessness in a male-dominated society. Women, having been excluded from power and thereby contamination by industrialism, militarism, science or politics, are uniquely placed to argue the case for the planet. Women's insight, nurturing and caring are called upon to liberate humanity, which in a patriarchal culture effectively means 'Man'.

Many male green writers stress the importance of ecofeminism – from Brian Tokar's claim that it represents 'the deepest current expression of a personal tie to the natural world' (1987, p. 85) to Rudolf Bahro's rather grudging argument for a 'slight dominance of the feminine element in human spirituality' (1986, p. 95). As against the destructiveness of Western industrial society and its spiritual impoverishment, Fritjof Capra sees women as the harbingers of a future green society (1983). All women's sufferings have not been in vain, as they carry the seeds of purity for the new order. Women are the *Dea ex machina* that is going to get men out of this mess.

Was the Western mechanistic scientific revolution, then, just an aberration? Can we somehow 'loop back' to a different age, and on what basis? Can men share in that journey, or are they too compromised and flawed? Ecofeminism is less than clear on this question. Irene Diamond and Gloria Orenstein, for example, see ecofeminism as embracing 'not only women and men of different races, but all forms of life – other animals, plants and the living earth itself' (1990, p. xi). If there is not a specific commitment to feminism, then on what basis will ecofeminists confront male power in all its forms: economic, political, sexual, physical and ideological, as well as spiritual and intellectual? At present male power is most strongly represented in patriarchal capitalism, militarism and religious fundamentalism. Because of the strength of the latter it is important that women do not abandon their worldly struggle for personal and political freedom on the strength of a mystical interaction with nature.

Equally, an emotional or spiritual identification with nature must not be a substitute for a political analysis of the relationship between humanity and nature. That is to replace one dualism by another. As Ynestra King points out, the nature–culture division is a product of our (male) culture. It is both an anthropocentric and an androcentric division. Women will not transcend that division by a one-sided identification with nature, nor will they achieve it by attempting to join men on an 'equal' basis in the nature-hating world they have created. Rather, women can:

> *consciously choose* not to sever the woman–nature
> connection by joining male culture. Rather, we can use it
> as a vantage point for creating a different kind of culture
> and politics that would integrate intuitive, spiritual and
> rational forms of knowledge embracing both science
> and magic insofar as they enable us to transform the
> nature–culture distinction and envision and create a free,
> ecological society. (1989, p. 23)

The strength of ecofeminist political action lies in uniting women's social, physical and spiritual experiences (Ruddick, 1990; Ynestra King, 1989; Starhawk, 1990). Although there is a danger that affinity ecofeminism could divert us from social and political questions, women's 'biological particularity' and spirituality are a tremendous source of empowerment. A clear example of the power of women's unified strength is the Chipko movement.

The Politics of Ecofeminism: Bringing it all together

The forest is our mother's home, we will defend it with all our might.
(Women of the village of Reni in the Garhwal mountains of the Himalayan Range, quoted in Anita Anand, 1983, p. 182)

What do the forests bear?
Soil, water and pure air.
Soil, water and pure air
Sustain the earth and all she bears.
(Song of the Chipko women, in Vandana Shiva, 1989, p. 77)

The Chipko movement of the Himalayas has been one of the most inspiring examples of women's affinity with nature, yet it is also an important example of the role of social and political action. The Chipko movement first came to public attention in 1974, when the women of Reni put their arms round their trees and hugged them to prevent them from being felled. In doing so they launched the Chipko (hugging) movement. They were not only expressing a spiritual unity with nature, they were demonstrating the way their daily lives depended on the trees for firewood and forage. While women in industrial communities may have to struggle to (re-)create their 'Earth-based consciousness', for poor rural women of the South this is the reality of their daily lives; all struggle is ecological struggle (Shiva, 1989).

Despite its inspirational example, the Chipko movement was not a spontaneous flowering of women's immediate physical and spiritual identification with the forest. It grew out of the long and purposeful struggle of politically committed followers of Gandhi in the Garhwal region (Shiva, 1989, pp. 67–77). Inspired by Gandhi, one woman, Mira Behn, settled in the Himalayas in the 1940s and began to study the ecology of the region. Other women, like Sarala Behn and Bimala Behn, started ashrams for the education of hill people. The movement grew out of a 'mosaic of many events and multiple actors' (ibid., p. 68). It combined the traditional relationship of hill people to their environment, the political and spiritual commitment of followers of Gandhi, and the very immediate material needs of local women. Irene Dankelman and Joan Davidson also tell us that in 1982–3 the Dasohli Gram Swaraj Mandal organisation set up twenty eco-development camps in the region (1988, p. 50).

However, political action alone is not enough; women did play a special role and exhibit a clear affinity with the ecological needs of their region. Although the camps and the whole Chipko movement were open to both men and women, it was women who responded with the most appropriate understanding of the ecological issue and undertook long-term committed action to defend the trees. The same pattern occurred in Africa. The Kenyan Green Belt movement was started by Professor Wangari Maathai and organised through the National Council of Women. As in the Indian example, a central part of the programme was political and ecological education. Women responded enthusiastically, and hundreds of local women's tree-planting groups were set up (Dankelman and Davidson, 1988, p. 51).

Clearly we need the insight of both social and affinity ecofeminism – it is not a case of one or the other. Those who overstress social and political relationships will miss the importance of threads of women's lives that run across eras and cultures. Those who stress biological and spiritual affinity may forget the importance of the traditional political triggers of education and collective action. Equally, if ecofeminism leans too heavily towards ecology and the needs of nature as against feminism and the needs of women, it is in danger of presenting women as the *solution* to the ecological and social problems of human society, thereby deflecting attention from men as the *problem* in their domination and exploitation of both women and the natural world. Men have not made a 'mistake' in their creation of nature and women as the dominated Other. The feminine is not the missing half of the masculine; the feminine is what men need to create the masculine in a patriarchal culture. The feminine has never been missing, as de Beauvoir pointed out – it is the source of male power. This is the insight that makes feminism truly radical. It is women's experience of oppression in patriarchal society that gives them a unique standpoint from which to analyse other forms of oppression and exploitation including that of the planet itself (Hartsock, 1984). However, in uniting the experience of women and nature we must not make the assumption that securing the future of the planet will also secure the future of women, that the green movement is inherently feminist. This may not necessarily be the case as the deep ecology movement shows.

CHAPTER 3

Back to Nature?
The Perils of Deep Ecology

Deep ecology encompasses the study of Nature's subtle
web of interrelated processes and the application of
that study to our interactions with Nature and among
ourselves. Principles of deep ecology are that the
well-being and flourishing of human and non-human life
on earth have inherent value, that richness and diversity
of life forms contribute to the realization of these values
and are values in themselves, and that humans have
no right to reduce this richness and diversity except to
satisfy *vital* needs.
(Charlene Spretnak, 1985, p. 233)

The deep ecology movement is shockingly sexist.
(Sharon Doubiago, 1989, p. 40)

The deep ecology movement embraces both a philosophy of
the relationship between humanity and the natural world and
a politics of direct action in defence of nature. In a sense, all
those who campaign on behalf of other species or the physical
environment are deep ecologists. They are – quite rightly –
saying that human activity has gone too far, that we have got to
call a halt to the destruction before it is too late. We must put a
boundary around human development that respects the right of
the natural world to its own autonomous existence. Many people
have been fearless in defence of this principle and deserve our
heartfelt thanks and support. However, there are elements of
deep ecology that go much further than redressing the balance

between humanity and nature. They move to a point where the human context becomes completely lost or, worse, rejected.

Without underestimating the importance of ecological struggle, I would like to put both humanity and feminism back into 'nature'.

Deep Ecology as Philosophy

In the Deep Ecology Movement we are biocentric or ecocentric. For us it is the ecosphere, the whole planet, Gaia, that is the basic unit, and every living being has intrinsic value.
(Arne Naess, 1990, p. 135)

Deep ecology goes beyond the so called factual level to the level of self and earth wisdom . . . to articulate a comprehensive religious and philosophical worldview . . . the basic intuitions and experiencing of ourselves and Nature which comprise ecological consciousness.
(Bill Devall and George Sessions, 1985, p. 65)

The basis of deep ecology lies in a rejection of the human-centredness of modern society in favour of ensuring the survival of both the biosphere (other plant and animal species) and the ecosphere (the non-biological environment). Arne Naess first drew a distinction between shallow environmentalism and deep ecology in 1972. Shallow environmentalism is a human-orientated concern with immediate environmental issues, such as pollution or resource depletion, which aims to reconstruct the relationship between human society and nature in a way that would ensure human survival. Against this Naess sees deep ecology as a nature-orientated desire to adjust human life in such a way that its destructive impact on the planet ceases.

Deep ecology celebrates the complexity and diversity of the

natural world *for its own sake*, not as something useful or even necessary for humanity (Naess, 1973). It argues that we need to replace our current science-based domination of nature with an approach based on 'biocentric equality'. Biocentric equality sees the human race as only one part of a wider planetary system, where all life forms have equal right to survival (Naess, 1990; Devall and Sessions, 1985). For Naess, the main difference between environmentalism and deep ecology is a spiritual/ philosophical one. Deep ecology starts from an Earth-based wisdom, which Naess calls an 'ecosophy', that is distinct from ecology, the science. Naess claims that technical knowledge will not help us to 'see reality', nor will a humanist ethics and morality. Ecosophy is a deeper form of 'knowing', an awareness of our oneness with the planet: 'world first, men [*sic*] not apart, friends of the earth, ecological responsibility, the forest for the trees, hug the trees' (Naess, 1990, p. 132).

Although Naess argues that every living – and, by implication, non-living – part of the natural world is 'intrinsically' equal, he still holds that the organisational principles of the natural world have priority over those of the social world. Within his 'ecosophy' is a timeless idea of balance and connectedness that we must 'understand' if we are to break through our destructive attitude to nature, represented in modern science and technology with its constant desire to conquer the natural world. Deep ecology means learning to open ourselves to nature, to accept that 'Nature is in control' (Spretnak, 1985, p. 234), to make 'the Earth as physical object' our foundation stone (Dobson, 1990, p. 15).

There are two fundamental contradictions in deep ecology. The first lies in the relationship between nature-centredness (ecocentricity) and the idea that all that exists, including human beings, has equal intrinsic worth (biocentric egalitarianism). According to Arne Naess there is no contradiction, as all species have equal merit in our relationship to the whole, to Gaia. However, there is a problem in the relationship between the parts and the whole, between an individual species (humanity) and the 'needs' of the ecosphere, of Gaia. The essence of deep ecology is that the needs of the whole, Gaia, must take precedence. In this context, ecocentrism quickly tumbles into antihumanism. Humanity is perceived to have less worth than the natural world – in fact to have a negative relationship with it. Humanity is seen not as part of nature, but against nature. Naess himself explicitly refutes this point of view. He rejects the ideas of what he calls 'natural ecologists', those who say 'save the whale' by getting rid of humanity. Nevertheless, antihumanism sits like a ghost on the shoulder of deep ecology and reveals itself in issues such as population control.

The second contradiction lies in the relationship between the idea of the intrinsic worth of nature and the aim of human self-realisation. This emerges most strongly in one of the main campaigning issues for deep ecologists, wilderness preservation. Seeing nature as having intrinsic worth implies that our campaigns are carried out for the sake of nature itself, not for any human-centred motivation. However, as is clear in the quotation from Devall and Sessions above, one of the aims of deep ecology is a deeper 'experiencing of ourselves' through our relationship to the natural world. This is a human-centred, not a nature-centred, motivation. For Devall conservation is 'self-defense' (1990, p. 70).

As a result of these two contradictions, deep ecology combines strong elements of antihumanism with an undercurrent of human-centredness. This comes down to 'keep nature for me' (wilderness preservation), 'there are too many of you' (population must be controlled). Such a position is potentially, if not inevitably, racist, sexist and class-biased.

Deep ecology's tendency towards antihumanism also means that it lacks an adequate political basis from which to address its ecological concerns. Placing the blame for the ecological crisis on an undifferentiated 'humanity' puts equal responsibility on North and South, rich and poor, Black and white, men and women. In order to build an effective politics of ecology, the insights of deep ecology must be combined with an understanding of the social and economic divisions within society. Without this, there can be no adequate politics of ecology to support the direct action movement.

Deep Ecology as Direct Action

Let your actions set the finer points of your philosophy.
(Dave Foreman, founder of Earth First! quoted in
Manes, 1990, p. 27)

Deep ecology as a direct action movement has emerged most strongly in North America and is best epitomised by the group Earth First!. Although some of its methods have been contentious – particularly the 'spiking' of trees by hammering in nails to make the use of chainsaws dangerous – in general Earth First! uses non-violent direct action to draw attention to the need to rescue 'nature' from human hands. Earth First! was formed in 1980 by a group of men disillusioned with the slow progress of existing environmental groups, particularly on the issue of wilderness preservation. The inspiration for the movement lay in Edward Abbey's 1975 novel *The Monkey Wrench Gang*, in which a group of 'ecosaboteurs' use 'ecotage' to protect the environment.

Earth First! had an estimated membership of 10,000 in 1989, with many sympathisers in other environmental organisations. According to one observer it brings together 'cowboy types, hippies, former businesspeople, students, scientists and academicians' (Manes, 1990, p. 76). Undoubtedly Earth First! has many women members – like the 12,000-strong Canadian direct action group Sea Shepherd, which has a majority of women – but Christopher Manes's history of Earth First! reflects an almost exclusively macho image. He describes the 'cowboy types' like the ex-Marine Dave Foreman and the oil-rig roughneck Mike

Roselle and celebrates the image of Earth Firsters, standing 6 feet 5 inches in cowboy boots and hats, with 'burly boyish faces', confronting – presumably equally macho – bulldozer drivers. The exploits he recounts – such as those of the tree-sitters who use their rock-climbing skills to shin up 300-foot trees – demand physical skill and strength. A history of women's participation in Earth First! remains to be written.

A primary aim of Earth First! is the protection of wilderness – those areas which, they argue, human culture has not yet 'contaminated'. Other direct action groups engaged in wilderness protection have emerged in countries from Scandinavia to Thailand and Australia. In Europe there is precious little wilderness left to protect, but the threads of deep ecology still run through much of the green movement.

According to Manes we live in a 'culture of extinction' as we hurtle towards 'biological meltdown'. Unlike the last global crisis that destroyed the dinosaurs at the top of the food chain, destruction is beginning at the bottom, with those organisms that sustain all life. If they are destroyed, new life cannot evolve. Manes argues that we have to make a choice between the natural and the cultural world. If we choose the natural world we must 'slow the technological beast down' by deindustrialisation, depopulation, stopping technology export to the South, elimination of multinationals and 'eco-wars' against the governments of countries like Brazil who want to deforest.

Although the early approach of Earth First! was deeply antihuman, particularly on the question of human population, there is evidence from the grass roots that it is evolving into a more Left-radical movement. Even in Manes's book there is a substantial criticism of economic growth, property rights and market economies; however, there is still little recognition of the issues of class, race and gender. Despite his assertion that it is just the 'ecological perspective that matters' (1990, p. 32), Manes does make one assertion with which I would wholeheartedly agree: 'the link between market economy and

environmental decline is an issue that will not go away ...
environmentalism may well become the template through which
we may finally perceive how power works in our society' (ibid.,
pp. 37–8).

Awareness of the issue of power in human society is essential,
even in what may seem to be the most pure aim of deep ecology,
the preservation of wilderness.

Wilderness Preservation

Wilderness is the preservation of the world.
(Henry David Thoreau, 1851, quoted in Paehlke,
1989, p. 21)

Wilderness and not civilisation is the real world.
(Dave Foreman of Earth First!, quoted in Manes,
1990, p. 21)

We did not think of the great open plains, the beautiful
rolling hills and winding streams with tangled growth as
'wild'. Only to the white man was nature a 'wilderness'
and only to him was the land 'infested' with wild animals
and 'savage' people. To us it was tame. Earth was
bountiful and we were surrounded with the blessings of
the Great Mystery.
(Chief Luther Standing Bear of the Oglala band of
Sioux, quoted in McLuhan, 1971, p. 45)

The five men who launched Earth First! formed the idea on a
hike across the Mexican Pinacate Desert, which Edward Abbey
had described as 'the wildest, least developed part of Mexico
and therefore the best' (Manes, 1990, p. 68). There are three
motivations for wilderness preservation in deep ecology. The
first is preservation for its own sake, for the intrinsic worth of
'untouched' nature. That is the only purely ecocentric motivation.
The other two motivations are more human-centred. One is to

enable us to learn from 'nature' in its purest form; the other
is to enable human beings to gain the aesthetic experience of
wilderness.

Bill Devall and George Sessions see in the experience of
wilderness an opportunity for 'self-realisation' and 'ecological awareness' in activities such as fishing, hunting, surf-
ing, sunbathing, kayaking, canoeing, sailing, mountain-climbing,
hang-gliding, skiing, running, cycling and bird-watching, if they
are performed with a 'proper attitude'. Generally these are
activities for the young and fit, usually male. To them a wild
place will not be wilderness; it is somewhere that excites them
and makes them feel free. As Edward Abbey expressed it:

> Why give up our wilderness? What good is a Bill of
> Rights that does not include the right to play, to wander,
> to explore, the right to stillness and solitude, to discovery
> and physical freedom? (in Manes, 1990, p. 3)

Despite the fact that ecofeminists such as Starhawk and Charlene
Spretnak also express an aesthetic and spiritual identification
with wilderness, other ecofeminists such as Marti Kheel sees
eco-masculinism in the deep ecologist search for an 'expanded
self' in wilderness activities. She argues that women and men
are looking for different things in the wilderness experience. For
men it is the search for an atomised egoistical experience rather
than the relational expandedness that women seek. Man against
the elements is much more satisying than woman against family
commitments (1990, p. 128). There is a danger that the idea
of wilderness embodies the same masculinist values of excitement, struggle and adventure that have destroyed the natural
environment. It is not nature-centred, it is human-centred, to
meet the needs of members of the dominant sex, race and
culture to escape from the world that they and their forebears
have created. As Sharon Doubiago has put it more pungently:
'where is the female on the bearshit trail?' (1989, p. 40).

There is certainly a strong whiff of the frontier in the battle
for wilderness preservation. Cowboys and Indians have been
replaced by the eco-warrior trekker, and the 'new settlers'
such as loggers or roadmakers. Both are predominantly male
and white, and both are reaching for the final frontier: one
as a source of raw materials to exploit, the other as 'virgin'
lands to experience. For many people wilderness is a place
where those who feel discontent with 'civilised' life can act
out their fantasies or their social dislocation, as in the case of
many Vietnam veterans who have taken to the hills and forests.
It is a place for men and some women to escape from the 'chains'
of responsibility.

Murray Bookchin argues (1989) that the search for wilderness
is a revolt against human society by misanthropes. It represents
their own personal escape from 'civilisation', and the most
important element in the designation of wilderness is exclusion of
'the mass'. According to Tim Luke (1988), support for wilderness
comes from the people who will most benefit from its creation:
biologists, mountaineers, hikers and backpackers. Although deep
ecologists claim that they are seeking to maintain the wilderness
as an end in itself, it is clear that it represents an opportunity
for aesthetic or religious experiences in the grandeur of wild
and empty places or in challenging physical activities. Richard
Grow points out that the search for spiritual experience may be
seen rather differently by those people to whom wilderness was
once home:

> There may be some sensitivity on the part of people
> of colour whose land and labour have already been
> expropriated when they see their philosophy and
> spirituality lifted and claimed, owned, by the white folks.
> (Grow, 1990)

Wilderness preservation is by no means a simple issue. Apart
from the feminist critique of masculinist bias there is, as Grow

points out, a potential racist element, and finally there is the question of class: who owns the wilderness?

Who Owns the Wilderness?

We are concerned that you have left us, the indigenous peoples, out of your vision of the Amazonian Biosphere. The focus of concern of the environmental community has typically been the preservation of the tropical forests and its plant and animal inhabitants. You have shown little interest in its human inhabitants who are also part of that biosphere. (Evaristo Nugkuag Ikanan, an Aguaruna Indian from Peru and President of COICA [the Centre for the Indigenous Organizations of the Amazon Basin], *Guardian*, 3 August 1990)

To declare land a wilderness is to assume that it is not home to human inhabitants (unless they are assumed to be wild as well). It has been estimated that in 1500 there may have been as many as fifteen to twenty million people living in the Amazon rainforest (*New Internationalist*, no. 219, May 1991). Presumably an equally large number of native Americans populated the northern half of the continent. There is hardly a part of the world where human remains cannot be found. If land is relatively uninhabited now it may be that its original population has perished, often at the hands of colonialists' weapons or diseases. The declaration that an area is a wilderness raises the problem of the rights of those humans who do live there. Evaristo Nugkuag Ikanan, for instance, points out that the million indigenous peoples of the Amazon 'never delegated power of representation to the environmentalist community', and argues that the best way of saving the rainforest is to recognise the traditional ownership rights of the Indians, who are the best people to maintain it.

The idea of preserving wilderness in the form of national parks is not new. In America it was pioneered by Henry David

Thoreau and John Muir in the nineteenth century (Paehlke, 1989). However, across the globe wilderness preservation has some unhappy associations. Nature reserves were supported by leading members of the Nazi regime in Germany (Bramwell, 1985, 1989), while European colonists in Africa, India and North America set up nature reserves by throwing indigenous people off their lands (Paehlke, 1989; Shiva, 1989). Today, the Maasai of the Serengeti Plain in Tanzania can no longer graze their animals on their traditional land, as it has been designated a national park. Throughout the African national parks controversy has arisen over an alleged 'shoot-to-kill' policy to deter poachers. A key issue is the identity of the poachers – are they well-armed ruthless criminals or local villagers following their traditional way of life?

The problem of access to nature is no less a problem for people in urbanised industrial societies. People trapped in cities find it increasingly difficult to get out into open countryside, and in both Britain and America national parks are coming under severe pressure from tramping feet. Common land, places where people can roam free, is severely restricted – particularly in Britain, where wildlife is more free to roam than people, particularly if it can be shot. In 1932 a mass trespass of Kinder Scout Fell in the Peak District was led by members of the Communist Party, with a young Ewan MacColl, who was then a member of the Young Communist League in Salford, Lancashire, as their publicist. In the postwar period, public ownership of land, particularly by water authorities, and the establishment of legal rights of way eased the situation a little. Since then, military use of large areas of moorland and privatisation of the water authorities have reopened the issue, and on 30 September 1990 a nationwide mass trespass took place, led by the 60,000 strong Ramblers' Association. The women of Greenham Common Peace Camp have also successfully challenged the legality of the suspension of rights of way across the Common to enable it to be used as an air force base.

Putting ourselves in touch with the natural world is not just about breaking the boundaries between human society and nature, it will also mean breaking the boundaries between those who own land and resources and those who do not. Land is wealth, and in Britain it is still largely in the hands of the old aristocracy, much of it distributed to victorious Normans after the conquest of 1066 or grabbed from the common people during the enclosure movements. Across the world land has not been stolen only from nature and other species, it has been stolen from indigenous peoples and from the poor. If wilderness is to be conserved, we need to know who is preserving it and on whose behalf. For deep ecologists the aim of creating wilderness is to let nature recover its own primeval condition before 'man' intervened. The irony of this aim is that if we do create a wilderness, we must never intrude upon it again: 'all conservation of wildness is self-defeating, for to cherish we must see and fondle, and when we have seen and fondled there is no wildness left to cherish' (Aldo Leopold, quoted in Collard, 1988, p. 150).

Even if the aim is to create a wilderness and abandon it, its very creation is a political process. Areas will have to be 'declared' wilderness; they will have to be policed and monitored in case people try to settle them, exploit them, mine them or hunt animals to extinction. To be a wilderness is not to be safe. The so-called last great 'natural' wilderness, Antarctica, has, after much international debate, been put under a mining moratorium for fifty years. This agreement will be effective only if it is 'policed' by all the signatories.

It is plain that the search for a 'biocentric' or 'ecocentric' deep ecology is doomed to failure. We can never escape from human society and its consequences, and to think that we can will introduce hidden biases of sex, race and class. This is not to detract from the aim of preserving those areas we describe as 'wilderness', as long as their social context is not ignored. In their search for wilderness and an Earth-based ecosophy, deep ecologists must first ask the fundamental question: Is nature natural?

Is Nature Natural?

History and nature, present history and past nature,
present nature and past history, are hopelessly entangled
with one another.
(James O'Connor and Barbara Laurence, nd, p. 5)

Central to deep ecology is the 'naturalness' of nature. If, as Arne Naess has suggested, we are to develop an ecosophy that looks deep into nature, to be 'far-seeing' and listen to its message, what are we seeing and what are we listening to? What is this 'nature' to which we are submitting? Is it nature red in tooth and claw or nature as a co-operative and symbiotic system (Kropotkin, 1955)? We are asked to reach out to the Earth, Gaia, not with our reason but with our faith. The problem for Gaia, as for all gods, is that she does not speak to us clearly; her messages are in the warming of the air and the death of fish. And as with all religions, it is humans who tell us what 'Gaia' is saying and what we must do. Central to the ideas of deep ecologists is the integrity of nature, that it has an existence and a voice, but what do we understand by 'nature' – was it ever natural?

Near where I live in Newcastle is a beautiful 'Dene', a wooded river valley running for more than a mile, but it is not natural. A painting of Newcastle in the sixteenth century shows it to be bare of trees; all the hills and valleys that surround it are smooth and bald. As early as the thirteenth century the people of Newcastle were given royal leave to mine for coal, as they had depleted all their tree cover. The Dene was replanted more than a hundred years ago by Lord Armstrong, the arms manufacturing magnate, as part of his estate, and eventually bequeathed to the city as a park. By the same token, farmland is not natural, heathland is not natural; the fens are the result of peat-cutting (Merchant,

1980). The human race has altered the face of the planet since the first tree was cut down, the first seed planted and the first river dammed. The landscape beloved of the English Romantic poets – protected waters, forests, salmon streams, lonely coasts and highlands, hedged and ditched fields, naturally fertilised rotational farming – was a product not of 'nature' but of a brutal expropriation of common land, the clearance of population and transportation of huge numbers to the colonies. Landless people were herded into the cities, and the number of offences punishable by death was trebled (Stretton, 1976). As both Marx and Engels pointed out, humanity is part of natural history and nature is part of human history.

A failure to understand its historical and social context leads to a hallowing of nature as it is *now* – or, worse, a socially constructed interpretation of how it could or should be (Bookchin, 1989). By the same token, the history of the human race is lost, particularly those who have suffered as 'nature' was created. As Grow has pointed out (1990), the Earth-orientated spirituality of the native Americans tends to be hallowed by deep ecologists in the past tense, while little or no attention is paid to the reality of the impoverished lives of their descendants.

At the same time, the human race has certainly been foolish to treat the planet as infinitely expendable. The message from the green movement is loud and clear: the world is finite, it is 'space-ship earth'. In an ecologically interconnected world, no action is without its reaction. Cutting down trees will reduce the stability of soil. Dredging will alter the shape of estuaries and coasts. Dams will mean loss of sediment on flood plains downstream. Monoculture increases vulnerability to pests. Chemicals in the soil will seep into underground water. Gases released will have effects upon the structure of the air.

A less spiritual understanding of the dynamics of the natural world is Jeremy Rifkin's analysis of 'entropy' (Rifkin, 1980). Entropy is a fundamental law of nature under which the physical world is gradually returning from order to disorder as the source of our energy, the sun, is used up. Although matter can neither be created nor destroyed, it can move from a usable to an unusable form. Burning a fossil fuel does not destroy the atoms of which it is made, but scatters them around as gases and particles which cannot be used again to produce energy without a new input of energy from another source.

In gaining technical control over nature, industrial society has speeded up the inevitable process of decay and dissolution by exploiting the world's 'once-and-for-all' stock of fossil fuels. Ultimately we cannot argue with Rifkin's position; the planet cannot live for ever. We are faced with an inevitable ecological decline that we cannot impede, but we can hasten. That is certainly a 'lesson' we can learn from nature, but apart from that, the idea of 'nature' as expressed in deep ecology is far too profoundly infused with social meanings to be able to 'reveal' to us any essential truth about how we should direct human society. This does not mean to say that we cannot feel reverence for the beauty of the natural world and recognise its destruction at our hands.

Rifkin does not offer us a mystical union with nature; in fact he warns against abandoning ourselves to reactionary religious forces. The worship of nature is not necessarily a force for progress; it can have deeply racist connotations. The Nazi movement in Germany adopted a quasi-mystical reverence for nature that was 'merely a rationalization for their murderous racial theories' (Tokar, 1987, p. 148). Deep ecology's aim of looking for an answer in nature will provide only human responses smuggled in under the guise of 'nature's will'. In North America deep ecology has sometimes taken such an antihuman turn that it has been accused of eco-fascism and eco-brutism (Bookchin, 1988; Tokar, 1990). For Bookchin, the appeal to 'nature' and its laws is a way of avoiding real social issues:

> 'Deep ecology' was spawned among well-to-do people
> who have been raised on a spiritual diet of Eastern cults

mixed with Hollywood and Disneyland fantasies. The
American mind is formless enough without burdening
it with 'biocentric' myths of a Buddhist and Taoist
belief in a universal 'oneness' so cosmic that human
beings with all their distinctiveness dissolve into an
all-encompassing form of 'biocentric equality'. (1989,
pp. 13–14)

Resolution into a cosmic oneness is a fundamental problem for
socialists and feminists – whose oneness is it? Who will control
the new ecocentric communities? Arne Naess hopes for the
emergence of a new aristocracy, by which he means 'the most
enlightened and far-seeing members of the society'. He argues
that at present we are 'occupied' by 'kind and well-meaning
people. They do things for our welfare but in reality we feel
completely estranged from the essence of the good life' (1990,
p. 130). There is more than a touch of authoritarianism in Naess's
idea of an aristocracy. What do they see, where will they lead
us? Are they to be the priests of a new religion, interpreters
of the mind of Gaia? For Murray Bookchin, that path leads to
servitude:

> To worship or revere *any* being, natural or supernatural,
> will always be a form of self-subjugation and servitude
> that ultimately yields social domination, be it in the name
> of nature, society, gender or religion. (1989, p. 13)

Without an awareness of the way human society has constructed
'Nature', the concerns of deep ecology will come to represent the
interests of those who have been best placed to create nature in
their own image. In determining the balance of the 'needs' of
nature as against those of humanity they will be reflecting their
own needs and interests as a race, class or gender. Awareness
of this fact is particularly crucial on the difficult question of
sustainable population levels.

Who Says How Many People?

Mass starvation is not a pleasant thought. But
recognition that human populations are subject to the
same ecological limitations as other living beings is
necessary if there is to be the possibility of adjusting
population drawdown with a minimum of suffering.
(Christopher Manes, 1990, p. 233)

An article in the *Earth First!* magazine under the by-line Miss
Ann Thropy argued that Aids was the sort of disease that would
'bring human population back to sanity' (quoted in Dobson,
1990, p. 64). Dave Foreman of Earth First! has reportedly said:
'the human race could go extinct and I for one would not shed any
tears'. Although Foreman has since recanted his more extreme
views on population, the issue of population represents a strong
theme in ecological writings and a crucial issue for green politics.
'The only real pollutant is people' is a phrase that can be heard
from the lips of (some) green activists as well as that ubiquitous
political touchstone, the 'man in the street' (I have heard men,
but not yet a woman, make this remark). The issues of population
and resources are intertwined in green thinking (Brown, 1981;
Porritt, 1984; Irvine and Ponton, 1988; Rivers, 1988; Icke, 1990;
McKibben, 1990). Emphasis varies from a low-key reference to
'overpopulation' in the *Global Policy* section of the Programme
of the German Green Party to the 'long-term aim' in the British
Green Party's 1987 Manifesto of reducing the UK population
from 55 million to around 35–40 million.

Human population is estimated to have been five million at
the time of the agricultural revolution in 8000 BC, rising to five
hundred million by AD 1650. Between 1650 and 1850 it doubled
to one billion (1,000 million), mainly concentrated in Europe,
America and China. Between 1850 and 1930 it doubled again
to two billion. By 1976 it had doubled again to four billion, with
most new population growth in the so-called Third World. By

1990 it was over five billion, but rising more slowly than thirty years ago (Erlich and Erlich, 1987). The older white industrial nations have stabilised both birth and death rates and settled into a high-density, low-growth pattern. Other parts of the world have not yet reached that stage. Death rates have been slowly coming down, but the population is still disproportionately young and fertile. Although childhood deaths are also falling, uncertainty about the future and lack of adequate access to contraception mean a high birth rate. World population will eventually stabilise sometime in the next century at around ten billion.

At present, population stability is correlated with a high standard of living and the world imbalance in population growth reflects the existing pattern of global inequality. The rich nations condemn the poor nations for not controlling their populations, while keeping them in the poverty that prevents them from doing so. If population growth is not seen in a historical and social context, any discussion of the issue invites an attack upon poor or disadvantaged ethnic groups. Rational debate is not helped by emotive references to a 'population time bomb' or the 'exploding birth rate' (Erlich, 1972; Irvine and Ponton, 1988). Debates about population size and growth have carried an implicit attack upon the poor since the days of Malthus.

Malthus's famous *Essay on the Principle of Population*, written in 1798, maintained that human population was growing faster than the land's capacity to feed it. His solution was quite simple: remove all forms of support to the poor in order to encourage them to restrict their numbers. Malthus's views were vigorously opposed by liberals and socialists, and he was proved utterly wrong as new agricultural technology dramatically improved production. The population question has been raised many times since, most notably by Paul Erlich and Garrett Hardin in 1968 (Paehlke, 1989). Hardin attacked Marx's vision of a society which would take from each according to their ability and give to each according to their needs. He argued that this was impossible, as resources were inevitably limited. Rather than seeing the world as a horn of plenty, we should adopt a 'lifeboat ethics' (Hardin and Baden, 1977).

According to Hardin, a lifeboat has provisions for only a specific number of people. These provisions are so finely balanced that even to take on one more person would threaten the survival of all. Hardin argues that the planet has a similar 'carrying capacity', and if this is exceeded all life is threatened. The way forward is for each nation to consider itself a lifeboat and decide how many people it can 'carry'. In the context of world inequality, poverty and the economic migration of peoples from South to North, Hardin's proposals have inevitable racist implications. The views of both Erlich and Hardin have been condemned as heralding a 'new barbarism' (Commoner, 1971), yet of all the issues raised by the ecology movement, this is the one that has produced the largest number of policy initiatives from organisations such as Zero Population Growth and Planned Parenthood. Population policy has also been a condition of aid from North to South, particularly in America (Adams, 1990).

The danger in Malthusian arguments about population is that they always have a mathematical logic at *any one point in time*. At any one level of consumption, at any one stage of technology, at any one audit of resources, a calculation can be made of the carrying capacity of the planet. The crucial issue is: Who sets the parameters, and on what basis? Christopher Manes's heartless scenario of mass starvation is based on his view that 'human culture is lethal to the ecology that it depends on and has been so for a long time, perhaps from the beginning' (1990, p. 22). For Manes the beginning of nature's downfall was agriculture, and he argues that the only ecologically acceptable lifestyle is the 'natural economy' of nomadic hunters and gatherers. By setting his parameters in the Stone Age, Manes reduces the carrying capacity of the planet to such a level that it can only mean a catastrophic drop in world population. Those doomed to perish are described as ecologically redundant in Manes's sinister euphemism. Perhaps it is hardly necessary to add that

Manes sees deep ecology as incompatible with social justice, as the needs of the poor and powerless must mean that human demands on the environment cannot be curtailed sufficiently. But the issue of social justice is inseparable from the question of population.

Too Many People or Too Much Consumption?

Either we reduce the pollution of poverty by fair means
while addressing our own excess of affluence, or we just
let the poor die.
(Richard Sandbrook, co-founder of Friends of the Earth,
Independent on Sunday, 13 October 1990)

We cannot begin to discuss how many people the Earth can carry, unless we know how much they will consume. One-sided attention to population growth deflects attention from the enormously high levels of consumption in the countries whose populations are stable or falling, a point acknowledged in the Brundtland Report. On average people in the richer countries of the world consume forty times more resources than those in poorer nations (Icke, 1990, p. 82). To put it another way: in consumption terms an average-sized family in the North has eighty children. Or to put it yet another way: the North consumes the equivalent of thirty-two billion poor people.

America has 2 per cent of the world's population but consumes one quarter of the world's oil, and in 1984 the two hundred million or so Americans alone consumed the equivalent energy resources of twenty-two billion people (Pepper, 1984). According to Sandy Irvine, in the last fifty years the USA has consumed more energy and raw materials than the rest of the human race has done in the whole of its history. If world population is likely to stabilise at ten billion, we seem to have a good deal of resources in hand in America alone. Given that one-third of Americans live in relative (if not absolute) poverty, an even smaller number of people are harnessing an inordinate amount of the world's resources.

At present one billion people in the world live on less than £4 per week (World Bank Development Report, 1990). They have a vast unmet need for housing, clean water and land. Many people in the world where populations are increasing consume very little; other countries consume very heavily with a near-stagnant population. In resource terms it makes much more sense to focus attention on the consumption levels of the richer nations than on the population growth of the poor. The green movement has been telling us loud and clear that we will all have to do with less, much less. It should follow that those who are absorbing most of the world's resources should make the biggest sacrifice. This would be a more fundamental challenge to power and wealth than the socialist movement in the West has ever managed to achieve. The unmet needs and population growth in the South reflects its poverty even down to the lack of adequate contraception, and it is women who pay the price. As well as being inseparable from the issue of poverty and social justice, the question of population is inseparable from women's equality.

Suffer the Women and Children

What works is increasing the security of life for those who are already alive, and especially increasing women's control over our own bodies and access to work and economic compensation independent of our role in procreation.
(Starhawk, 1990, p. 83)

If most unwanted pregnancies in the Third World could be prevented it would reduce population growth in the less developed world by as much as 40 per cent.
(1985 World Fertility Survey, quoted in Icke, 1990, p. 86)

Discussion of birth control is always in danger of developing authoritarian overtones, especially when academics, politicians, scientists and demographers, nearly all of them men, declare that a particular group, class, race or nation is too populous. Sometimes it has been directly expressed in racist or class terms: the poor, the 'ignorant', the South, will 'swamp' the rich, the 'intelligent', the North. This is particularly the case where policies for population control do not have as their main focus a woman's right to control her own fertility. At their worst, population policies can mean female genocide (gynocide). Throughout history, when population has to fall, it is female children who are left to die on hillsides or, in the more modern technological version, identified by amniocentesis and aborted. In India it has been estimated that between 1978 and 1983 78,000 female foetuses were aborted (Mies, 1986). In 1988 a survey of aborted foetuses in Bombay found that all except one of 8,000 were female (*Guardian*, 4 December 1990).

Often, techniques for population control show very little concern for women's physical or psychological health. In rural areas intrauterine devices are inserted in situations where there is no proper sanitation or aftercare. Often heavy bleeding results in already undernourished women. Contraceptives such as DepoProvera, considered too dangerous for women in the North, are administered widely to women of the South (Sen and Grown, 1987; Mies, 1986).

Abortion can be carried out in inhumane circumstances, as when China imposed its much-praised population policy in Tibet:

> Women nine months pregnant had their babies taken out. We saw many girls crying, heard their screams as they waited their turn to go into the tent and saw the growing pile of foetuses build outside the tent. (*Guardian*, 1 August 1990)

Tibetan women were also subject to forced sterilisations and even infanticide. Additional children were social outcasts:

> Third children have no legal right to attend school, work,
> travel, own property or receive a ration card. There are
> thousands of such children in villages. Their economic
> and social exile is complete and is rapidly producing a
> generation of illegal children who must collect refuse or
> dung to earn a living. (ibid.)

The fate of children under Chinese rule in Tibet is little different
from that of the seven million street children of capitalist Brazil.
Despite the fact that Brazil is the world's eighth largest industrial
power, with a *per capita* income of $2,437, thirty-three million
people live on less than $370 a year, and it is their children
who drift on to the streets and into petty crime. Amnesty
International has drawn attention to the torture, mutilation and
death of street children at the hands of death squads, often led
by police officers. The older industrial countries have treated
their children with equal contempt; for a long period Britain
transported its unwanted children to the colonies.

These cruelties are inflicted on women and children despite
the fact that it is common knowledge that poverty and a high
birth rate are closely connected. In the Sahel a couple have to
bear ten children on average to be 95 per cent certain that a
son will survive to support them in their old age (Asian and
Pacific Women's Resource Collection Network, 1989, p. 70).
In poor countries children are an asset to the family – a child
in Java earns an income for the household by the age of nine,
and in Bangladesh boys produce more in income than they
consume by the age of ten. Women also need female children
to help them carry out their very large burden of domestic
and subsistence work, and male children to satisfy patriarchal
demands for descendants (Harrison, 1987).

A policy for population control must take account of the impact
of poverty on family size and place birth control firmly in the
hands of women. One of the biggest problems for women
controlling their fertility is access to contraception. It is not

wilful ignorance that leads an Ethiopian or a Malaysian woman to have several pregnancies, it is the four-hour round trip to the local clinic that she has to make each month. Each time she may lose half a day's pay out of her pittance as a labourer. In the absence of contraception, women risk death through informal systems of abortion. Guaranteed easy access to contraception and abortion will remove this perilous issue from the agenda once and for all.

A very successful birth-control programme in Kerala, India, has halved the birth rate in ten years. Thirty years ago Kerala produced the first freely elected communist government and has continued to have comprehensive social and land reform policies. Unionisation and a minimum wage have improved the conditions of the poorest workers. Literacy is two or three times the national average, and all children go on to secondary school. Each community has a health centre within walking distance, and there is an extensive programme of inoculation and childcare. Children in Kerala are three or four times more likely to survive than the average Indian child. A positive programme of women's rights and equality of opportunity has meant that girls are as valued as boys as future wage-earners. Against this background, even the poorest families have felt confident about limiting family size.

Socialists have quite rightly accused the greens of class and race bias in their attitude to population growth. This problem was acknowledged early on by Herman Daly, but he concluded that it was 'hopelessly utopian' to expect the 'simple' solution of the rich cutting consumption while the poor cut their population growth so that a 'steady state' could be achieved of a common level of 'capital stock' per person (1973). In the face of massive global inequality, the issue of population can be discussed only in the context of a commitment to ending global inequality and injustice and a guarantee of a woman's inalienable right to control her own fertility.

Going Deeper

Deep ecologists and ecofeminists share a core vision:
we are doomed if we do not change and change fast.
We also share the terrible despair at times that the
work is hopeless. The understanding of who and what
is to blame is the same in both: feminists call it the
Patriarchy; ecologists evading the gender issue call it
Western Culture, Science and Technology, Capitalism,
Materialism etc. . . .
(Sharon Doubiago, 1989, p. 43)

Despite profound reservations about deep ecology as presented by some representatives, we cannot ignore the fundamental green issue at its centre. Human society will have to renegotiate its relationship with the natural world. Deep ecologists are quite right to raise the needs of the planet in the face of the destructiveness of human activities, as long as they do not tip the balance towards becoming antihuman in the process. It is also right for deep ecologists to argue that we have to change our whole attitude to the natural world, but in saying this humanity cannot be treated as an undifferentiated whole. Human society is fractured by race, class and sex. It is not right to hold the poor or people of the South responsible for developments by the rich white North. Women cannot be held responsible for the actions of men. The ecological unsustainability created by the grabbing and exploitation of land by dominant groups in dominant nations must not be paid for by population control imposed upon the poor and landless.

It is also important that a male-dominated deep ecology movement does not engage in a battle for the planet with other men over the heads of women. It does not help women if a male-dominated scientific culture is rejected in favour of a male-dominated idea of 'natural' culture, such as the atavistic 'warrior society' that Dave Foreman and others has called for.

Civilisation is not just juggernaut technological machines tearing down 'virgin' forests, it is hospitals, sanitation, birth control, clean water, food-grinders – things that have made women's lives tolerable. At the same time, both feminists and socialists must take account of the deep ecologists' argument that we can no longer hope to achieve equality in human societies by a process of 'levelling up' our material standard of living. The whole world cannot share the standard of living of California, and even that state has found itself reverting to desert as water supplies dry up.

So how are we to balance the insights of deep ecology with an awareness of the social causes and consequences of the ecological crisis? Murray Bookchin points us in the right direction by seeing humanity and nature as in a dialectical relationship, where each affects the other.

Social Ecology: Balancing Humanity and Nature

> Ecology . . . firmly rooted in *social* criticism and a vision of *social* reconstruction, can provide us with the means for remaking society in a way that will benefit nature *and* humanity.
> (Murray Bookchin, 1989, p. 13; original emphasis)

Murray Bookchin argues for a 'social ecology' which sees the solution not in an uncritical embracing of nature but in a 'remaking' of society. He argues that human domination of nature stems from human domination within society; if society could eliminate such dominations as racism, sexism, capitalism, homophobia and the centralised state, our relationship with the planet would be resolved (Bookchin, 1982, 1988, 1989; Clarke, 1990).

Bookchin argues that the natural world cannot be understood as a timeless entity. He sees both the deep ecologist's idea of a steady-state Gaia and the scientist's mechanistic view of nature as lacking an awareness of the historical evolution of nature. Human society is a part of this process; there is a *'natural* continuity between biological and social evolution' (quoted in Biehl, 1991, p. 118). Human activity and development is not a 'sick aberration' of the 'natural' process:

> Human beings can no more be separated from nature and their own animality than lemmings can survive without their skins. What makes the human animal a product of natural evolution is not only its physical primate characteristics; it is also the extent to which humanity actualises a deep-seated nisus in evolution toward self-consciousness and freedom. (Bookchin, 1989, p. 203)

This echoes Marx's observation that while human beings are part of natural history, so is nature part of human history. Marx also saw human development as a process of evolution towards self-realisation. For both Bookchin and Marx, human emancipation is achieved only through a social struggle to gain conscious human control of what would otherwise be the 'incoherent aspects of an evolution left to its own wayward unfolding' (Bookchin, 1989, p. 203). For Bookchin, nature needs the rational intervention of humanity to help it to achieve its full potential, which he sees as the development of complex and differentiated life-forms. Humans, as part of nature, must open up a dialogue with nature which will enable an 'emancipated humanity' to become the voice of a 'free nature'. We must not abandon human reason and technological development, as deep ecologists urge, but use them to comprehend the wider ecological context.

Despite his sometimes vitriolic attacks on deep ecology, Bookchin shares with it a view of nature as having an inherent 'ethic' – albeit achieved only through active human intervention. He echoes Kropotkin's view of nature as – at least potentially – non-hierarchical, diverse yet unified, with a biological predisposition to interdependence and mutual aid (Bookchin, 1982, p. 26).

As with Kropotkin, Bookchin's description of nature just

happens to reflect his anarchist philosophy. Bookchin also shares the deep ecologist's preference for decentralisation, in advocating egalitarian face-to-face self-governing municipalities.

For Bookchin the enemy of nature is hierarchy in all its forms, from the centralised state to the business monopoly. By grouping all the ills of society under the heading of 'hierarchy' he is, in effect, asking us to be against sin. In asking us to rid ourselves of our 'hierarchical mentality' he does not help us to differentiate sources and types of domination; a centralised state based on representative democracy is presented as the hierarchical equivalent of racism, sexism or class exploitation. Bookchin's campaign against hierarchy makes the same political error as the deep ecologists who ask us to blame all humanity for the ecological crises. In condemning all hierarchies, Bookchin leaves us no means of deciding which is the worst, or where to begin our struggle against them.

While Bookchin's social ecology is an important corrective to the antihumanism of some deep ecology, he tips the balance between humanity and nature too far the other way. By seeing the resolution of the ecological crisis in resolving the problems of humanity, he loses the most important thrust of green thinking: that the ecological framework of our lives is not just an adjunct of the failures of human society; ecology is a reality in itself. It is a reality that offers a radical challenge to the present military, political and economic structures of society by pointing to the artificial way in which they have been constructed. Social boundaries have paid little or no attention to natural boundaries. One of the most helpful ideas in understanding the natural boundaries of human society is bioregionalism.

Living within Natural Boundaries: Bioregionalism

Bioregionalism means learning to become native to a place, fitting ourselves to a particular place, not fitting a place to our predetermined tastes. It is living within the limits and the gifts provided by a place, creating a way of life that can be passed on to future generations. (Judith Plant, 1990, p. 158)

The essence of bioregionalism is beginning from where we are. By learning to live within the tolerances of our own ecological framework, we will be able to 'grow out' towards a more sustainable world. Judith Plant sees a strong relationship between bioregionalism and ecofeminism in the bioregional emphasis on returning to the 'home': 'the bioregional view values home above all else, because it is here where new values and behaviours are created' (1990, p. 160). She also stresses the importance of regional cultures. In view of deep ecology's tendency towards both antihumanism and a celebration of masculine values, we need to be certain, in welcoming the insights of bioregionalism, that the new bioregional boundaries do not create or enhance ethnic antagonisms or constrain women even more firmly to the domestic sphere.

Kirkpatrick Sale identifies a number of bioregional boundaries that take both ecological and human communities as their base. He sees the largest division as ecoregions that share a common ecology, such as native vegetation and 'soil contours' that could cover thousands of square miles. The second level is a georegion that might be a river basin, desert or mountain range. The largest of these could, of course, run through several ecoregions. The local level, which Sale calls the vitaregion, is defined more by human needs. According to Sale, the vitaregion must of necessity provide for the needs of its inhabitants, as 'the most elemental and elegant principle' of the natural world is 'self-sufficiency' (Sale, 1991, p. 79). Sale claims that if we leave nature to find its own 'steady state' within our own localities, it will be naturally fecund and biodiverse.

Like Judith Plant, Sale sees the idea of 'particularity' as central to bioregionalism. According to the principle of 'particularity', people should become 'dwellers in the land' in order to:

come to know the earth, fully and honestly, the crucial
and only all-encompassing task is to understand the
place, the immediate specific place where we live ... We
must somehow live as close to it as possible, be in touch
with its particular soils, its waters, its winds ... (in Sale,
1991, p. 77)

There is a strong thread of human-centredness in Sale's idea
of bioregionalism, as illustrated by the relationship between
the eco- or georegion and the local vitaregion. The first two
are defined on the basis of ecological principles, the last is
human-scale. There is also a human-centredness in Sale's
assumption that each local area will 'naturally' sustain all the
needs of its human population. This does not necessarily
follow; there is no reason why a particular locality should
meet *all* the needs of the people who live there. There are
huge areas of the world where the climate and geography are
very inhospitable to local communities. Sale's argument rests on
the assumption that all nature's anomalies are human-produced
through 'giantism, centralisation and hierarchy'. While these
could be resolved by local communal self-management, it is
less clear how we are to respond to the naturally created limits
of natural resources. It is perhaps noteworthy that bioregionalism
has developed most strongly in the ecologically resplendent North
American continent, not in more ecologically and economically
troubled Africa.

As a result, perhaps, of its North American origins, there is a
tendency in bioregionalism to confuse arguments for a decentralised administration for human-centred reasons of democracy and
autonomy with arguments for decentralisation on the grounds of
ecological sustainability and self-sufficiency. In practice these two
demands may mean very different things, particularly in terms
of desirable size. A vitaregion that could sustain the majority
of the needs of its human population may prove much larger
than the face-to-face communities the decentralists desire. If

these two aims are conflated, it brings us back to the deeply reactionary issue of the size of a 'sustainable' population in a particular area.

There is also a tendency in bioregionalism to see local ecological knowledge as 'organically' evolving into a wider ecological awareness (Devall, 1990). Kirkpatrick Sale, for example, assumes that local knowledge of our 'particular place' helps in understanding the wider ecological context. The implication is that global bioregional understanding is the sum of the many parts of local ecological understanding. This claim seems to make the same mistake as the mechanistic science that many greens condemn. Knowledge of small parts of the whole does not necessarily mean that we grasp the implications of the whole. Why should someone who fishes a local stream *necessarily* understand the ecology of the whole river basin without some conscious attempt to do so? Deep ecology claims that because all *things* are connected, our minds are connected in the same organic way. By knowing the 'stones' of our immediate surroundings we will embrace the whole of Gaia (or Gaea, as Sale calls it). Our connection with the planet and each other is a combination of the biological and the spiritual. Being is Knowing.

Those who do not share the spiritual faith of the deep ecologists would, perhaps, prefer to build the connections in a more material form. The ecological basis of human life on a regional and global level would need to be understood through a conscious process of learning. Knowing the particularity of one's own 'place' would need to be accompanied by local, regional and global *political* action. From this perspective the injunction to think globally and act locally is too limited. If we want to understand the global ecosystem we will have to raise our eyes from our particular cabbage patch to study the material reality of Gaia in its global context. In addition, we need to understand the reality of Gaia in its social context. In the light of that understanding we will need to think and act both globally and locally and *politically construct the relationships in between*.

Living within Natural Boundaries: Global Politics

The Earth was created by the assistance of the sun,
and it should be left as it was . . . the country was made
without lines of demarcation and it is no man's [*sic*]
business to divide it.
(Hin-mah-too-lat-kekht, Leader of the Nez Perce
Indians, quoted in McLuhan, 1971, p. 54)

The radicalism of bioregionalism lies in its claim that the
'natural' boundary for human social organisation is not the
nation-state, nor the political boundaries that have been drawn
within states, regional states, counties, cities, districts, wards.
Ecological problems cannot be 'contained' or repelled at national
or local borders. An ecological region, such as a river basin or a
rainforest, may cover a huge area of land and thousands, if not
millions, of people. In fact, the whole world is one ecological
region; it represents a 'natural' internationalism. To make the *first*
point of political decision-making the ecological framework of our
lives must undermine the artificial boundaries of nation-state
or any other non-ecologically based units of administration or
economy.

If we are to adopt a bioregional approach on a global level,
the political problems we face are horrendous. Every inch of
the globe is straddled by a militarised nation-state or jealously
guarded within a 'sphere of influence'. Failure to 'think globally',
or even ecoregionally, means that limited economic or national
interests create or threaten wide ecological damage. The Gulf
War was one example of political and military interests totally
overriding ecological, or humanitarian, considerations. Even so,
this was nothing compared to the ecological and human holocaust
a nuclear war would unleash.

The Middle East is, however, a good example of the minefield
of bioregional politics where water as well as oil is a source of
conflict. The 1967 Arab–Israeli War and the Israeli occupation

of the Golan Heights and West Bank were as much about the security of water resources as military considerations. Equally, Turkey's proposals for damming the Euphrates are likely to have a profound effect on Syria and Iraq, and may be the source of future military conflicts. Many other large river systems such as the Nile, Ganges and Brahmaputra cross both national boundaries and national interests. National self-interest leads countries to put dangerous installations like nuclear power stations on their borders, hoping to protect the majority of their own population in case of accident. The same limited approach means that Britain continues to churn out sulphur dioxide, safe in the knowledge that prevailing winds will take the poisonous effects to Scandinavia. On a global or even a regional scale, such activities are an ecological delusion.

The interconnectedness of the planet is an ecological reality that we are only just beginning to recognise politically. The United Nations has made some tentative moves. Following the Basle disaster in 1986 when the chemical company Sandoz accidentally poured toxic chemicals into the Rhine, polluting the river through several countries, a UN treaty was proposed to secure the ecology of international rivers. The seas, which are already overfished in many areas, are equally a potential source of dispute. The United Nations has been trying since the early 1980s to get a universally agreed 'Law of the Sea' to cover both mining and fishing. Under UN pressure, countries like Japan have agreed to stop drift-netting, but the United States and Britain have so far led the opposition to a unified approach to the oceans through their commercial interest in deep-sea mining.

The self-interest of the nation-states is more than matched by the self-interest of transnational capitalist corporations that often operate beyond any national or international control. Perhaps most importantly, ecology does not figure at all on the military agenda apart from the tactical benefit of ecological destruction, as in the United States's use of Agent Orange in Vietnam.

Greens have put the security of the future of the planet firmly on the agenda, but this will not be achieved by a decentralised 'communing' with the soil. It will require collective political action at a global level. Resources are not evenly spread across the globe. Despite the claims of bioregionalists, bioregionalism would not of itself create diverse self-sufficiency for local human communities. Although needs would be met as far as possible from local resources, there would also need to be a non-exploitative basis for exchange or transfer of resources. This would require *increased* co-ordination and monitoring at a regional and global level, a *concentration* of political and economic control, rather than the devolution to the small, self-reliant communities that many greens desire.

If we are to sustain the future of the planet without risking neo-Malthusian authoritarianism or the formation of militarised national ecological lifeboats, greens must link up with the political internationalism inherent in socialism and feminism. I say inherent because for a time the internationalism of Western socialists and feminists contained an unacknowledged cultural imperialism that obscured differences of class, race, ethnicity and nationality (hooks, 1982). At the same time, radical social movements will need to embrace the ecological insights of the greens in order to help build an international movement that can challenge divisions of class, race and nation and begin to dismantle the militarised states.

Living Naturally?

To demand organised political action at a regional and global level is not to ignore the question of the political organisation of local communities. To say that decentralisation will not *of itself* produce a global response is not to deny the importance of returning control of their lives to people at grass-roots level. What is important is the basis upon which this is done.

Throughout the green movement, there is a desire to return to a more 'natural' way of life. This is often associated with what Thomas Jefferson called the 'communal anarchism' of the native

Americans. As I have said more than once, it is deeply ironic that representatives of a culture that destroyed the very basis of the life of the native Americans are now trying to scrabble in the embers to rescue their lifestyle for themselves. The yearning for the lifestyle of an earlier age runs profoundly through green thinking, from deep ecologists to ecofeminists. It has also attracted some socialists. All see something in the past that is lost in the present. For deep ecologists ancient society was closer to nature and ecological sustainability; for ecofeminists it was more sexually egalitarian; for socialists more socially egalitarian. At a much deeper level they are all asserting the 'naturalness' of original human society and 'attempting to rebuild human and *natural* community' (Plant, 1990, p. 160; emphasis added).

In arguing for a feminist green *socialism* I will argue against the idea of a 'natural' community in favour of the need for conscious *human* construction of society *at all levels*, from the local to the global. But first I will examine both the claims and the evidence about the nature of earlier forms of human society. Were they more benign towards the natural world, towards each other and towards women? Are they a suitable model for communal life in a feminist, green and socialist future?

CHAPTER 4

The Search for Innocence

The native American became a symbol in the ecology
movement's search for alternatives to western exploitative
attitudes.
(Carolyn Merchant, 1983, p. 106)

Modern archaeologists and those who have gone to
study some of the few remaining tribal peoples are
telling us ... of people that lived for thousands of years
in harmony with nature and each other ... We find
accounts of people needing to work less than half-time
to satisfy their basic survival needs, leaving many
more hours and days for creative pursuits, celebration
and rest ... Primitive peoples had a highly evolved
understanding of the world around them and of their
place within it. They knew how to live from the earth
without destroying it.
(Brian Tokar, 1987, p. 11)

According to the German writer and political activist Rudolf
Bahro, human beings have remained essentially unchanged for
ten thousand years. Modern human societies, with their emphasis
on material possessions, are not developing the human race, they
are destroying it. Bahro argues for a return to pre-industrial,
small-scale agricultural communities. He is so committed to this
vision that he has resigned from the German Green Party because
of what he sees as its compromises with the antinature systems of
modern industrial society (Bahro, 1986).

Disillusionment with the destructive cruelty and inequality of our present world is often represented as a sense of loss: nostalgia for a 'Golden Age' that is the mirror opposite of our present ills, when people were not competitive, destructive, selfish or cruel. For greens, in particular, a critique of the destructive power of the modern industrial system implies that human communities once lived in peace and harmony with each other and with the natural world. The ecological, spiritual and social organisation of early human communities is an important inspiration for their politics. Jeremy Seabrook is concerned that the search has come too late:

> At the very moment when the need for sustainable alternatives is becoming apparent, the examples, the living embodiments of harmonious and stable ways of living, are being extinguished. (1988, p. 7)

Judith Plant is also concerned that 'man's world' is 'spreading across the face of the earth teasing and tempting the last remnants of loving peoples with its modern glass beads, televisions and tanks' (1989, p. 2). Looking for a time when things were better than they are now is an expression of optimism; it is a declaration that within ourselves, within our society and its relationship to the natural world, exists the capacity for innocence, in its original Latin meaning: *innocentia*, doing no harm. For greens it seems that in order to move forward we need to go back, recover our 'real' selves, return to our roots in the natural world, rediscover a sense of community, balance, harmony.

The opposing point of view is that things have always been the same, cruel and unfair, with human beings exploiting each other and the natural world. Ironically, the blame is often laid upon nature itself: the human condition is a reflection of 'nature red in tooth and claw'. Human development represents a long and dangerous crawl from the primeval slime. Our progress is shaky and uncertain, civilisation is merely a rickety compromise, a façade that can collapse at any time, pushing us back into the 'state of nature' where life, in Thomas Hobbes's often-repeated phrase, is 'solitary, poore, nasty, brutish and short'. Such a view leaves us with only the hope that by some miracle we can tame all the forces, human and non-human, that threaten us. Survival demands eternal vigilance and control.

Most socialists, on the other hand, follow Marx in having a progressive view of human history and modern industrial society, a view that conflicts sharply with both green images of ecological decline and fall and the Hobbesian survivalist idea. It is anarchists who tend to look to the past to claim that there were once societies in which all people shared power and all property was held in common, where even the weakest were sustained by a spirit of mutuality and co-operation (Kropotkin, 1955), and it is anarchism rather than socialism that has most influenced green politics. Feminists are perhaps the most ambivalent of all about the past. Some have claimed that there were once societies in which women were not oppressed, where they were valued for their wisdom and nurturing, where they were worshipped or might even have ruled (Eisler, 1987; Stone, 1979).

Others argue that such a search would be not only fruitless but diversionary, wasting time that feminists could better spend tackling women's immediate experience of male power (Delphy, 1984; Walby, 1990). On the other hand, Maria Mies sees it as an important weapon in women's liberation:

> The search for the origins of unequal and hierarchical relationships in society in general, and the asymmetric division of labour between men and women in particular . . . is part of the political strategy for women's liberation. (1986, p. 44)

Given green assumptions about the benign social and ecological nature of clan society and the way in which feminism has become attached to green thinking, it is important to look at the evidence of women's experience in the earliest form of human community.

Before women can wholeheartedly share the green assumption that small was – and will be – beautiful we need to know if it was – and will be – patriarchal. If we can prove that women have throughout history suffered badly at the hands of men, then feminism needs to go to the heart of green politics in creating a template for an egalitarian and sustainable future.

Learning from the Past

Understanding our own history as a species is an
important tool in the development of a social vision that
can, this time, consciously reflect ecological values.
(Brian Tokar, 1987, p. 14)

Greens draw inspiration from historical and actually existing clan societies. From the traditions of peoples like the Gourounsi of Burkina-Faso, now struggling in the Sahelian drought, who appointed a Chief of the Greenwood whose job was to protect the forest and ensure that valuable species were not felled. From the present-day struggle of indigenous peoples to save their environment from modern commercial and technological developments: the Western Shoshone Indian Nation of Nevada, who opposed nuclear testing by encircling the testing grounds; the Mohawk Indians of Canada, protesting against a plan to turn their ancestral burial grounds into a golf course; the Indian peoples of the Amazon, campaigning to save the rainforest.

In a Schumacher Lecture, Helena Norberg-Hodge described villages in the Ladakh region of the Northern Himalayas that remained unchanged for hundreds of years (Norberg-Hodge, 1990). In a harsh and difficult environment the Ladakh people were resourceful and self-sufficient. Precious fruit-bearing wood was not cut for fuel (cow dung was used instead) and each household had a composting lavatory to create night-soil fertiliser. Everyone was well fed and healthy, despite bitterly cold weather and a short growing season of only four months. The rest of the time was spent in leisure: weddings, monastery festivals, story-telling and music-making. Women had an 'almost equal' position to men! Norbert-Hodge reports that the people smiled a lot, reflecting their deep sense of peace and contentedness. Unfortunately, Ladakh society is now under threat from tourism and the invasion of the 'cash economy'. The Ladakh young are more interested in consumer goods than in the traditional way of life.

While the position of women among the Ladakh is a little unclear, the agricultural Lepcha people of Mount Kinchenjunga in the Himalayas would seem to embody sexual equality in the 'age of innocence' (Sanday, 1981). The Lepcha were peaceful, with little contrast between rich and poor. Work was amicably shared: women would sometimes weave baskets, men would sometimes spin, although these were traditionally segregated tasks. If a woman performed a task better than her husband (e.g. climbing trees) he was considered lucky rather than shamed. Men were closely involved in childcare, and all adults responded to the demands of infants and young children. Men nursed children, held them in their laps and carried them on long journeys. Children were taught to be co-operative and pacifist. Although individual differences were acknowledged, people were not competitive or egotistical because the Lepcha did not recognise social goals that were achieved at the expense of others. I do not know if the Lepcha have gone the way of the Ladakh as the market economy creeps closer.

Murray Bookchin has described such societies as 'organic', united by blood and a common willingness to let no one fall below the 'irreducible minimum' necessary for survival (1982, 1989). Social relationships based on tribes or clans produced an intensive communal solidarity that was reflected in the relationship of organic societies with the natural world. Quoting from the anthropologist Dorothy Lee's study of the Wintu Indians, Bookchin claims that for them, 'equality exists in the very nature of things'. The Wintu language did not even have words for concepts like having, taking or owning. Bookchin claims that in organic communities people operated upon the principle of 'usufruct' – that is, possession of a tool or plot of land was based upon need and use, not upon ownership.

The clan societies of North America have provided considerable inspiration for the green movement. They were mainly matrilineal (i.e. children 'belong' to their mother's family and daughters still retain that relationship even on marriage). A study of the Huron people in seventeenth-century Canada, for example, showed them living in long houses made up of several families, all related through the mother. Grain was stored collectively and anyone could draw on the resources if they were accepted as a family member (Karen Anderson, 1987). The native American way of life was destroyed by European colonisation. Terry McLuhan's collection of Indian speeches (1971) records the sorrow and anguish of the Indian peoples at the advent of the White man [sic]. She has caught for ever the poetry of their language as they describe their love of the natural world:

> The White people never cared for land or deer or bear.
> When we Indians kill meat, we eat it all up. When
> we dig roots, we make little holes. When we build
> houses, we make little holes. When we burn grass for
> grasshoppers, we don't ruin things. We shake down
> acorns and pinenuts. We don't chop down the trees. We
> only use dead wood. But the White people plow up the
> ground, pull down the trees, kill everything . . . They
> blast rocks and scatter them on the ground. The rock
> says 'Don't. You are hurting me'. But the White people
> pay no attention . . . How can the spirit of the earth
> like the White man? . . . Everywhere the White man has
> touched it, it is sore. (McLuhan, 1971, p. 15)

This speech was by a Wintu holy woman, one of only four women recorded by McLuhan as against around eighty men. The message of the Indian people is still with us; a contemporary

Clan Chieftainness expresses the spirituality, poetry and reverence for nature that have so attracted people to their culture:

> From Mother Earth a sacred energy is rising, and
> when heaven and earth meet within our hearts and we
> acknowledge ourselves in good relationship with creation
> and when we keep the precepts of dignified human
> behaviour, of caretaking the earth and one another, then
> a great energy is generated from our hearts ... The
> voice of the indigenous people has really been whispering
> in your heart for a long time because you eat our food,
> and you are sustained by the bones of our ancestors and
> the water that you drink we have blessed and prayed over
> it that all human beings may recognise peace of mind
> and come again to caretaking the earth and one another.
> (Speech of the Venerable Ugowiyuhi Dhyani Ywahoo,
> Clan Chieftainness of the Etowah Cherokee Nation,
> addressing the World Goodwill Conference in 1989)

Greens argue that the main thing the native American relationship with nature can teach us is that human society must work *with* nature, not against it. Modern society has lost this message. By taking inspiration from early communities we can, as Brian Tokar suggests, begin 'consciously' to build a new relationship with the natural world. Neither he nor Bookchin thinks that we can go back in any literal sense to ancient ways of life. The question that socialists and feminists need to ask of the greens is whether harmony with nature *necessarily* implies harmony within the human community. Peggy Sanday, for example, argues that early societies did live in a relatively egalitarian and non-sexist way, *provided they were not put under pressure* from invasion, migration or environmental stress (Sanday, 1981, p. 136).

The Emergence of Domination

I take the discovery of nothing but female figures [from
the Palaeolithic Age] as evidence of gynocentric societies

or matriarchy. By matriarchy I mean not that women
were 'the dominant sex' – the notion of dominance is
patriarchal – but that female experience determined
culture.
(Andrée Collard, 1988, p. 11)

I would flatly assert that we find women subordinated to
men in every known society. The search for a genuinely
egalitarian, let alone matriarchal, culture has proved
fruitless.
(Sherry Ortner, 1974, p. 70)

There is still considerable debate over the existence or non-
existence of women-orientated communities in early human
history. Those feminists who do argue for a matriarchy see it
as an egalitarian, peaceful society. What went wrong?

For Bookchin, harmony in organic clan societies broke down
with the emergence of hierarchy and the increased domination
of human by human. 'Primordial equality' was destroyed, kinship
groups disintegrated into classes, tribal communities dissolved
into the city, and finally all political control passed to the
state (Bookchin, 1982, p. 43). For Bookchin, hierarchy first
emerged through domination of the community by the elders, and
increasingly by male elders. As populations grew and encroached
upon each other's land, power extended to the (male) warriors.
The exact historical period and geographical location of this
process are vague, as Bookchin extends his praise to societies
variously described as pre-capitalist, pre-literate and tribal.

Alarm bells will ring for women when they find that Bookchin
ascribes male dominance over women to their physiological difference: 'that males are born into a special status in relationship
to females becomes an obvious social fact' (1989, p. 55).
According to Bookchin, men's superior physical strength and
greater quantities of haemoglobin and testosterone give rise
to 'behavioural traits that we associate with a high degree of
physical dynamism'. This 'dynamism' was reflected in hunting

and war-making. Bookchin assures us that this power was not used to intimidate women in 'organic society'; male domination of women was a by-product of men's domination over each other, particularly in war-making. This contrasts with the view of the anarcho-communist Peter Kropotkin, writing more than half a century earlier. Kropotkin traced the beginning of hierarchy to the emergence of the patriarchal family, with its stress upon individual accumulation of wealth and power and hereditary transmission of both (Kropotkin, 1955).

Bookchin's image of man-the-hunter/warrior as the agent of destruction for organic communities reflects the same male-centred view of history as that which sees man-the-hunter/warrior as the source of civilisation. Women have strongly challenged this claim and have put forward their own version of the history of human society (Slocum, 1982; Reed, 1975; Morgan 1985).

The male reading of human history in much of twentieth-century archaeological and anthropological literature is that human society originally developed through the social organisation and communication necessary for the hunt or the battle. Bookchin gives men credit for the earliest organisation of 'civil' society. Emphasis on the overwhelming importance of war-making in human social history continues, despite repeated feminist critiques (Mann, 1986). Feminist anthropologists and historians have challenged the male-dominated history of the human race. Peggy Sanday sees the man-the-hunter assumptions of twentieth-century anthropology as a reflection of patriarchal Western colonialism, with its desire to enhance the power of men and oppose (or not recognise) the power of women (Sanday, 1981).

Nineteenth-century anthropologists adopted an evolutionary theory that stressed the original power of women. Bachofen in 1861 and Lewis Henry Morgan in 1871 stressed the importance of women's mothering role. Both argued that early societies were matriarchal (i.e. dominated, if not ruled, by women) because the biological relationship between sexual intercourse and birth was not understood. Drawing on an analysis of Greek mythology, Bachofen argued that the most basic social relation was between mother and child, and the first types of social organisation were based on mother-right – i.e. family groups were organised around the mother. Morgan made the same case, based on an analysis of kin names among native Americans (Reed, 1975, 1978). However, these theories are still male-centred in that they see human society evolving through male realisation of their paternal role and their desire to gain control over women's bodies.

Feminist historians have emphasised the importance of woman's economic role as well as her mothering. There is considerable evidence that 'woman-the-gatherer' was the primary source of food in early human society (Dahlberg, 1981). Re-examination of archaeological evidence indicated that Stone Age men were not big and hairy. Hairy they might have been, but they were not very large; survival for the early hunter depended on speed and agility, not on muscle-bound aggression. Hunting was not normally dependent on direct physical force; often it relied on cunning, laying traps or driving animals over cliffs or into boggy ground. Often the weaker, older animals were captured (Miles, 1988).

Given the centrality of woman's child-rearing and food-gathering to early society, it follows that she would have invented some of the earliest tools: the digging stick, slings to carry food and babies, the means of making food edible, the pots to cook in, the fire to heat the food. She would also have developed knowledge of plant types, their uses and dangers, distances and geography of food sources, the round of the days and the seasons, and particularly the lunar cycles that matched her own menstrual cycle (Shuttle and Redgrove, 1978). As animal predators would make it very dangerous for women to gather alone, weighed down by nursing children and gathered food, they almost certainly went as a group. Although male-stream history argues that men first developed co-operation and communication during the hunt, it is equally likely, if not more likely, to have developed among women gatherers as they discussed the best direction in which to go and how long it would take. For example, the eighteenth-century Abipon women of the South American Gran Chaco plain travelled long distances in groups of up to one hundred to gather food. A Jesuit observer noted: 'I never heard of a single woman being torn to pieces by a tiger, or bitten by a serpent, but I knew many men who were killed in both ways' (quoted in Sanday, 1981, p. 122).

If an age of innocence did exist, it was one in which women played a major part, but did woman's role as mother, food-producer and religious symbol give her a predominant, or at least equal, share of power with men in early human societies?

Women's Work in Clan Societies

The men went to war, hunted, fished, provided the raw
materials for food . . . women cared for the house and
prepared the food and clothing . . . Each was master in
his or her own field of activity; men in the forest, women
in the house.
(Friedrich Engels, 1970, p. 567; originally written
in 1884)

Sexual differences, also biological in origin, defined the
kind of work one did in the community and the role of a
parent in rearing the young. Women essentially prepared
and gathered food; men hunted animals and assumed a
protective role for the community as a whole . . . none
of these gender differences . . . initially conferred a
commanding position.
(Murray Bookchin, 1989, p. 52)

Although they are separated by over a century, Engels and Bookchin share the same assumption that there is a 'natural' and egalitarian division of labour between the sexes. In early human societies, there were distinct 'fields of activity' between the sexes that were separate and equal. In fact they were neither. Feminist anthropologists have shown that woman's total responsibility for food preparation was almost matched by her role in food production (Boserup, 1970; Moore, 1988; Waring, 1989). Even today it has been calculated that half of the world's women live and work on farmlands and are responsible for from 40 per cent to 80 per cent of agricultural production, depending on the country and the way in which food is produced.

Women were undoubtedly the workhorses of gatherer-hunter societies and gardener-hunter societies. In the early 1970s among the !Kung bushpeople of the African Kalahari Desert, women's gathering provided two-thirds of food consumed (Lee, 1979, p. 310). This is little changed from the Huron people of seventeenth-century Canada: women's corn production provided 65 per cent of calorific intake, whereas male hunting provided only 5 per cent. According to a seventeenth-century observer, women led a life of constant toil:

> Among these tribes are found powerful women of
> extraordinary stature; for they till the soil, sow the corn,
> fetch the wood for the winter, strip the hemp, and spin
> it, and with the threads make fishing nets . . . they have
> the labour of harvesting the corn, sorting it, preparing it
> and attending to the house and besides are required to
> follow their husbands from place to place, in the fields,
> where they serve as *mules* to carry the baggage . . .
> (quoted in Anderson, 1987, p. 128)

As gathering changed to gardening and gardening changed to agriculture, men gradually took on a greater share of the work. In her survey of 186 anthropological studies, Peggy Sanday found that women worked hardest in societies that relied primarily upon hunting or animal husbandry, and they were also more likely to be solely responsible for childcare. In societies which relied primarily on gardening, fathers were much more involved with their children and work was more evenly shared (Sanday, 1981). There did seem to be some relationship between women's predominance in food production and their economic/political power or authority. Sanday found that women had recognised authority and/or economic power in 67 per cent of foraging societies as against 52 per cent of non-foraging societies.

In his study of the !Kung bushpeople, Richard Lee found that although men spent more time hunting than women did gathering, gathering produced the majority of calories consumed. However, as !Kung women were primarily responsible for child-care, gathering was an arduous task. For two or three days a week a !Kung woman walked anything from two to twelve miles (3–20 km), carrying on her return from 15 to 33 pounds (7–15 kg) of food. In addition she carried her youngest child on her back and her older child (two to four years old) on her shoulder. She may also have been pregnant.

When she returned, the food would have to be processed, although Lee pays very little attention to this task and does not record how many hours it took (Lee, 1979). A recent estimate of the working hours of African women reports that grinding or pounding food takes around one and a half hours and collecting fuel and water anything up to seven hours each day (Harrison, 1987, p. 60). Lee found that even !Kung men's commitment to hunting was patchy. They did not hunt for more than a certain number of days, even if they caught nothing, and 'their work rhythm was, to say the least, erratic' (Lee, 1979, p. 248). Sanday found that native American women sometimes took up hunting because of the failure/incompetence of the men or because they were widowed (Sanday, 1981, p. 125).

Women's experience does not seem to square with the claim that gatherer-hunter communities were the original 'affluent' societies where a substantial material abundance could be gathered in a couple of hours a day (Sahlins, 1974). In view of women's primary role in food production and childcare, what were men doing?

What Did Men Do?

As is now well-known, with very few exceptions, the
spheres of religion and politics have been dominated and
controlled by men.
(Gita Sen and Caren Grown, 1987, p. 27)

My young men shall never work, men who work cannot
dream: and wisdom comes to us in dreams.
(Smohalla, Nez Perce Indian and founder of the
Dreamer religion, quoted in McLuhan, 1971, p. 56)

Women exercised full control over the domestic world:
the home, family hearth, and the preparation of the most
immediate means of life such as skins and food. Often
a woman built her own shelter and tended to her own
garden ... Men, in turn, dealt with what we might call
'civil' affairs ...
(Murray Bookchin, 1989, p. 52)

Bookchin assures us that this division was not hierarchical or
exploitative. It represented a complementary, respectful balance.
He is more concerned about the balance of power than the
balance of work. For Bookchin, the fact that women provided
the majority of the food while men handled 'civil' affairs was
not 'problematic', as domestic matters were the primary focus
of society and there was very little that we would now identify as
'politics'. But it is clear that men had much more time on their
hands and, as Bookchin himself goes on to note, the fledgling
'civil' affairs of an isolated clan can soon turn to war and warrior
associations or more entrenched political institutions. The very
fact that women were responsible for the basic sustenance of
the community creates an imbalance in the social development
of the sexes. Peggy Sanday argues that that imbalance turns on
the essential nature of women's work and male expendability.

In her survey of anthropological studies, Sanday found that

wherever there was a division of labour it tended to follow a general pattern that men did tasks that involved danger or distance: hunting, war-making, trade. Because males are expendable, both as worker and as parent, their absence or death is not essential to group survival. Men's political dominance grew from their very *lack* of centrality to the nurturing and development of society. Men also tended to do tasks that required short-term exertion such as land-clearing, leaving routine tasks to women. In all societies women were responsible for food preparation, and in most for childcare. Overall, men do tasks that are not essential to immediate subsistence; this leaves them with considerable periods of free time for political, ceremonial and ritual activities (Sanday, 1981). Frances Dahlberg argues that although the evidence on gatherer-hunter societies is thin, women do partake in ritual and ceremonial activities more than in pastoral and agricultural societies (Dahlberg, 1981). However, men still predominate, for example, among the !Kung:

> In the political sphere men do more of the talking
> than women, and it is my impression that their
> overall influence in 'public' matters is greater. (Lee,
> 1979, p. 454)

Among the Huron people of Canada, hunting was more important as a ritual than as a source of food. The meat was either eaten by the men themselves during hunting expeditions or presented to the matrilineal family (i.e. the long house of the hunter's mother). The main bulk of Huron food came from women's gardening (wives, sisters and mothers), which was so much women's role that once the land was cleared men did not even stay around for the growing season but took off on trading, war-making or hunting expeditions. Despite this, men were entitled to share in communal food stores and women did all the food preparation. According to a contemporary chronicler, the Huron males passed their time in:

> fishing, hunting and war; going off to trade, making lodges
> and canoes ... The rest of the time they pass in idleness,
> gambling, sleeping, singing, dancing, smoking or going to
> feasts, and they are reluctant to undertake any other work
> that forms part of the women's duty except under strong
> necessity. (quoted in Anderson, 1987, p. 128)

The life of men in the 'age of innocence' seems quite idyllic.
Apart from going to war, the life of the Huron male is very
similar to the ideal of communist society set out by Karl Marx
in *The German Ideology* in which it is possible 'to hunt in the
morning, rear cattle in the evening, criticise after dinner' (Marx
and Engels, 1970, p. 54).

   However, idle men could undermine the harmony of a community; among the Chambri people of the South-West Pacific:

> Men are plunged into perpetual competition with
> other men in which each seeks to achieve worth both
> by demonstrating the extent of his existing power and
> augmenting his power from that of other men. The
> realm of male activity was thus characterized by a
> considerable elaboration of strategy and political form
> as each man attempts to succeed at the expense of the
> others. In contrast, because women are able to achieve
> worth in a more reliable and less competitive fashion,
> their strategies are relatively straightforward and can be
> independently pursued in a less complex social context.
> (Errington and Gewertz, 1987, p. 13)

Giving Men Time

Men in hunter/gatherer societies do not command or
exploit women's labour.
(Rosalind Miles, 1988, p. 16)

At face value, Rosalind Miles's statement is true. Men do not own
the 'means of production', and women were directly responsible

for producing the food for themselves and their children. They could care for themselves and their children with very little input from men. Bookchin argues that women's central role in food production prevented male violence against women (1989, pp. 55–6). Putting it colloquially, they knew which side their bread was buttered, or their roots dug and cooked. Karen Anderson also records that Huron women's control of food resources made them more autonomous. They could deny men access to food if their behaviour was unacceptable, and women's control of food also meant that their marriages were very loose relationships. Divorce was common, and women felt no compulsion to be monogamous or to have large numbers of children (Anderson, 1987).

There is no doubt that women gained autonomy through food production, but there is another side to that coin. Men could not prevent women gaining access to food for themselves and their children, and therefore could not demand women's services in return for food or access to land. However, the division of labour was still exploitative. The imbalance of production meant that women, through their labour, were giving men both *time* and *surplus*. Exploitation is taking from a worker what s/he produces over and above what they need to reproduce themselves. This is exactly what was happening in gatherer-hunter and gardener-hunter societies. Women produced more than they themselves needed to reproduce themselves and their children; the surplus was available for the (relatively) non-producing men to consume. The contradiction for women is that while they obtained their autonomy from their access to the means of subsistence through their work, that same work gave men time and surplus to conduct 'civic affairs'.

If there is one universal 'gift' that women have given men, it is time. In addition to their gardening or gathering work, women had long and arduous domestic duties. Marilyn Waring gives the contemporary example of Tendai, a young girl in Lowveld, Zimbabwe, who starts her day at 4 a.m. by walking twenty-two kilometres to collect water. From 9.00 a.m. until lunch time she collects firewood. She then cleans the breakfast utensils and prepares lunch. All afternoon she collects wild vegetables and then cooks supper. After supper she does another round trip to the borehole to fill a thirty-litre can with water. Childcare and agricultural work are additions to this punishing schedule (Waring, 1989). Compare this with the life of the male and the time he has to spend on ritual, ceremony and 'civic' affairs. Women could, however, use their relative independence and central kin positions to form mutual aid groups and be at least as assertive as men (Tanner, 1974). However, even this independence is being undermined by so-called 'development'.

Women and 'Development'

The penetration of capitalism and the money economy
has led to a marked and devastating erosion of the
productive power of land and the power of women.
(Vandana Shiva, 1989, p. 113)

One of the major impacts of Western intervention on subsistence economies has been a catastrophic effect on women's control of their own subsistence. Although in the South women are still responsible for a good deal of subsistence food production, they are increasingly losing access to land or being pushed into less fertile areas. Where women are directly dependent upon the land for their food, fuel and water, anything that pollutes, degrades, destroys or denies them access to the land takes away their livelihood. In the face of patriarchal colonialism and a male-dominated market economy it is difficult for women to sustain their usufruct rights to communal land (Afshar, 1985, p. xiii). If there was a strong matrilineal system and women held formal title to land, as in Negeri Sembilan in Malaysia, women managed to improve their position slightly (Stivens, 1985), but where formal ownership was not clear or lay with men, they were rapidly dispossessed (Fruzzetti, 1985).

Development projects ignore women's right to land. The Indian government has offered five acres of land to any male displaced by the huge Narmada dam project, even if he previously owned no land; there is no similar provision for women. Women are not affected only when communal land passes into private ownership or is destroyed through 'development'. Common land is also lost or enclosed, and often this increases the burden on women as they have to walk further afield to gather firewood and collect water (Sen and Grown, 1987; Rao, 1989). Women's main responsibility for food production in subsistence economies also meant that when the 'outside world' came to call in the form of missionaries, traders, settlers, colonialists and development workers, men were more readily available to be converted, to look for waged labour or to emigrate to the towns. This was reinforced by the fact that the invaders themselves came from patriarchal cultures. They demanded that men pay the taxes and work on the plantations. Development workers from industrialised patriarchal cultures did not recognise women's central role in agriculture and directed their attention inappropriately to men (Chambers, 1983; Dankelman and Davidson, 1988):

> Male extension workers often carry an ideological image of households with male heads, the man tilling the land and the woman rocking the cradle and keeping the home fires burning. Unable to obtain help in the form of cheap loans and improved seeds, and subsidized fertilisers, sooner or later many women abandon the unequal struggle for survival on the land. (Afshar, 1985, p. xiii)

Paradoxically, loss of land may also reduce women's independent access to the cash economy. Throughout the world many women are petty traders, selling their surplus produce at the local market. Losing land means not only losing an independent source of food, but losing income as well. Women have little choice then but to become agricultural labourers at grossly exploitative rates of pay. Wage rates are set *on the assumption* that women are providing the basic subsistence for themselves and male wage labourers (Afshar, 1985). This is what Maria Mies describes as 'super-exploitation' (1986, p. 48). However, Vandana Shiva argues that the development process has not only destroyed the economic independence of rural women and turned men into labourers or migrant workers, it is threatening the ecological future of the planet.

Seeds of Destruction

The green revolution is in reality a western patriarchal anti-nature model of agriculture which shifts control of food systems from women and peasants to food and agri-business multi-nationals and disrupts natural processes. (Vandana Shiva, 1989, p. 97)

Shiva argues that traditional forms of agriculture based upon principles of sustainability are being destroyed by new developments such as the so-called 'green revolution'. As women were primarily responsible for traditional agriculture, to break the women's relationship with the land not only reduces sustainability, it also destroys all the knowledge that women hold. Such knowledge was reflected in the many words used to record the differing conditions of the soil and trees and the many forms of food preparation and growing, herbal remedies and craft skills. Traditional agriculture rested on a close relationship between forestry, animal husbandry and agriculture. Animal husbandry produced organic fertiliser for the land, while the forests trapped water and produced 'green fodder'. Several different types of grain were planted so that no matter what pests or climatic conditions occurred, some crops would survive. This genetic diversity has been lost as subsistence and small peasant farmers are swept away by cash cropping and the new monoculture of the green revolution.

N. Shanmugaratnam argues (1989) that the green revolution was launched by the North in the 1950s to avoid the possibility of hunger leading to revolutions in the South. New strains of plants were developed that attached heavy-yielding crop strains of wheat and rice to dwarf plants. This maximised food production and minimised wasted energy in growing the stem of the plant. Food production worldwide increased by 50 billion tonnes, but at the expense of being taken out of the hands of Southern peoples, particularly women, and handed over to the predominantly male scientists, agronomists and agribusinesses of the West. Multinational corporations helped to fund the new development because the new seeds demanded high inputs of fertilisers and pesticides. The result of the green revolution has been to pass control of seeds from South to North, thereby robbing the South of its genetic diversity (Shiva, 1989; Mies, 1986). Farmers could no longer be independent; seeds, fertilisers and pesticides all had to be bought in fresh each year – mostly on credit, which only the richer farmers could afford. Land became concentrated in fewer and fewer (male) hands, and women were pushed aside.

As the green revolution plants demanded very high inputs of water, fertiliser and pesticides, the early high yields soon gave way to smaller yields as soils became depleted and pests became resistant to insecticides. Excessive use of water led to land becoming waterlogged or saline (in previously arid soil, water draws up excess salt which rises to the surface and is left there when the water evaporates). The 'once-and-for-all' resource of ground water that had collected over millions of years was also rapidly depleted. Vandana Shiva argues that ecological balance will return only when the natural fertility of the soil is seen as the capital to be accumulated and not as the short-term cash gain that can be obtained by rapidly depleting it through cash cropping. Shiva argues that if the future of the fertility of the planet is to be secured, women must be given back their traditional role as guardians of the soil. Anything that puts a barrier between women and the land acts against the interests of the planet and of women.

The weakness of women's historical relationship to land lies in male domination of the political, ceremonial and ritual aspects of clan societies. Why was the political role of women so weak? Did they not have power as mothers, particularly in matrilineal societies?

Mother Power?

Women certainly have rights in kinship systems, but systems of marriage, residence, descent and inheritance are rarely organized in such a way as to guarantee women's access to resources and/or to allow them to secure access for other women. It has long been argued that matrilineal systems are no different in this respect from patrilineal ones. If patriliny creates ties between the 'father' and his wife's sons, then matriliny creates ties between the mother's brother and the sister's sons. (Henrietta Moore, 1988, p. 60)

'Mothers bring Warriors to heel' claimed a newspaper headline as clan mothers avoided bloodshed during a protest by Mohawk Indian men and boys by threatening to 'kick your asses' (*Guardian*, 3 September 1990). Another contemporary example of the continuing importance of women in matrilineal societies is Palau (Belau) in Micronesia. Mothers are powerful figures in Palau, and men must listen to their point of view. In 1979 this tiny island declared itself a nuclear-free zone. To overturn this declaration, a 75 per cent majority would be required in a referendum. At present Palau is under United Nations trusteeship, but the United States has put it under sustained pressure to form a Compact of Free Association.

This Compact is a euphemism for neo-colonialism. Under its provisions the USA would provide half a billion dollars' worth of aid and gain in return access to one-third of the island for military bases, airfields, weapons storage and jungle training. It would be free to commandeer any other part of the island at sixty days' notice, and has long-term plans for a deep-water Trident base if the US bases are expelled from the Philippines. Despite overwhelming US pressure, the resistance and political strength of women led the people of Palau to refuse to accept the Compact in repeated referenda.

There is a sting in the tail, however. Despite the fact that Palau is a matrilineal society, the women's wishes have to be passed in the last instance through discussions in men's houses, from which women are excluded. Women are also heavily involved in food production and have little time to organise their protests. In the mid 1980s a Palauan woman reported to a peace meeting in Britain how women travelled by boat at night to different scattered communities, galvanising resistance. Men were the Achilles heel of their struggle, as they were very vulnerable to American bribes and particularly to the penetration of the Coca-Cola economy. At that time this Palauan woman was uncertain how much longer the women could hold the men in line.

Powerful women 'behind the scenes', with formal power in the hands of men, is a common feature of matrilineal societies. The matrilineal Iroquois, for example, have never had a female political office-holder, although women wielded substantial kinship and economic power, especially when men were absent for long periods engaged in war, hunting and interclan diplomacy (Sanday, 1981, p. 117). The Iroquois were a confederacy of five native American nations with a strong emphasis on female symbolism of Earth, fertility and bounty of nature. They lived in woman-headed family long houses, and much of their economic and ceremonial life centred on the agricultural activities of women. Women owned the land and soil and had the right to nominate the Chiefs, who ruled only by the consent of leading Iroquois women who could veto war-making. However, the social and economic power of Iroquois women was rapidly undermined by nineteenth-century Christian missionaries who convinced the men of the importance of the patriarchal nuclear family. Women were denied the right to own land, or even to tend their own plots. Those who insisted on their traditional rights were accused of witchcraft and occasionally executed (Sanday, 1981, p. 142). In this, the experience of the Iroquois women was not unlike the persecution of the witches in Europe.

Although Karen Anderson describes the Huron people as 'astonishingly egalitarian', with a kinship and political structure that provided a 'formidable obstacle to women's subordination' (p. 136):

> It was men who were clan leaders; men sat on councils, made decisions, were charged with realising them. It was men too who had direct relations with foreigners, who traded, went to war, and forged political, military and economic alliances with other nations. (Anderson, 1987, p. 131)

Peggy Sanday also found no evidence of any societies where women clearly predominated in the sense of political power (controlling decision-making outside the household), economic power (controlling economic resources outside the household), or authority (right to make a particular decision and command obedience). However, women were relatively more powerful where there were female creation myths and female religious symbols:

> Females *achieve* economic and political power or authority when environmental or historical circumstances grant them economic autonomy and make men dependent on female activities. Female economic and political power or authority is *ascribed* as a natural right due the female sex when a long-standing magico-religious association between maternity and fertility of

> the soil associates women with social continuity and the
> social good. (Sanday, 1981, p. 114)

Equally, the power of men rested upon magico-religious symbols
that created institutions of male power that are still with us.

The Brotherhood

> Male dominance and female power are consequences
> of the way in which peoples come to terms with
> their historical and natural environments and develop
> their separate identities ... Power is accorded to
> whichever sex is thought to embody or to be in touch
> with the forces upon which people depend for their
> perceived needs.
> (Sanday, 1981, p. 11)

Male domination of the public world in clan society is achieved
by two institutions that are still with us today: the men's house
and the warrior band. The men's house of the matrilineal Palau
is little different from the public school, the gentlemen's club,
the Masonic lodge or even the rugby club locker room. It is
a place where men gather together to initiate new members,
rehearse their rituals, allocate public positions and declare their
brotherhood against other men's houses and all women. The
warrior band is only a smaller version of the modern military. It
too has its initiation ceremonies and its rituals, its brotherhood
and its misogyny. Joan Smith records the way in which images
of humiliated women and war are intertwined in the songs
of USAF fighter pilots. A pamphlet published by a group of
pilots at Upper Heyford camp records their 'favourite things'
in predictable barrack-room humour:

> Reading our porno and picking our asses
> Checking our forms out and passing our gasses
> Silver sleek B-61's slung below

Nuclear war and we're ready to go.
(quoted in Smith, 1989, p. 100)

These guardians of the Western world sing of a woman whose 'tits were all a floppin', her cunt ate out with clap', and of fucking 'a dead whore by the roadside' whose 'skin was all gone from her tummy, The hair was all gone from her head' (ibid., p. 103).

The humiliation of women to establish the power of men is equally important in clan societies. In fact, Joan Bamberger argues (1974) that this might be responsible for the 'myth' of the existence of matriarchal societies. Far from recording a historically existing situation, it is a justification for male rule. Male brotherhood is built upon a 'tale' of powerful women who have been defeated and/or humiliated. Another common theme with the men of Upper Heyford is that the women deserved it. Bamberger argues that all myths of matriarchy are accompanied by a fall or a push in which women are removed from power. The classic mythological attack upon women is the story of Adam and Eve, where a vengeful male God lays responsibility for all the sorrows of the human race on the shoulders of the woman Eve and puts her under the control of Adam. Bamberger finds similar examples of stories that justify male power and proclaim women's fallibility from her study of South American Indians of the Amazon basin in early 1960s. Typical is the Yamana origin myth.

Among the Yamana-Yaghan people, the Kina is a ceremony that focuses on the men's hut (also called a Kina). The Yamana myth claims that the Kina was once women-only. Women played all the major roles in society; they sat in the bow of the canoe and gave the orders. All the work was done by men, including childcare. The women then tried to fool the men into thinking they were spirits and came out of the Kina hut wearing masks and with painted bodies. The men were terrified of them and hid in the huts doing their work. One day the Sun-man who hunted game for the women happened to see women washing off the paint in a lagoon. He forced their secrets out of them. The men, realising that they had been fooled, defeated the women in a fierce battle and took over the Kina and its secrets. The women then had to take the men's place and do all the work.

The myth of the Selk'nam-Ona Hain is even more misogynist. Women are accused of originally ruling over men by witchcraft until men killed them all. To prevent the women re-establishing themselves, the men themselves called upon demons, and in masked ceremonies impersonate those demons and show the men's power to keep the women in place. Similar myths occur in various parts of the world (MacCormack and Strathern, 1980; Gewertz, 1988).

A common theme between these early myths and ceremonies and present-day men's organisations such as the Freemasons is the emphasis on keeping secrets and hiding secret regalia. Bamberger found that the penalties inflicted upon women who 'discovered' the secrets were by no means mythical, and women throughout the Amazon area were punished by gang rape for viewing sacred male paraphernalia. Keeping male secrets justifies women's subordination, as women are deemed either incapable of keeping secrets or dangerous to men if they discover them. Women were portrayed in the myths as morally lax or likely to abuse power if they could obtain it. They were seen as unclean, likely to undermine men's fertility or success in their activities such as hunting or fishing. Often this is expressed by a male fear of women's sexuality, or of menstruation or birth.

Many feminist anthropologists see this male fear of women's bodies and sexuality as deep-seated fear of women's power as mothers (Gillison, 1980). Particularly important is the image of blood and menstruation, which is often mimicked in male rituals (Lidz and Lidz, 1977; Gillison, 1980). This theme travels through history to the pilots of Upper Heyford USAF, who sing of 'a bloody Kotex in my toilet bowl' and 'syphilitic scabs' (Smith, 1989, p. 104). Unlike today, the taboos about women's bodies often made men reticent about intercourse. Marie Reay reports that the Kuma men of Papua New Guinea concentrated their sexual energies on periodic impregnation to achieve pregnancy, and the women complained that they were otherwise sexually deprived (1988, p. 132).

Bamberger interprets male attitudes towards women as reflecting their need to establish reasons why women should not rule, given their obvious biological right through the ability to produce children, and I would add their massive economic contribution to the survival of the community. To charge women with being unclean and unworthy ('can't keep secrets', 'always gossiping') justifies their exclusion from public office. The myths and stories are culturally controlled by male imagery and male determination of women's role in society, and reflect a male domination of what passes for 'public life' in the community. Bamberger concludes pessimistically:

> Whatever the justification for it, the sacred male order
> laid down in myth and reenacted in ritual continues
> unchallenged in many societies throughout the world.
> One may surmise from this state of affairs that the
> Rule of Men proceeds unchanged because women, its
> potential challengers, have been trapped for so long in
> a closed system that they are unable to perceive how
> otherwise they might break down the successful methods
> used to inculcate them in an ideology of moral failure.
> (Bamberger, 1974, pp. 279–80)

Bamberger's work has stirred up a good deal of controversy since it was first published nearly twenty years ago. In 1984 a symposium was held in Australia to consider it in relation to the societies of the South-West Pacific (Gewertz, 1988). Once again, study after study talks of initiation ceremonies, male cults, rituals, male houses, male myth-tellers. In the Papua New Guinea Highlands, male cults based on ceremonies and secrets were used to build a community of warriors and to help individuals gain personal and clan prestige and political and economic power (Hays, 1988, p. 115). Hays argues that the rituals and secrets also met the psychic and social needs of men in response to the natural (rather than the social) power of women. Women's role in child-rearing and nurturing was the source of many male anxieties – women already had a virtual monopoly on all matters relating to fertility and growth; they fed and reared both boys and pigs (both socially important to men): 'if it were not for men's control of the flutes and associated rites, would they have been excluded completely from these vital spheres?' (ibid., p. 105).

The cults surrounding sacred flutes and other associated secrets, ceremonies and seclusions are 'nothing more than the fears of insecure men' (Hays, 1988, p. 106). Is the same true of Masonic ceremonies, the sanctity of the gentlemen's club or the camaraderie of the barrack or locker room? Hays did get the men of Kuman Chimbu to admit that the veil of secrecy is to hide the rather prosaic nature of men's activities from women: 'they would laugh at us and we men would lose all authority over them; they would no longer cook food for us or rear our pigs' (ibid., p. 106). The Chambri women of Papua New Guinea were well aware of the secrets men were so carefully imparting to each other, but did not undermine the rituals as they considered them a 'harmless' indulgence (Errington and Gewertz, 1987). Are rolled-up trouser legs equally silly? Initiation into institutions such as public schools and military establishments is often built on routine humiliation. Is it possible that men then and now used humiliation to make sure *men* kept the secrets and didn't break with the brotherhood in favour of their relationships with women?

On this evidence, male power is built on a mixture of exclusiveness, secrecy, solidarity and humiliation. Is it the same secrecy and solidarity that produces old boy networks and insider trading? Is it the same exclusiveness that stops women from becoming priests, using the same arguments about women as unworthy (unclean) vessels? While greens may argue that modern industrial society has made us lose touch with a socially and sexually egalitarian past, and socialists may argue that modern society offers us the chance to get control of the industrial cornucopia, for women there is no 'break' in history. Male power and male contrivance, and the *dangers* of male power, still exist. Even the origin of the medieval guilds, much praised by anarchists such as Kropotkin, have been traced back to 'fraternities of young warriors practising the cult of heroes' (quoted in Black, 1984, p. 3). Interestingly, Black does point out that women became involved when the guilds were based on a whole community rather than a trade (ibid., p. 6). This may mean that communal organisations are inherently less divisive. More pessimistically, it might be because 'their activities focused upon the communal feast', with women playing a supportive 'domestic' role.

It would seem that for women there was no age of matriarchy, nor even an age of innocence. However, we have one more continuity between clan societies and today: violence against women.

Violence

The threat of sexual violence to restrict women's physical mobility and to punish women who flouted social norms was practiced in most societies. Rape and other forms of sexual abuse are not individual acts; they have often received social sanction.
(Gita Sen and Caren Grown, 1987, p. 27)

If there is a basic difference between the sexes other than differences associated with human reproductivity, it is that women as a group have not willingly faced death in violent conflict. This fact, perhaps more than any other, explains why men have sometimes become the dominating sex.
(Peggy Sanday, 1981, pp. 210–11)

Clan societies may have had a harmonious relationship with nature, but this did not necessarily apply to each other or to women. In some cases war-making and violence towards women were directly connected. The Shavante men of lowland South America:

> display a we/they mentality in which all human beings who are not part of the initiated men's club are enemies. While waiting for the imagined attack, they sharpen their teeth upon women . . . Hunting and warfare are activities that interest the Shavante male above all else. Boys are trained in men's houses in the virtues of co-operation, manliness and bellicosity. The Shavante have ceremonies of aggression in which initiated men ritually attack uninitiated boys. In the most important ceremony of all, women are ritually raped in a demonstration of the twin powers of sexuality and aggression. (Sanday, 1981, p. 155)

Bookchin's claim that men were not violent towards women in clan society is not confirmed by the facts. Clan societies were suffused by a male fear of women's power, their sexuality and their mystery. Sex was seen as a powerful force that could sap a man's strength and bring him bad luck in the hunt. Failure in the hunt could lead to sexual violence, particularly where men practised sexual abstention to improve their hunting prowess. Often the consequent sexual tension resulted in gang rape (Sanday, 1981, p. 144). Matriliny was no guarantee against male violence, even among the nature-loving native Americans, particularly where an emphasis on warfare led to the formation of military societies that increased male power. Sanday found evidence that military societies used gang rape to create a bond of male solidarity. The military society was also used to discipline women. The Cheyenne husband of a 'strong willed, flagrantly adulterous woman' had the right to invite all the unmarried men of his military society to rape his wife. One woman was raped by more than forty men (Sanday, 1981, p. 151). Among

the Northern Saulteaux of Canada, a woman risked gang rape
if she rejected a man.

Olivia Harris found that the men of the Laymi Indians of
the Central Bolivian Highlands controlled their wives through
male ownership of land and physical violence (Harris, 1980).
The Laymi were a peasant community, but even among the
forest-dwelling Kaulong of Papua New Guinea, women's destiny
was violently linked to that of men. Men controlled more
resources than women, and on a man's death his wife was
strangled and buried with him until colonisation made this
illegal (Goodale, 1980).

There are a number of similar reports from Papua New
Guinea. Gardner records that he found it hard not to be
shocked by many aspects of the husband–wife relationships
among the Mianmin people. He collected a number of accounts
of women being killed and had witnessed wives being beaten by
their husbands (Gardner, 1988). From the age of six or seven,
women worked in the gardens providing food for their male kin
(fathers, brothers, husbands). Women who did not work hard
enough to provide for their husbands' needs were beaten and
sometimes killed (ibid., p. 155). Marie Reay reports similar
findings for the Kuma people: 'this is a society which men rule
by physical force and the threat of it' (Reay, 1988, p. 129). Even
if a man is physically weaker than his wife, he can call upon his
clansmen to 'come to help him injure her badly' (ibid., p. 129).
She records that until the 1950s a brother could trade his sister
for a wife, regardless of her wishes. By the 1980s young men
were offering their sisters for gang rape in exchange for beer or
petrol (ibid., p. 125).

These examples do not imply that *every* clan society is violent
and warmongering, but they are sufficiently numerous to dismiss
any ideas that such societies represent a sylvan age of harmony
and peace. Nor, of course, do they mean that only men were
violent or warlike. Peggy Sanday argues that men's lack of an
essential nurturing role 'freed' them to risk death in war, and if

women did fight, they first abandoned their mothering role. For example, when ten thousand Igbo women declared war against colonial taxation policy in Southern Nigeria, one Igbo woman recalled that they were:

> different from any other crowd of women I have ever seen ... There were no children with them. As they had no children with them that also made me afraid ... I was very much afraid of them and did not look at their faces. (Sanday, 1981, p. 139)

Women have also been complicit in violent acts of control against women, in particular clitoridectomy and infibulation. Clitoridectomy is the removal of all or part of the clitoris and labia; infibulation is the sewing up of the vaginal area to prevent intercourse. The practice is fraught with danger from infection, and women often suffer long-term pain and discomfort. It has been estimated that eighty million women have suffered some sort of genital mutilation. Opposition to the control of women's sexuality through genital mutilation, particularly from women in the North, is made more difficult because it is in the hands of women defending the cultures of the South (Thiam, 1986). At the same time, women cannot ignore violence against women in other cultures. In reading anthropological literature I have regularly been surprised by the way even women writers record appallingly violent acts against women without even a word of comment or concern. It is hardly surprising, therefore, if green writers who eulogise clan societies are not aware that many are far from sexually benign.

Some Things Never Change

I cannot rise from the haggard load of childbearing
I cannot free myself from the clutches of poverty firmly grasped
In the skeletal touch of my malnourished children.

I cannot escape
The inescapable trappings
Of my husband's desires
Born out of ignorance
And senseless dominance.
I cannot understand
why I cannot. . . .
(Noumea Simi, Western Samoa, quoted in Asian and Pacific
Women's Resource Collection Network, 1989, p. 100)

At a meeting of the Women's League of the African National
Congress in 1991, one of the women declared: 'it's a combination
of apartheid legacies and tribal traditions that we have to fight
to overcome here' (*Guardian*, 30 April 1991). While it would
be wrong to assume that women's experiences in clan societies
were all as gloomy as those I have recorded here, there is enough
evidence to show that male domination of women is one of the
oldest forms of oppression and exploitation in human history
(Coontz and Henderson, 1986).

Unless green and socialist thinking begins to understand at
a deep and fundamental level how corrosive patriarchal power
is, there is little hope of any progress to a sustainable and
egalitarian future. It is all the more important to understand
the role of patriarchy now, because it is meshing with capitalism
across the globe to destroy the lives of women and the viability
of the natural world.

CHAPTER 5

The Profits of Doom:
Nimble Fingers and Burning Forests

When the economies of the world, based on the
masculinist paradigm of wealth, start to crash, women
and children will be first – not the first to be saved, but
the first to fall into the abyss that is poverty. The modern
creation myth that male western minds propagate
is based on the sacrifice of nature, women and the
Third World.
(Vandana Shiva, 1989, p. 221)

The global industrialisation process not only devours
and destroys its own preconditions, but also the natural
foundations of human life, of the very biosphere that
sustains us. The completion of this process on a world
scale would be the ultimate natural catastrophe. It cannot
be continued for a further 200 years and it must be
braked and stopped much earlier.
(Rudolf Bahro, 1986, p. 12)

For more than two hundred years the 'masculinist paradigm of
wealth' has been based on industrial production, first developed
within a capitalist economic framework and then mimicked by
state-sponsored industrialism. The economic power of each
system was tested in a ten-year arms race between 1979 and
1989, which the West conclusively won. Private accumulation
of wealth and the unfettered operation of the 'free' market' in
both labour and goods constitute a system to which, we are told,
'there is no alternative'. Both capitalism and industrialism are

male-dominated and have exploited and marginalised women and the South.

The green movement has been ambivalent about the relationship between industrialism and capitalism. While industrialism is roundly condemned, capitalism is less often specifically identified as the motor of environmental destruction. The Programme of the German Green Party refers to both 'destructive economic growth' and 'limitless industrial growth'. In the 1970s and early 1980s greens often criticised industrial growth by reference to Gross National Product (GNP). Later it was argued that this did not necessarily represent industrial growth, as it was a measure of the money value of all activity within an economy, industrial and non-industrial, from wholefood shops to the manufacture of nuclear submarines. Although there were good arguments for making this distinction, it had the effect of separating criticism of industrialism as a process from criticism of the capitalist market system and the way it defined and measured human activities. Some ecologists have even claimed that capitalism could 'go green' (Elkington and Burke, 1987) – an assertion I will examine later.

The industrial system that the greens attacked was 'Fordist' production. In 1908 Henry Ford produced the first 'motorcar for the great multitude' at his new River Rouge plant in Detroit. Into one end of his great factory went workers and raw materials, and out of the other came Model 'T' Ford cars. This was the beginning of a sixty-year explosion of mass production and mass consumption. Working-class people started the period as underprivileged and poorly paid factory workers and servants to the rich, and ended it as mass consumers. In the green attack upon Fordist industrialism, the specific role of capitalism became just one of many aspects of modern society that needed to be grappled with (Schumacher, 1973; Herman Daly, 1973; Ophuls, 1977). Modern industrial society was seen as centralised, obsessed with growth and based on an anti-nature scientific and technical rationality.

Greens could hardly be blamed for seeing industrialism as the main enemy of the environment when the environmental catastrophe of state-owned industrialism in Eastern Europe became clear. In Poland it has been calculated that pollution has reduced average life expectancy by ten years, in Hungary 44 per cent of the air is polluted by traffic fumes, and the total cost of cleaning up Eastern Europe has been calculated at $200 billion (BBC 'Woman's Hour', 26 November 1990). In 1990 what was formerly East Germany emitted three times more sulphur dioxide than any other European country, and industrial diseases are rampant (*Green Line*, no. 77, 1990). The USSR has equal horror stories to tell including Chernobyl, the death of the Aral Sea and the release of poisonous gas from a nuclear plant at Kazakhstan. A revulsion of the population of Eastern Europe at the environmental squalor in which they were forced to live was one of the triggers of political change. It seemed as if the green movement would have a lot of new allies. Unfortunately, the newly emerging green movements quickly got swallowed up in the surge towards market systems and economic 'growth'. Eastern Europe, like the countries of the South, has been seduced by the Trojan Horse of capitalism, development.

North and South: Exporting Inequality

The perspective of poor and oppressed women provides a unique and powerful vantage point from which we can examine the effects of development programmes and strategies.
(Gita Sen and Caren Grown, 1987, p. 23)

For the past two decades the main development strategy for the South has been its incorporation into the world capitalist market economy through export-led growth. South countries have been urged to link themselves to the world market by selling their labour, manufactured goods or primary products from fishing, farming, mining and logging. In so doing the South has found the 'free' market economy a very difficult club to join. Under the General Agreement on Tariffs and Trade (GATT), international trade is to be conducted in an open and unrestricted way. However, when low-wage economies of the South try to export their goods to the richer countries of the North they are met with 'non-tariff' restrictions such as the Multi-Fibre Arrangement on textiles. At the same time the North uses the South as a place to dump unwanted production, particularly of food. This may seem like a good idea, but it undermines local production and self-sufficiency. If local producers in the South are to compete with dumped food, they have to try to match the industrialised agriculture of the North, further increasing the pressure on the local ecosystem. The industrial countries of the North have been able to use their accumulated wealth to draw in raw materials and labour from the poorer countries of the South, while the latter have not been able to jump on to an economic bandwagon that has already rolled out of their sight.

For most countries of the South, the promise of 'development' along the yellow brick road to Western-style capitalism proved to be a chimera. Apart from the relative success of the 'four tigers' of South-East Asia, Singapore, Hong Kong, Taiwan and South Korea, submission to world markets has been a disaster for the South. Gross inequalities have continued unabated and been made worse by massive debt. This burden has fallen particularly heavily on women. The United Nations declared 1975–85 a Decade for the Advancement of Women, but Sen and Grown found that this decade produced a worsening of the situation for women in the South. While the burden of their work increased there was a decline in their relative access to economic resources, educational status and relative and absolute health (1987, p. 16). Although there have been some general improvements in literacy, life expectancy and childhood survival in the past thirty years, the situation for the poor across the globe has worsened, and women predominate among the poor.

Over the years several attempts have been made to get the North to engage in multilateral action to help the South 'develop'. In the early 1980s a United Nations Commission chaired by Willy Brandt of former West Germany argued that the South could be 'brought up' to the level of the North by a transfer of resources in aid and investment. This proved a false dream, and instead the South has been asked to hand over its resources to private (often foreign) ownership and restrain the needs of its own people on the promise that some day they will share in the process of 'development'.

Development, industrial or otherwise, is inseparable from the capitalism economic system. The worldwide capitalist market has emerged in an already grossly unequal world divided by sex, race and colonial expansion. Profits can be maximised by exploiting those inequalities. Capital has gone where people and resources are cheap, and the cheapest and most vulnerable human resource is women, particularly in the South. The cheapest and most available natural resources are those held by women. Capital is seeking out both. Industrialism, capitalism, colonialism, racism and patriarchy are the different manifestations of a many-headed Hydra that has its fingers around the throat of women, poor people and the planet.

Gambling on the World

Today wealth comes from *unproductive* and fictitious commodity exchange. It is based not on exchange of industrial commodities but on servicing a paper and electronic money system . . .
  Entire countries, ecosystems and communities are vulnerable to instant collapse in this game of speculation which bids on them and their produce and then abandons them as waste – wastelands, wasted people.
(Vandana Shiva, 1989, p. 221)

The capitalist system rests not on the intrinsic worth of any resource or human activity but on its money value as determined by 'the market'. Capitalism is a spider's web which has at its centre a huge financial system. This has been one of the biggest growth areas in the North, as the 'free enterprise' system has run rampant across the globe. With the greatest of ironies, the world financial system has been grossly inflated by the huge influx of petrodollars from the oil price hike in the early 1970s. It is this money, passed on in loans to the South, that has given rise to the colossal debt crisis.

Financial speculation has become an increasingly important means of economic 'growth': share-dealing and company takeover; currency and interest rate speculation; trading in commodities and insurance; industrial contraction and asset-stripping of land, machinery, property and cash. In Britain today around 2.8 million people work in banking and insurance alone which, together with business services, account for nearly 20 per cent of GNP. The growth and influence of the financial sector has become so dominant that it is common to hear reference to 'the real economy' to remind us that excited young men (and a few women) in shirtsleeves, wheeling and dealing, do not represent the reality of most people's lives.

In immediate ecological terms a casino economy may seem harmless, like a giant amusement arcade for those who are willing to play for high stakes. But financial speculation has very real social and ecological consequences (Nicholas Costello *et al.*, 1989). Lying behind the deals are the resources of the planet and the livelihoods of people across the world. Most countries of the South are dependent on the export of primary products from mining, forestry, agriculture and fishing, and are very vulnerable to a drop in price or fluctuation in exchange or interest rates. One obvious example is speculation on worldwide agricultural production in the so-called 'futures' market, where crops are bought in advance and traded on to other speculators. This brings little benefit to the grower, as only 5 per cent of futures transactions relate to the actual delivery of produce; the other 95 per cent represent swapping of futures among speculators

(Shiva, 1989). Treating a precious resource like food purely as a commodity can have catastrophic consequences. Gita Sen and Caren Grown argue that during the severe Indian drought of 1972–3 as many as a million people may have died because the Indian government could not compete with China and the USSR for American grain. Worse, international grain merchants had opposed the setting up of a global reserve of grain to meet such a contingency, as this would make the market less volatile and reduce the opportunity for speculative profits (Sen and Grown, 1987, p. 53).

Local food supplies have also been seriously undermined through much of the South by the widespread conversion of the most fertile land to 'cash cropping' – i.e. crops that can be sold to earn foreign exchange such as tea, coffee, cotton, soya, tobacco, flowers or fruit. In 1985 the Earth Resources Institute reported that although the five hundred million-plus people in Africa had been self-sufficient in food in 1970, by 1984 a hundred and forty million had to be fed with grain from abroad. Submission to the global market was so great that it was even seriously suggested at one point that India should stop producing food and rely on imports from the United States (Shiva, 1989). Conversion to cash cropping was encouraged by the old colonial powers – often with substantial initial cash incentives, such as in the notorious groundnut schemes launched by the British and the French in Africa (Shanmugaratnam, 1989).

Cash cropping is detrimental to both local people and the environment. Land becomes a commercial asset rather than a community resource and traditional subsistence farmers, many of whom are women, are driven off it, while the new owners are either richer members of the indigenous community (usually men) or colonists. Unlike in the North, privatisation and the enclosure of common land are rarely accompanied by alternative employment in new industries. As a result, the highly productive and commercially successful cash crops carry the hidden costs of poverty in the cities and the erosion of marginal land by those who have been displaced from more fertile areas. In the absence of an alternative source of income, poor people have no choice but to find alternative land on which to grow enough food to survive. The only available land tends to be in marginal areas where soil fertility was low, such as hillsides or areas of low rainfall, which are also very vulnerable to erosion. Meanwhile, the better land is equally threatened by the agribusiness methods of manufacture based on monoculture, high levels of water consumption and huge imputs of fertilisers and pesticides (Shanmugaratnam, 1989).

Ownership and control of land has become a key battleground in many parts of the South as capitalist penetration increases and indigenous peoples are struggling to retain or regain control of their traditional land, from the Chipko women of the Himalayas to the forest peoples of the Amazon basin. Their livelihoods are threatened by the 'quick buck' of the market economy and international capital:

> Instead of a sustainable reproduction of wealth, the
> global economic system, led by commercial capitalism,
> has started to focus on instant wealth creation through
> speculation at the cost of the future – and the poor.
> (Shiva, 1989, p. 220)

The capitalist world market exists not to meet the needs of the world's peoples but to maximise profits (Frankel, 1987). The speculative force of international capitalism is huge: around $500 billion in 'hot money' sloshes round the world every twenty-four hours, playing havoc with currencies, commodity and share prices. World banking systems 'vacuum' out local savings that could be used for local investment (Henderson, 1990). Hazel Henderson argues that this has led to a 'plantation' mentality whereby countries compete for the attention of the eight hundred or so multinational companies that handle the bulk of world trade, offering them tax-havens, unregulated free trade zones, and cheap labour. It is a casino economy in which the wheel has been fixed and the cards marked, where poor people, women and the environment pick up the tab.

Nimble Fingers: Women and the Global Market

We hire mostly women because they are more reliable than men, they have finer fingers, smaller muscles and unsurpassed manual dexterity. Also, women don't get tired of repeating the same operations nine hundred times a day.
(Personnel manager of a Mexican 'free trade' factory, quoted in Mitter, 1986, p. 48)

Women remain the most poorly paid, badly organised, and vulnerable group of industrial workers in the Third World and elsewhere, and the record of the trades unions in this regard continues to be a sorry one.
(Gita Sen and Caren Grown, 1987, p. 36)

The decline in industrial production in many of the older industrialised countries over the past twenty years has not meant that it has declined worldwide. Industrial production is now scattered across the globe in free trade zones and the newly industrialising countries such as Korea and Brazil (Sen and Grown, 1987; Mitter 1986; Mies, 1986; Elson and Pearson, 1984). Multinational companies have been helped in their search for easy profits by the export-led development policies of many Southern governments, encouraged by the World Bank and the International Monetary Fund. Companies have been offered tax-free, union-free and regulation-free havens where pollution controls (if any) are minimal. There is now a world market for both labour and goods, where wages are determined by the standard of living in poorer countries while the price of goods is related to the standard of living in wealthier countries.

Cheap-labour countries are being effectively used as outworkers, a system that existed long before industrial capitalism. Components or ready-cut material are taken to factories in the South to be made up, and the finished product is returned to the country of origin for sale. This exploits not only people but the resources of the planet, as millions of gallons of fuel are wasted transporting goods around the world.

One of the features of the 'new international division of labour' is the large number of women who are employed (Frobel *et al.*, 1980). These are mainly young women between the ages of fourteen and twenty-five, concentrated in the textile and electronics industries where their 'nimble fingers' and docile behaviour are prized. Both represent aspects of patriarchy (Mitter, 1986; Mies, 1986; Elson and Pearson, 1984). Women are claimed to have 'nimble' fingers because of their domestic work in sewing and weaving, which makes them suitable for repetitive assembly work, although this does not appear to qualify them automatically for equally dexterous male-dominated jobs, from technical drawing to brain surgery. In a patriarchal culture that prizes female submission, women's docility represents their fear of physical, sexual and social repression at the hands of men. Fear of their fathers and of losing their 'respectability' in the eyes of a future husband deters women from engaging in industrial action. Husbands are equally repressive:

> I wanted to go for a [union] course. It was a leadership course and was to last for three days. [My husband] told me point-blank that if I went for the course, I could consider our marriage finished . . . I didn't go to the course and I haven't tried again . . . (in Ariffin and Lochhead, 1988, p. 71)

Women's docility in the workplace is enhanced by their lack of industrial experience and the fact that labour turnover is high through marriage and because the very detailed work, particularly in the electronics industry, ruins their health. In 1990 the Traidcraft organisation reported that Bangladeshi garment workers, 80 per cent of whom were women, were forced to work up to sixteen hours a day with no rights to join a trades union. The Asian and Pacific Women's Resource Collection Network reports a Bangladeshi factory that had only one toilet for two hundred women (1989, p. 107). Women working in the Free Trade Zone of Sri Lanka put out the following plea:

> We are being made to work both day and night, like
> buffaloes tethered to trees. Not a single moment of
> the day is there for rest, both the machines and the
> workers . . . the supervisory staff and the management
> are never satisfied, however much work we produce.
> Please focus your attention on the sufferings of the poor
> female workers who are being subject to harassment and
> harshness by supervisors and the management. (quoted
> in Mitter, 1986, p. 51)

Women also suffer chronic health problems through their employment. Textile work can lead to lung disease, exposure to toxic chemicals, hearing loss from high noise levels and physical injury from high-speed machinery. Electronics work can lead to eye injuries. The Asian and Pacific Network reports that 95 per cent of workers in one American-owned firm in Korea had eye problems after one year, as did up to half the workers in similar firms in Malaysia, the Philippines and Hong Kong (ibid., p. 108). Swasti Mitter reports that in the Philippine export-processing zones the working 'life' of a woman worker is about four years. Women are sometimes asked to work for forty-eight hours at a stretch and are fed stimulants to keep them awake. Some companies offer incentives for women to be sterilised. There are no worker benefits such as sick pay, maternity benefits or paid holidays, which form a substantial part of the labour costs in the older industrialised nations, and trades unions are repressed (1986, p. 55). This does not mean that women workers in the South are not trying to fight back.

Waking up to Women Workers

Once I started work, it was obvious that we were under a
lot of pressure from the bosses. We had to meet targets,
had to work through our rest time . . . When I asked a
friend if anything was being done about it, she told me
about the union . . .
(in Ariffin and Lochhead, 1988, p. 61)

I tell you, being active in the union is no joke. I have
lost count of the number of times I have been switched
around in my department . . . always given the lousy
jobs . . .
(ibid., p. 66)

It is really difficult to talk to the union officials. Meet
them in the coffee shop and they'll make jokes. Meet
them in the office and they're not interested . . .
(ibid., p. 75)

These statements by women workers in Malaysia illustrate the
problems they face as women and as workers. Such highly
exploitable and exploited workforces have received little sympathy from workers in the older industrial economies. The
old, strongly unionised male labour force has been very slow
to respond to changing structure of the labour market. New
technologies have replaced much of the older, heavier labour
associated with a male workforce, and computerisation has
allowed firms to be run more flexibly, holding fewer stocks.
In the North the huge industrial plants and large profit margins
in expanding markets that proved such a very fertile ground for
industrial struggle are disappearing. Firms no longer have large
amounts of capital tied up in huge stocks of finished goods, raw
materials and components. Workforces are increasingly being
divided between 'core workers', who are predominantly male,
and women, ethnic minorities and displaced male workers who

are pushed into peripheral, casual, part-time work (Wheelock, 1990; Jenson *et al.*, 1988).

Trades unions are slowly beginning to acknowledge the problem of marginalised Black and women workers, but industrial struggle is still riddled with sexism, racism, ethnicity and nationalism which can easily be used by capitalism to fracture solidarity. The worldwide manipulation of labour by capitalism makes it difficult for workers to unite against poor wages and conditions as they are divided by race, nationality, gender, religion and ethnicity as well as physical distance. If workers are to regain any of their collective strength, women are going to have to be recognised as the backbone of the new proletariat. Socialists are barely beginning to acknowledge that if an alienated and exploited working class is going to overthrow capitalism, it is as likely to be composed of young women in South-East Asia or Black women hospital cleaners in Europe as white, European males in heavy industry.

In 1988 more than half the members of the Electrical Industry Workers' Union in Malaysia were women. In India 40,000 women home-workers, some of the most exploited workers in the world, have formed a union. In Mexico 5,000 people, mainly women, formed a Union of Garment Workers. Organisations of women workers are springing up across the globe, and many are building links between North and South (Mitter, 1986; Sen and Grown, 1987). Unlike the workers of the North in the first wave of industrialism, the workers of the South cannot be bought off with cheap goods from the colonies. The workers of the South have no 'periphery' to cushion their exploitation, and women are doubly exploited as women and as workers.

Docility Grows out of the Barrel of a Gun

Militarization of the host states has been one of the major consequences of export-led growth in Third World countries.
(Swasti Mitter, 1986, p. 58)

Military expenditure has become the Pandora's Box of
the twentieth century.
(Gita Sen and Caren Grown, 1987, p. 67)

The pliability of the workforce (male and female) of many
nations of the South is ensured by their staggeringly high
military expenditure; political and economic stability is enforced,
in the last resort, through the barrel of a gun. The newly
industrialised countries of the Pacific rim such as Malaysia,
South Korea and Indonesia have had a huge increase in their
defence budgets.

A large number of South countries are ruled by military gov-
ernments or civilian dictators with military backing – Thailand,
Indonesia, Singapore and, until recently, the Philippines. Latin
America has an equally sorry history of military repression.
Global inequality and militarism are locked into a vicious circle.
Capitalist exploitation of the labour of the South and strip-mining
of its resources leads to poverty as people are pushed from their
land and denied the resources to support themselves adequately.
When the poor turn to popular protest, guerrilla struggle or
crime, governments resort to military repression, imposing horrendous hardship and cruelty. The expansion of 'free trade' is
almost inevitably supported by a privileged elite who will defend
capitalism's interests by whatever means are necessary: financial
inducements, bribes, torture, repression, dictatorship.

Maintaining the power and loyalty of the military costs money,
and a good deal of the petrodollar loans released through the
exploitation of the once-and-for-all resource of oil was spent on
the military. The proportion of arms expenditure in the South
went from 6 per cent in 1965 to 20 per cent in 1982. In 1985
military 'assistance' by the North accounted for 43 per cent of
aid to the South, with the added benefit of swelling the coffers
of the arms manufacturers of the North (Maycock, 1989). As the
poor got poorer, the army got larger and better equipped. An
increasingly dominant militarism reinforces the macho culture

of patriarchy and increases the sexual and physical oppression of women. Human rights disappear under the gun and the baton, as do many of the population – to which the mothers of the disappeared in El Salvador, Guatemala and Chile stand testimony.

While Latin America has suffered some of the most repressive effects of unbridled capitalism, particularly the horrific monetarist experiment in Chile, the whole South has suffered under the drive towards export-orientated development over the past decade. Capitalism stalks the globe like an international terrorist, threatening the livelihood of anyone who does not obey its commands. As Dr Peter Draper pointed out in a letter to the *Guardian* (7 December 1990), if free trade is such a good thing, why does it have to be imposed by gunboats and marines? In the United States the 1988 Trade Act declares that reprisals may be taken against countries who 'unfairly' impede the activities of American corporations.

Exploited Workers and . . .

Brazil has been one of the most successful of the export-led economies in terms of rapid industrialisation and growth of GNP, although this is somewhat marred by a four-figure inflation rate. However, Brazil's experience shows how interaction with the capitalist world system can socially and ecologically devastate a naturally rich country. Apart from its rainforest, Brazil has millions of acres of unploughed arable land. There are two or three harvests a year and plentiful supplies to urban markets. Sugar, soya beans, orange juice and cacao are exported, and Brazil has the world's largest cattle herd. Despite this wealth, one-third of all Brazilian children under the age of five suffer from malnutrition. According to a Food and Agriculture Organisation (FAO) seminar held in São Paulo in October 1990, malnutrition causes the death of 60 per cent of the 350,000 children who die each year. One-third of the population do not get enough to eat, and those in the north-east suffer from stunted growth. The major cities have huge *favelas* (shantytowns), and millions of children from poor families sleep on the streets. Women, who already suffer from the cult of machismo, head many of the poor families in the *favelas*.

This distress is directly related to the need to provide cheap labour for capitalist companies. Cheap labour is achieved by a very repressive policy towards trades-union organisation and the concentration of land in a small number of private hands. Ninety per cent of the land is owned by 10 per cent of the population, a system inherited from the Portuguese colonialists. The result is to reproduce the conditions of early-nineteenth-century Britain: large numbers of landless people, denied their own means of subsistence, are forced to move to the cities to look for work (O'Connor, 1989). If they fail to find work they have no money to buy food, and starve. In desperation people turn to crime, or go to the rainforest in the hope of finding gold or clearing a few acres of land to grow crops. The poor are caught between the feudal landowners and the demands of international capital for cheap labour, and all three – the poor, landowners and capital – threaten the future of the forest and its inhabitants.

... *Burning Forests*

The indigenous peoples of the Amazon have always lived there; the Amazon is our home. We know its secrets well, both what it can offer us and what its limits are. For us there can be no life if our forests are destroyed. We want to continue living in our homeland. We have no interest in taking everything the forest has to offer and moving to the city to live in material comfort from the profits of our plunder ... Our forest today is a land of violence. Poverty, corruption, injustice, and lack of the most basic security, all generate violence.

(Evaristo Nugkuag Ikanan, President of COICA, the
Centre for the Indigenous Organizations of the Amazon
Basin, 1990)

Ikanan gives a horrific account of life – or rather death – for the
Amazonian peoples, reporting that six million have been killed.
Random assassinations are common, and the forest is effectively
beyond the law. In Colombia an assassin, when brought to trial,
declared that he did not know it was a crime to kill an Indian.
Ikanan points to the racism of those who see the Amazon as
uninhabited: 'the Amazon is empty for those who don't want
to see us, for those who continue to think it is a great act of
pioneering heroism to clear us from our territories dead or alive'.
He tells how timber is cut by slave labour and young women are
subject to the landowner's domestic and sexual demands. The
authorities know that the timber is cut by slave labour, 'but they
close their eyes, because . . . if the lord had to pay for the labour
the local economy would collapse . . . This is the price we pay
for Amazonian development' (Ikanan, 1990, p. 12).

The main cause of Amazonian rainforest destruction is not
logging which, according to Richard Sandbrook, accounts for
only 10 per cent of forest clearance (*Independent on Sunday*, 13
October 1990). In 1978 a Peruvian forestry expert calculated
that only 6 per cent of Peruvian timber reached the market,
while 250–300,000 acres a year went up in smoke (Ikanan,
1990). Land cleared for ranching or logging represents a very
short-term economic view. Ikanan calculates that each hectare
cleared produced only 25 kilos of meat before it became infertile
as against the 'nutritional value of the animals, birds, grubs, fruit
and nuts and plants the original forest contained'. Nor do the
benefits of clearance accrue to the government. In Brazil a
government subsidy for clearing the forest caused the rapid
destruction of primal forest, with massive amounts of money
being invested in land clearances, but the short-term profits
accrued to the rich. One area of five million hectares given over to

livestock *cost* the Brazilian economy US$5.6m, although it yielded vast profits to the private owners (Shanmugaratnam, 1989).

An article in *Nature* calculated that one hectare of Peruvian rainforest would produce an income of $650 each year as against a once-and-for-all income of $1,000 for the cut timber (reported in Tickell, 1989). Chico Mendes, the Brazilian rubber-tappers' leader and head of the Forest Peoples' Alliance, calculated that rubber-tapping and gathering brazil nuts was twenty times more profitable in the long term than land clearance (Mendes, 1989, p. 62). But defending the forest meant death for the rubber-tappers, as for the Indians, and Mendes was murdered in December 1988 by local ranchers. In December 1990 a rancher and his son were sentenced to nineteen years' imprisonment for the murder, the first time a *mandante*, or planner of a murder connected to land disputes, was tried and sentenced. It was hoped that this conviction would set a precedent and help to reduce the carnage in Brazil that has claimed 1,500 lives in the past twenty years.

The President of Brazil, Fernando Collor de Melio, has also appointed a radical green, Jose Lutzenberger, as Environment Secretary. Lutzenberger is a green convert who once promoted chemical fertilisers for a multinational company. Subsidies for land clearance have ended and agricultural production is being taxed, while the gold-diggers have been refused diesel to work their pumps. The Indian leaders are still quite cynical and think that Brazil's rampant inflation will continue to drive people into the forest. An alliance has been formed between Indians, rubber-tappers and riverbank communities to 'protect and preserve this immense but fragile life-system that involves our forests, lakes, rivers and springs, the source of our wealth and the basis of our cultures and traditions' (Mendes, 1989, p. 85).

Logging is a much greater problem in South-East Asia, where energy-efficient Japan gobbles up 40 per cent of the world market in woodpulp while maintaining its own huge forests intact

(Shanmugaratnam, 1989). Indonesia's rate of deforestation is second only to Brazil's, but there were some small victories for rainforest campaigners when Scott Paper withdrew from a plan to cut down a forest area the size of Cyprus, and the mangrove forests of Irian Jaya were saved from a Malaysian timber company by a campaign of the indigenous peoples. The government had argued that the mangroves were uninhabited, whereas the University of Malaysia's Wetland Bureau found 11,000 inhabitants (Leonard, 1990). The logging contractors have now moved on to Papua New Guinea, where a National Commission has described them as 'robber barons roaming the country'. Logging companies bribe officials or promise a cash income to local village heads in order to gain access to the forest.

Although Papua New Guinea has imposed an environmental tax on logging, companies avoid this by understating the value of the timber by as much as $10 per cubic metre. A similar practice occurs in Sarawak, where tribal peoples have been struggling against Japanese logging firms. Logging operations have also moved to Burma, where the military government is grabbing the opportunity to earn foreign exchange in order to increase its military grip on the country which, according to Amnesty International, has already tortured and killed thousands of people (Leonard, 1990).

In 1987 the Forestry Department of the UN Food and Agriculture Organisation headed up a Tropical Forest Action Plan under which countries would be encouraged to exploit their rainforests commercially with minimal environmental damage. In fact, according to environmentalists, the $8 billion plan has become a 'logger's charter' channelling aid into commercial schemes to rip up the forests. Governments ruthlessly took the opportunity to gain foreign currency, as tropical timber sold in international markets generates substantial amounts of foreign exchange. Even so, only 5–10 per cent of the timber reaches the market, whereas 40–50 per cent is destroyed by the mechanical means of extraction (Shanmugaratnam, 1989). Governments are willing to sacrifice such huge areas of forest for such limited and short-term economic benefit because timber, unlike the sustainable economies of the indigenous peoples, is a highly visible export commodity which they can control:

> Non-wood resources, on the other hand, are collected and sold in local markets by an incalculable number of subsistence farmers, forest collectors, middlemen [*sic*] and shop owners. These decentralised trade networks are extremely hard to monitor and ignored in national accounting schemes. (Tickell, 1989)

Much of the discussion of the problems of the rainforest is conducted entirely by men – from government leaders to ranchers, gold-diggers, rubber-tappers and the male leaders of the indigenous peoples. It is almost as if women do not exist in the rainforest or among the landless poor. Feminist geographers Janet Townsend and Jennie Bean have tried to redress the balance by studying the role of women in planting cleared land. They found that in one area of Mexico women had planted gardens on cleared land, but that in doing so they had retained some useful forest products. The study revealed over three hundred plants cultivated and grown by the women. However, their 'gentle touch' on the land was very tenuous and they were under threat from the male-dominated ranch economy (*Guardian*, 4 January 1991).

Within the older industrial nations there are active campaigns to unite with rainforest peoples to save the forests. These have been greeted with suspicion by both rainforest governments and indigenous peoples themselves. Governments have pointed to the fact that Western countries have historically denuded themselves of all their broadleaved forests and gained the economic benefit of doing so – why should this 'once-and-for-all' wealth be denied to South peoples? Why should rainforest countries maintain the 'lungs' that let the richer countries continue to pollute? Indonesia, for example, earns $4 billion from its forestry industry, which employs between one and three million people.

Rainforest people are also concerned about proposals for debt-for-nature swaps and other schemes to maintain the forests by putting ownership into 'friendly' hands. They claim that the land belongs to them, and governments, banks or supportive environmental groups have no right to buy it from under them. Indigenous peoples argue that they received no benefit from the debts their governments incurred, so why should they have to pay for them with their lives and their land? Debt-for-nature swaps are particularly invidious, as ownership of the land passes to banks which are getting 'good assets for bad loans'. Although the land purchased is theoretically to be preserved, it passes from local control and becomes subject to the 'dictates of the centres of political and economic power' (*Green Line*, no. 77, 1990, p. 6). Debt-swap schemes are effectively a means by which banks can recoup some of their losses from aid agencies or other sources while imposing a form of ecological colonialism that ignores the need to sustain the livelihood of local people (Cartwright, 1989). In order to resolve the problems of the rainforest, we will first have to resolve the issue of the debt crisis.

The Debt Crisis

This war is tearing down Brazil, Latin America and
practically all the Third World. Instead of soldiers dying
there are children; instead of millions of wounded there
are millions of unemployed; instead of destruction of
bridges there is the tearing down of factories, schools,
hospitals and entire economies. It is a war by the United
States against the Latin American continent and the
Third World.
(The Brazilian trades unionist Luis 'Lulu' Silva, quoted
in *Green Line*, no. 77, 1990, p. 6)

The war to which Luis Silva refers is the debt crisis which he sees as a 'Third World War'. The escalating debts of the Third World countries to which he refers were part of the global expansion of international capitalism, and by 1990 they totalled around one trillion dollars. Easy credit from banks in the North enabled South countries to obtain the things they needed (medical equipment, technology) or thought they needed (arms or luxury goods for rich elites). Military governments, in particular, spent huge amounts on arms, which poor people and the rainforests are being exploited to repay. Financing escalating debts becomes even more difficult when the North forces down the price of agricultural products or raw materials and poorer countries have no choice but to expand production by increasing the exploitation of both people and land. Effectively, the debt crisis is 'financing ecocide' (George, 1988, p. 155).

Crippling debt repayments are also forcing countries to impose austerity measures on their populations, pushing them even deeper into poverty:

> The recent history of 'development' processes is replete
> with the struggles of the poor against policies that
> reduce their access to resources, destroy and pollute
> their environment, or mortgage their jobs and food
> consumption to the requirements of debt repayments.
> (Sen and Grown, 1987, p. 39)

As women form the majority of poor people in the world, the social and economic effects of the debt crisis fall most heavily on them.

The debt crisis has been made much worse by the monetarist policy of forcing up interest rates in the North (Nicholas Costello *et al.*, 1989). In the early 1980s interest rates in America rose to nearly 20 per cent, while commodity prices fell by 20 per cent. At the same time the profits of the seven biggest United States banks rose from 22 per cent in 1970 to 55 per cent in 1981 to 60 per cent in 1982 (Shiva, 1989, p. 220). The poorest countries of the South became net exporters of capital to the rich North: the imbalance rose from $7 billion in 1981 to $74 billion in 1985. In 1989 Latin America paid one-third of its export earnings in debt repayments. The casino economy almost shuddered to a halt when Western banks pushed the developing countries too far and payments began to look uncertain. An immediate crisis was averted by rescheduling debts, but the situation is still unresolved.

The debt crisis has increased the exploitation of both the environment and women. The environment is being mined, degraded and eroded by the desperate drive to achieve export-related growth. Women are used as cheap labour both in factories and in their homes. In her classic study of lace-making in Narsapur (1982), Maria Mies found that one hundred thousand women using their so-called 'leisure' to make lace were a major export industry for the region, even though they were paid only a pittance. In some countries women are even more directly exploited as an 'export': poverty, patriarchy and the debt crisis have conspired to exploit them as a human 'cash crop' – as slaves and as prostitutes.

Women – the Ultimate Cash Crop

Prostitution in the Philippines . . . was more than just tolerated under the 20-year dictatorship of President Marcos; it was actively encouraged as an important source of foreign revenue for a country crippled by external debt.
(Tonette Raquisa, 1987, p. 218)

Taking a girl here is as easy as buying a package of cigarettes . . . little slaves who give real Thai warmth.
(Dutch travel brochure, quoted in Truong, 1990, p. 178)

We vehemently protest the use of Filipino women as
commodities; packaged and marketed by profit-seeking
enterprises in the commercialised marriage circuit . . .

STOP THE TRAFFICKING OF WOMEN BY MALE-ORDER!
STOP RACIST EXPLOITATION OF FILIPINO WOMEN!
(Statement by GABRIELA [Filipino Women's Organisation],
8 July 1986)

The anthropologist Claude Meillassoux has argued (1981) that
women were the first commodity, the first 'good' to be marketed
and exchanged as bride and labourer. A similar trade in women
still exists in Asia, Africa, Latin America and China, where women
are sold or trapped into marriage or slave labour. Worldwide there
are at least two hundred million slaves, many of them women and
children, and it has been estimated recently that there are at least
three thousand female domestic 'slaves' in London alone. Many
have no legal status and suffer appalling hardship. One maid to
two Kuwaiti princesses was eventually awarded £300,000 damages
in the High Court in 1990 for the abuse she had suffered.

There is a racist twist to the commercial trade in women for
marriage, as it is white men from the North (mainly Norwegian,
German and Australian) who 'import' women from the South,
mainly from South-East Asia. Women are advertised through
'male-order' catalogues at a price which even an unemployed
West German can afford (Mies, 1986, p. 138). In many cases
these women ended up being forced into prostitution by their
new 'masters' or turned into domestic and sex slaves (Mies,
1986; Raquisa, 1987). Women are 'marketed' not only for
export, but also as an attraction to male tourists. In South-East
Asia women have been trapped in an exploitative interaction
between capitalism, patriarchy and militarism. In Thailand, the
growth of sex tourism reflects a traditional cult of militarism and
male domination of women under which the accumulation of
wives and mistresses was seen as evidence of military prowess

(Truong, 1990). This was reinforced by the Buddhist view of women as more earthly than and inferior to men, and therefore a source of their pleasure. These patriarchal and religious views, common throughout the region, were compounded by American economic and military domination of South-East Asia, enhanced in the 1950s and 1960s by the Korean and Vietnam wars.

The huge American bases of Clark and Subic Bay in the Philippines and the popularity of Thailand for 'R & R' (Rest and Recreation) created a demand for sexual services (Raquisa, 1987). The reputed 'docility' and 'willingness to please' of South-East Asian women contributed to a dramatic growth in tourism. In 1986 Thailand's income from tourism was double that of its traditional export of rice, whereas in 1970 earnings were approximately equivalent. Women became increasingly important to Thai foreign exchange earnings – in 1986 the income from tourism was equal to that of the textile industry, which also employed large numbers of women.

In both Thailand and the Philippines prostitution has been condoned, if not actively promoted, by the government and tourist agencies, from the 'delicious hostess' of Thai Airways advertisements to the explicit sex-tourism brochures that list services, prices and addresses. The 'attractions' of the sex industry contribute to the profits of the airlines, hotel chains and package tour operators who, wittingly or unwittingly, transport the disproportionately large number of male visitors to the region. As many as 800,000 Thai women may be working as prostitutes, representing around 8 per cent of all women between the ages of fifteen and thirty-four (Truong, 1990). Maria Mies reports that 200,000 to 300,000 women are working in the sex industry in Bangkok alone. Child prostitution is also common, and both women and children are sold into sex-slavery. Virgins are particularly prized as, by Thai tradition, men gain virility and increased life expectancy by deflowering a virgin.

Prostitution is justified by the machismo culture that places great significance on male sexual domination of females, the assumed sexual availability (and willingness) of Thai women, and the argument that it is a better life than the rural poverty that women would otherwise suffer. These justifications mean that the wishes and right to self-determination of the women themselves can be ignored:

> By locating prostitution in the culture of poverty and the exotic, the question of human dignity becomes obscured and neutralized while Thai women become qualified as a 'new pasture' in which local entrepreneurs can invest and make profits, and over which rich clients can exercise their social and economic power by pursuing their sexual fantasies without guilt. Hidden behind the culture of poverty and the glossy image of the exotic is a process of accumulation from prostitutes' labour facilitated by a dubious juridical structure and the direct and indirect participation of members of the ruling class in the recruitment and utilization of prostitutes' labour. (Truong, 1990, p. 180)

In drawing attention to the exploitation of women's bodies by countries in the South, it is important to remember that prostitution is just as rife in the North and has been equally associated with militarism and male domination of women's sexuality. 'Red light' districts are also a tourist attraction in many Northern cities. The situation in South-East Asia and other parts of the world is only an extension of the 'oldest profession', compounded by the inequalities produced by international capitalism and the economic interests of governments and ruling elites, who are desperate to keep their toehold within the international economy. Women's bodies are exploited to enable men to pay for their military uniforms, huge estates and stretch limos.

Women are uniting against the sex industry by building links between women's organisations such as GABRIELA in the sex-exporting countries and women's organisations in the sex-importing countries. However, the sex industry cannot be destroyed without the destruction of all the exploitative institutions that promote and sustain it.

Common Cause

The struggle for the human essence, for human dignity,
cannot be divided and cannot be won unless *all* [the]
colonising divisions, created by patriarchy and capitalism,
are rejected and transcended.
(Maria Mies, 1986, p. 230)

The world capitalist economy has not proved to be a 'magic machine' that will bring everyone the goodies in the end. Quite the opposite: some people and countries are rich *because* other people and countries are poor. As Hazel Henderson has argued (1990), industrial capitalism has proved to be a 'one time historical process', and an unstable one at that. For the South it has brought the mining of natural resources without industrial development, a growing circulation of capital with no capitalist transformation of the economy (Shanmugaratnam, 1989). The world market works directly against the arguments of bodies like the Commission for Africa, which claims that 'if hunger is to be averted, Africa must start producing what it consumes and consuming what it produces'. The World Bank, which was one of the sponsors of the policy of export-led growth in 1980, admitted in 1990 that the market solution had not worked for poor countries and proposed that there should be a move away from financial support to the commercial sector and towards public-sector and labour-intensive employment, and more finance for basic services such as health, education and nutrition.

In 1987 the United Nations Commission on Environment and Development published the Brundtland Report, which envisaged environment and development linked in a new international economic system geared to sustainability. The Report argued that the environment must be taken into account in economic decision-making. Technology should be orientated towards conserving resources and meeting essential needs: jobs, food, energy, water and sanitation. None of this is compatible with a 'free' profit-orientated market. Like the Brandt Commission in 1980, the Brundtland Report looks to initiatives coming from the North, and if the response to the Brandt Commission report is any indication, the Brundtland Report is unlikely to have any impact on the world economy in the foreseeable future. While the Brundtland Report has tried to show that South and North have a 'Common Future', that does not necessarily mean an equal one.

In 1990 the United Nations Human Development Report calculated that one billion people were living in absolute poverty, nearly two billion without safe drinking water. Eight hundred million went hungry every day and one hundred million were homeless. Fourteen million children still died each year before their fifth birthday. It acknowledged that the situation had worsened for many people in Latin America and Africa since 1960. In 1990 a group of British Labour MPs found that the number of people living in countries with a declining GNP had increased twelvefold in that period, and there was no evidence that wealth was 'trickling down' to the poor. In 1981 the United Nations launched a campaign to give two billion people access to safe drinking water in ten years, but by 1991 1,977 billion people were still waiting, and the situation on sanitation had deteriorated. Allowing for population growth, the clean-water campaign had reached 700 million people and sanitation 250 million.

In fact, far from being a 'trickle down' from North to South, a sluice-way ran from South to North. Aid programmes had transferred some resources to the South, but this could not compensate for the $32.5 billion the North was extracting from the South by 1988. This represents a vast transfer of wealth from the poor to the rich that can only increase pressure on the poor, women and the environment. Government aid programmes were also often tied to the economic interests of donor countries. One study found that European Community aid to Bangladesh, one of the poorest countries in the world, had been underspent by 20 per cent in nine years, and that European suppliers were favoured over cheaper local sources. Food aid that did reach the country was disproportionately allocated to government and public-sector officials (*Guardian*, 4 January 1991).

There are no financial reasons why the peoples of the South should continue to live in poverty or ecological devastation. The trillion dollars a year the world spends on arms would wipe out nearly the whole of their debt. It would take only $9 billion a year to secure the world's topsoil, $3 billion to restore the forests, $4 billion to halt the deserts, $18 billion to provide contraception, $30 billion for clean water (Myers, 1990). Commitment of resources to military expenditure has meant that nuclear missiles can go from Europe to Moscow in minutes, while a woman in Africa must walk for several hours a day to fetch water. These priorities are not the 'neutral decisions' of a market; they are the priorities of powerful men in powerful nations. It is their sex, race and class interests that drive the capitalist system and its worldwide network of accumulation and deprivation (Wallerstein, 1983).

Women, greens and socialists have common cause in opposing the development of worldwide capitalism. Both industrialism and capitalism are enemies of the planet, but they have united with other powerful forces – feudalism, patriarchy, colonialism, imperialism, militarism, racism – to form a monstrous global structure of economic, social and political power. Just abandoning industrialism, as some greens have suggested, will not end the torment of the planet or its peoples. There is a much larger system to deconstruct, and the battle is going to be long and hard.

The beneficiaries of the global market have been the people in the centres of the world economy who obtain cheap goods and services, and the multinational companies who provide them. It has been a bonanza for the rich, white nations of the North (latterly joined by Japan) and for the rich within those nations. It has been a bonanza for many men and some women.

The losers are the low-paid and unemployed of the older industrial nations, the workers in the newer industrial nations, those who have no access to markets and no means of subsistence, and the planet itself. International capitalism has brought wealth to around one-seventh of the human race and absolute poverty to another seventh; it has enabled the 'haves' to accumulate, while the 'have nots' have been robbed of what little they had. The agony of the South is that it is locked into an economic system driven by the North, without being able to find any mechanism with which to control and influence it. The North needs the South as a larder for its raw materials and a dustbin for its waste, as a source of cheap labour and a ready dumping ground for surplus goods. If the South were to 'develop', these economic advantages to the North would be lost. However, the North now needs the South in a more fundamental sense. It needs the underdeveloped South as a green 'lung' to replace the blackened lungs of the North. The North has an ecological as well as an economic interest in maintaining the South's underdevelopment.

While the peoples of the South are engaged in many struggles over land, work and resources, we in the North will also have to work here to undermine the structures of power that threaten women, the poor, the South and the planet. If the South is to get off the treadmill of international capitalism it will have to 'transcend the boundaries set by the international and the sexual division of labour, and by commodity production, *both* in the developed and the underdeveloped worlds' (Mies, 1986, p. 232). At present, political systems in the North have, to varying degrees, capitulated to the blandishments and promises of capitalism and the competitive market system, and that is where we must begin our challenge.

CHAPTER 6

Challenging the Market

The modern creation myth that male western minds
propagate is based on the sacrifice of nature, women and
the Third World. It is not merely the impoverishment
of these excluded sectors that is the issue in the late
twentieth century; it is the very dispensability of nature
and non-industrial and non-commercial cultures that is
at stake. Only the price on the market counts.
(Vandana Shiva, 1989, p. 221)

Socialism, as an economic theory . . . is dead. The
argument now is about what kind of capitalism we want.
(John Elkington and Tom Burke, 1987, p. 252)

For Vandana Shiva, the capitalist market economy is a modern 'creation myth' spawned by the Western male mind. For
Elkington and Burke, it is the only alternative. I would agree
with Elkington and Burke that both state socialism and welfare
socialism have capitulated to the market: the former because it
could not match the productivity of industrial capitalism, the
latter because it always relied parasitically on capitalism to
produce a wealthy tax-base. The final decades of the twentieth
century have seen the ascendance of the so-called 'free' market,
not only to economic domination of the global community but
to a dogma of near-religious proportions, particularly in Britain
and the United States.

To say that the ideology of the market has triumphed is not
to imply that the market system in practice is an undifferentiated

universal model. Quite the contrary – there are many different ways in which the market operates, from the welfare systems of Scandinavia to the social market system in Germany. The economists' model of the classical market system was always an 'ideal' model of how things could be in perfect conditions of knowledge and competition. While the market system itself has many alternatives, with the collapse of socialism there seems little alternative to the market ideology, as Elkington and Burke point out. Where there are compromises between the market and social considerations, what matters is which principle will rule in the last instance, the social principle or the market principle? This question becomes particularly important given the way the ideology of the classical market has become such a dominant dynamic in political and economic decision-making, particularly in the global context.

As Shiva points out, the ideology of the market has been created by men in the industrial capitalist economies. The capitalist 'free market' is based on the private ownership of resources, factories and businesses, with profit-making as the only basis for the production or exchange of goods. For the majority, who do not own or control any productive resources, the only compensations are the possibility of waged labour and the pleasures of consumption. As Hazel Henderson has pointed out:

> The conspicuous consumption of surplus has been a
> continuous theme of human behaviour since the building
> of the pyramids. What is relatively new today is that the
> excesses of kings and emperors now provide a general
> model for emulation by large numbers of people.
> (1978, p. 340)

Greens are divided on their attitude to the capitalist market. Some have argued that capitalism can 'go green', or be induced to do so. Others maintain that the consumer society is corrosive of non-material human values, and anything but the most basic level of consumption is unsustainable on a global scale. Feminists are also ambivalent. For some, the main issue is equal opportunities. The market is condemned not in itself, but for the fact that men benefit disproportionately from it. Others stress that woman-orientated values are collective and egalitarian, and incompatible with a competitive, exploitative system. Socialists who have not succumbed to the blandishments of the market point to the inevitable inequalities it produces.

The most important feature of the capitalist market system is the boundaries it creates and the boundaries it destroys. As Shiva argues, in the form of the cash economy it overruns traditional cultures and resources, destroying the economic autonomy of local communities. At the same time capitalism places a boundary around economic activity and excludes from the market those who do not have the resources to participate in the form of waged work or a product to sell. It is a boundary that excludes many women and, by definition, the poor, North and South. The market also draws boundaries around costs it will acknowledge. For the most part environmental costs have been seen as lying outside the market, as is much of the work carried out by women in reproducing and maintaining the human population.

A feminist green socialist challenge to the capitalist market would demand that it should: be able to secure the future of the environment; take account of women's work and be responsive to women's needs; reduce the inequalities both within and between nations. I will argue that it fails on all three counts. To start with the first challenge: Can capitalism go green, or be induced to do so?

The Challenge of Ecology: Can Capitalism Go Green?

The exponential growth argument in my view has gone out of the window. All the trends point towards smaller more efficient plants. Our most important task is to get more and more out of less and less. This is the

industrialist's mission ... not because we are boy scouts
... but for very good business reasons.
(John Harvey-Jones, then Head of ICI, quoted in
Elkington and Burke, 1987, p. 179)

Business and the environment are on a collision course.
(Sir James Goldsmith, *Independent on Sunday*, 21 October
1990)

In contrast to Harvey-Jones's optimistic view of the responsive
flexibility of capitalist industry, Goldsmith announced his retire-
ment from industry in October 1990 in order to 'save the planet'.
He declared that the 'ecological bill' for industry would come
due in the next generation, and that the main culprits were the
car and nuclear industries. Despite Goldsmith's pessimism, in
November 1990 the Chair of IBM, Prince Charles, the then
Tory Environment Secretary Chris Patten and Jonathon Porritt
jointly launched a guide for businesses that declared that green
was good for them (Business in the Environment, 1990). The
message of the launch was that there was no fundamental
incompatibility between the environment and the interests of
business. Money could be saved through energy conservation,
ranging from millions for IBM to £70,000 for St Thomas' Hospital,
London. It argued that businesses should look at the possibilities
for savings by carrying out environmental impact assessments,
redesigning products to save raw materials, finding substitutes
for harmful substances, recycling and waste reclamation.

John Elkington and Tom Burke had already announced the
arrival of 'green sunrise' capitalism in 1987, claiming that
industry could 'make money – and protect the environment'.
Drawing on evidence of an awareness and willingness to embrace
environmental issues in the boardrooms of several multinational
companies, they claimed that capitalism was ready and able to
respond to the ecological crisis. New technologies would be
the basis of a green capitalist future: fibre optics, ceramics,

biotechnology, electronics and alternative energy. Firms would produce more with less. Japan, after the oil shock of 1973, reduced the energy needed to produce a tonne of steel by 85 per cent and also achieved its 'economic miracle' with half the energy consumption per head of the United States. Pollution control would itself become big business; in the United States it was already a $70 billion industry that had created 167,000 jobs. By 1990, 225 'green consultancy' companies had been set up in Britain and firms were responding to consumer concern about the safety of food, household products and packaging. Industries from toilet-roll makers and peat-cutters to nuclear power and oil have advertised their commitment to the environment.

Elkington and Burke offer us a picture of benign creativity and goodwill among far-sighted industrialists who know that unbridled capitalism will destroy both itself and the planet. They claim that green capitalists are ready to acknowledge that present and future generations are also 'stake-holders' in their businesses. Green capitalism is epitomised by Anita Roddick's Body Shop, which has captured the public imagination as well as its money. Elkington and Burke's green capitalists would never create a Bhopal, a Seveso, or kill everything for 200 kilometres in the Rhine. They would never declare, as Alan Sugar of Amstrad is alleged to have done, that if there were a market in mass-produced portable nuclear weapons they would be selling them. Elkington and Burke do, however, acknowledge that new technologies are not entirely ecologically unproblematic – from the contamination of ground water by chemicals in America's Silicon Valley to the enormous consumption of paper by computers, which, in America, use enough paper to go round the world twenty times every day. Even service industries such as hairdressing involve the disposal of millions of gallons of chemical residues.

According to Elkington and Burke, such pollution is not a long-term problem, as 'environmentally unsound activities are ultimately economically unsound' (1987, p. 210). If the market is left to find its own balance, environmental questions will be resolved. There was some evidence to support this assertion when the British government's attempt to privatise the nuclear power industry was thwarted because the cost of decommissioning power stations and disposing of waste made it commercially unprofitable – something the American nuclear industry had already discovered. American power companies also found it more profitable to encourage people to use less power rather than build new conventional power stations (Paehlke, 1989). The French nationalised power industry, on the other hand, has an aggressive policy of building new nuclear power stations, as did the Soviet Union, despite Chernobyl. However, it was not the market that first 'discovered' these costs, it was the near-catastrophe at Three Mile Island and the long campaigns of antinuclear groups that put the issue of pollution costs on the economic agenda. Nuclear power is also a highly visible national industry; its polluting effects could not be hidden away in some poor and distant country. A nuclear power station was always on somebody's doorstep, favourite beach or river valley.

Market solutions also got another boost in 1990 when the eco-optimist Julian Simon won a long-standing bet with the eco-pessimist Paul Erlich. In 1980 they had laid a bet about the exhaustion of metals such as chrome, nickel, tin and tungsten as measured by their price. Erlich had thought that they would become scarce and the price would rise. Simon had thought that human ingenuity would come up with alternatives. Simon won; the price had not risen. Of course, if the price had risen that would have been because the resource was *already scarce*; the market cannot anticipate for future scarcity or the needs of future generations (Jacobs, 1991).

Even when scarcity is imminent, the market may not respond. Drought-induced inflation in the South has been slow to produce Simon's 'human ingenuity' in creating drought-reducing technological innovations (Shanmugaratnam, 1989). The market does not necessarily respond, even if the necessary technology is in existence. In Ethiopia it was not 'economic' to make fuel brickettes out of coffee-stalk waste, although the technology was available, *until* all the trees had been burnt down and the people were forced to burn dung instead, which could no longer be used to replenish the soil. The market may respond in the long run, but as someone once said, in the long run we are all dead. In the shorter term it would seem more sensible to give the market a nudge in the green direction. One of the most immediate policy responses to the environmental crisis has been to try to bring the costs of ecological destruction within the marketplace by making the polluter pay.

Making the Polluter Pay

We demand the immediate application of the principle
that the causer of pollution must pay its costs.
(Programme of the German Green Party, 1983, p. 30)

In his analysis of capitalism, Marx pointed out that the Earth and the worker were 'the original sources of all wealth'. The Earth was the 'workshop and repository of raw materials', which were provided by nature 'gratis', a 'free gift' to Capital. Marx was concerned about the 'exploitation and squandering of the vitality of the soil' and complained that moving people to the towns meant that their waste products could not be recycled into the Earth. He noted that the waste products of the four-and-a-half million people of London were dumped in the Thames at 'heavy expense'. He went on to argue that raw materials would be recycled only when their price rose sufficiently, an early criticism of 'leaving it to the market'. Making the polluter pay is an acceptance that the market is not likely to respond to ecological dereliction until the air is fouled and the water lifeless.

Pollution has traditionally been treated by firms as an 'externality' – that is, something for which the firm is not responsible and which does not appear as an expense on the balance sheet

(Kapp, 1978; Sagoff, 1988). As a result, the penalties of pollution and depletion have been paid by the environment and the people directly affected by it. Being able to use the environment 'freely' as a dump for waste increases the profits of privately owned firms. As long as a business can get away with externalising costs, it has no economic incentive to stop degrading the environment. A public industry may equally well ignore externalities in the short run, but the costs will eventually have to be borne by the government in the form of clean-up operations or the ill-health or early death of the present or future population.

Professor David Pearce and his colleagues, in their report *Blueprint for a Green Economy* (1989), argue that failure to take account of future environmental costs gives a false picture of a nation's wealth. To obtain a truer picture we should deduct from measures of national income (GDP, GNP) the costs of coping with pollution. This would give us a measure of sustainable income – i.e. the level of income that can be achieved without adverse ecological impact.

Some countries have already tried to adjust their national accounts to allow for environmental impact. Japan has tried to develop an environmental measure of national welfare. Norway, Canada and France have attempted to measure physical levels of depletion and dereliction (number of tonnes of coal used, amount of lead in the air, etc.). Pearce argues that all products should reflect in their price their 'true' environmental costs, both now and for future generations. Governments could achieve this by imposing a pollution tax or issuing a 'tradeable permit', – i.e. those who wanted to discharge waste or use raw materials could bid against each other for the right to do so.

Certainly it is possible to influence the market through taxation. When the British government reduced the tax on unleaded petrol, the number of cars converting from leaded to unleaded fuel increased dramatically. Sweden, Norway and Denmark have already imposed environmental taxes. However, taxes can only tinker with the problem. A report to the European

Commission in 1990 calculated that a carbon tax of 421 per cent would be needed to reduce greenhouse gases by 20 per cent, as use of fossil fuel dropped by only 2 per cent for every 10 per cent increase in tax (*New Scientist*, 3 November 1990, p. 38). It has also been calculated that for the United States the cost of cutting consumption of greenhouse gas to safe levels would be equivalent to the whole country's national income – not something that could be achieved by a carbon tax.

The effectiveness of a tax also depends on how essential the product is and the different spending patterns of the poor and the rich. Long after the poor have been priced out of the market, the rich may be able to continue consuming, possibly to ecologically unsustainable levels. Higher prices may not even stop the poor consuming in the short term if it is an essential item such as fuel for travel to work, cooking and basic heating. They may cut back on other less polluting consumption such as housing, leisure activities or food. The policy of 'making the polluter pay' through taxation would succeed in shooting prices sky-high with grave social effects, particularly if it meant that badly needed goods would be available only to a wealthy minority.

The idea of tradeable permits has also been condemned by many greens as 'buying the right to pollute'. The British Association of Nature Conservationists has suggested that a better approach would be to look at ways of technically overcoming environmental problems, with strict rules for conservation (BANC, 1990). The same argument has been applied to pollution taxes: 'pollution needs to be stopped not taxed' (Wall, 1990). Even fines are not very effective instruments unless they are very high. In 1990 a report by the Women's Environmental Network, sponsored by the World Wide Fund for Nature, found that despite a fine of £10,000 and damages of £200,000 to restock a river poisoned by a chemical spill, a paper mill still found the fine and damages cheaper than buying new equipment to deal with the problem. Although the 1990 Environmental Protection Act in Britain substantially raised fines for pollution, it allowed that firms need not introduce less polluting technology if 'excessive cost' was involved; a 'coach and horses' clause that will give lawyers a field day.

Even with inducements, the capitalist market cannot resolve the problems of the environment. It is geared to short-term profit-making, not to long-term conservation. Imposing permits, regulations or taxes undermines the capitalist idea of a free market; they are not compatible with the maximisation of profit. In a competitive market there would always be an incentive to undercut other producers by ducking environmental taxes, quietly discharging effluent or moving to a more impoverished country that could not afford to be too fussy. At present governments across the world are falling over themselves to 'attract' the transnational corporations, promising enterprise zones, tax-free holidays and no questions asked. Equally, goods that are deemed to be too dangerous to use in the North – such as pesticides or the contraceptive Depoprovera – are still sold to the South.

Under any market solution, be it *laissez-faire* or interventionist, it would not be the polluter who paid, it would be the consumers. High prices for raw materials, taxes, the expense of new equipment or fines would eventually filter down the line in higher prices to the consumer. Taxes or any other cost added to a product must penalise most heavily those who are least able to pay (Elson, 1988; Stretton, 1976; BANC, 1990). The market solution will mean that consumers (mainly women) and poor people (mainly women) will pay the price for decisions made by those (mainly men) who create polluting products and activities in companies, laboratories and governments. Productive decisions will continue to rest in the hands of men, while women juggle domestic budgets to try to cover the increased costs of basic items such as fuel.

Greens who advocate intervention or regulation in the market-place vary in their awareness of the social implications of their proposals. The same is true of greens who advocate direct consumer action to influence the market.

Consumer Activism

It's not just because consumers are worried about their
own personal health that they want to buy 'green'.
Women especially are also worried about the planet
and the potential effect pollution will have on future
generations.
(Alison Costello, Bernadette Vallely and Josa Young,
1989, p. 88)

In 1991 a Mintel survey found that 63 per cent of the British
public wanted to buy green products. Bernadette Vallely of the
Women's Environmental Network (WEN) argues that as 87 per
cent of shoppers/consumers are women, consumer activism is a
major source of empowerment for women and a way of bringing
together the women's movement and the environmental movement. WEN has turned women's generalised concern into positive
action around the issues of bleach in nappies and sanitary wear,
promotion of recycled paper and rejection of excess packaging.
Other environmental groups such as Friends of the Earth have
also campaigned around consumer issues such as non-returnable
bottles and food safety.

Green consumer pressure has undoubtedly produced positive
results, particularly in such campaigns as those opposing the
use of CFCs or chlorine-bleached paper products. Goods with
'additive-free', 'environmentally friendly' and 'natural' on their
labels have sprung up like mushrooms. Consumer awareness
has also been raised by numerous 'scares' over the safety of
food, from salmonella in eggs and chicken to BSE in beef; from
chemical residues in salmon and bran to listeria in fruit and
chilled food. Wholefoods have also made their way on to the
supermarket shelves, often at the expense of the small co-
operatives who first pioneered them. The fast-food companies
are gradually moving to less damaging packaging, although in
general excessive packaging is a huge problem. The demand for

cruelty-free soaps and cosmetics has brought huge commercial success for the Body Shop. Green consumers have built upon a long history of consumer activism championed by such people as Ralph Nader in America or Michael Young (founder of the Consumers' Association) in Britain.

Green consumer action varies from a marginal choice between different products to a much more political use of consumer pressure. Without a strong political focus, the present concern for environmental issues can easily be turned to the advantage of the market and may well increase rather than reduce consumption. Green consumerism has created vast new markets for goods as companies fall over themselves to show their green credentials and glossy green magazines help people 'shop wisely'. Friends of the Earth has responded by creating an annual 'Green Con Award'. In 1990 it was won by the Eastern Electricity Company for a letter which claimed that using more electricity would reduce global warming. The runner-up was Scott, the paper company, which claimed that paper-making helped to counter the greenhouse effect.

A much more effective use of consumer power is the consumer boycott. Boycotts have been used successfully against companies which invest in South Africa by campaigners against apartheid, and against Californian grape-producers in protest at the inhumane treatment of grape-pickers. In South Africa consumer boycotts have been an important part of Black struggle; Black women consumers have been encouraged to use their 'immense power' by the writer Ellen Kuzwayo, who since 1984 has been president of the Black Consumer Union.

Maria Mies calls on middle-class consumers in the North to help the struggle of producers in the South by building a 'consumer liberation movement'. She argues that such a movement must be led by women, as they are the vast majority of consumers. Mies acknowledges that this would be a movement open only to better-off women in powerful economies, but she argues that it is women's 'work' in consumption that helps to keep the whole international capitalist show on the road (1986). She claims that rich women are as much trapped in their housewife/consumer role as the poor housewives/producers who may well have made the products the former consume in factories, in sweatshops or as home-workers. Mies sees liberation from consumption as an important aspect of the liberation of women. She argues that we can start immediately by deciding what not to buy, given that 'perhaps more than 50% of what is bought and consumed in households in overdeveloped countries and overdeveloped classes is not only superfluous, but also harmful' (1986, p. 225). Greens have made much the same case.

Voluntary Simplicity

The good society cannot be an affluent society.
(Ted Trainer, 1985, p. xii)

Some greens have suggested that the market system could be broken from within by changes in personal lifestyle, placing the emphasis on the quality rather than the quantity of life (Elgin, 1981). Voluntary simplicity is underpinned by the idea that the creative and spiritual development of human beings is blocked by an excessive preoccupation with material things (Schumacher, 1973). Large claimed (1981) that fifteen million Americans had already adopted an ecological lifestyle by the late 1970s. Yankelovitch (1983) also found evidence of an emerging post-materialist culture in the older industrial nations. The former West Germany has a flourishing alternative movement in which people work for lower incomes and higher personal satisfaction by reducing their standard of living, and there is a similar alternative sector in many Western economies (Mary Mellor et al., 1988).

The dilemma for advocates of voluntary simplicity is that it is very much the province of the well-educated middle class, as socialists have been quick to point out (Weston, 1986). This is the same group who launched the 1960s rebellion, those who are 'future-assured', who can always return to the fold and the profession. Voluntary simplicity and the move to post-material values is a reality only for those who are already materially well endowed. A message of self-denial and self-sufficiency for those who have very little means something very different. To 'abandon affluence', as Ted Trainer suggests, we must already have it. By its nature, voluntary simplicity implies a choice; it would not be what Marx called 'the unnatural simplicity of the poor' – quite the opposite, it would be the unnatural simplicity of the rich.

All consumer actions – voluntary simplicity, consumer choice or boycotts – are undoubtedly powerful weapons, but they will succeed only if they stop the market functioning, or at least substantially obstruct it. Any interaction with the market must operate within its assumption that the only measure of value is price, and the only motivation for economic activity is profit. A feminist green socialist would challenge that proposition; it would show that some things are beyond price.

Life Beyond Price

Our land is more valuable than your money. It will last
forever. It will not even perish by the flames of fire. As
long as the sun shines and the waters flow, this land
will be here to give life to men and animals. We cannot
sell the lives of men and animals; therefore we cannot
sell this land . . . You can count your money and burn
it within the nod of a buffalo's head, but only the Great
Spirit can count the grains of sand and the blades of
grass of these plains.
(Blackfoot Chief, quoted in McLuhan, 1971, p. 53)

[New Zealand's] pollution free environment: its mountain
streams with safe drinking water, the accessibility of
national parks, walkways, beaches, lakes, kauri and beech

forests; the absence of nuclear power and nuclear energy
– all counted for nothing . . .
(Marilyn Waring, commenting on how the wealth of a
nation is calculated: 1989, p. 1)

The essence of the capitalist market system is commodification:
the turning of human activities and natural resources into
commodities to be bought and sold in the marketplace. People,
actions and resources are not valued for their intrinsic worth, or
even for their immediate benefit to people, but by their market
value. By allocating a money value to a resource, capitalism
effectively excludes it from common use. As resources fall
under private ownership and control, only those with money can
'afford' to buy. As Robert Tressell warned in his *Ragged-Trousered
Philanthropist*, if we do not challenge capitalism it will bottle
the air we breathe and sell it back to us. Perhaps air is a little
far-fetched, but land and water are not.

One of the latest targets of international trade is the genetic
heritage of the South. In 1991, under the current round of GATT
talks, it was proposed that the biotechnological development of
genetic material should become subject to a global patent. This
would mean that even the original genetic material used to
develop, for example, new seeds could become 'private property'.
Given that the vast majority of the world's genetic varieties are
in the South, there is wide scope for their 'privatisation' by the
biotechnology companies of the North. Countries of the South
would then have to buy back their own local species from seed
companies in the North if they wanted to compete in world
agricultural markets.

It is essential that we establish that some things are beyond
price: clean air, fresh water, a beautiful view, peace, silence, love.
There are many things in human life that are already beyond
price, that lie outside the market. One of the most important of
these is women's domestic, subsistence and caring work. How
can a market tell us it cannot 'afford' readily available clean water

when it expects women to produce it every day by fetching and boiling it? Women throughout the world are a living indictment of the market system:

> Indian women . . . have challenged the western concept of economics as production of profits and capital accumulation with their own concept of economics as production of sustenance and needs satisfaction. (Shiva, 1989, p. xvii)

Outside the Boundary: The Challenge of Women's Work

If human maintenance, mental and physical, and the nurturance of human beings are not taken care of, no other economy is possible.
(Hilkka Pietilä, 1987, p. 11)

[For Moroccan women] life is played out around the struggle for food, for wages, for some living, however minimal . . . earning one's living is the essential concern and purpose in life. Women exist above all as economic agents, as sources of income, energy and work, ceaselessly struggling against poverty, unemployment and insecurity . . .
(Fatima Mernissi, 1988, pp. 1–2)

I once asked a class of students if it would be a good idea to pay women the 'family' wage, as they were mainly responsible for home and family, while men carried out their present work for nothing. The male students were flabbergasted, as they could see no reason why men should be willing to do unpaid work for the benefit of their family, yet this is the reality for most women. One of the most important boundaries that the market has constructed is between men's and women's work. The market is not just capitalist, it is male (Armstrong and Armstrong, 1988). Male definition of what type of work is to be valued, and therefore waged, means that women who do unpaid domestic work have no independent right to resources except through a male wage or a welfare system.

For women in the South, there is a constant struggle to gain access to resources. In rural villages and shantytowns they continue to strive to support themselves and their families when men have gone to war, migrated to look for work, disappeared or taken to the bottle. According to Fatima Mernissi, in the view of the Moroccan women she interviewed 'men play no role at all in the daily battle that women wage to earn a living' (1988, p. 5). Women are the backstop of the world. If all else fails, they sell their own bodies to feed their families. Women have also agreed to be sterilised for money or food, particularly in the spring, before the growing season begins (Asian and Pacific Women's Resource Collection Network, 1989, p. 75). Most of women's work is unpaid because it is never bought or sold as a commodity on the market. Crops grown, meals prepared, clothes made are used directly, so that women do not produce a tangible 'product' other than a healthy child, a well-cooked meal, or a few gallons of water fetched from a distant well. On this basis most of women's work counts, quite literally, for nothing.

The large number of hours women spend in domestic and subsistence labour outside the marketplace is a vast resource to societies all over the world. In 1985 the Greater London Council calculated that 280 million hours were worked in London each week, but only 100 million of them were paid, and in America it has been calculated that the money value of childcare alone could be up to 50 per cent of GNP (*New Internationalist*, no. 181, March 1988). Across the globe women are engaged in a variety of tasks from agriculture to industry, from water-carrying to teaching, for little reward. According to the well-known and often-quoted statistic, women do two-thirds of the world's work for only 5 per cent of world income, and own less than 1 per cent of the world's assets. If we reverse the figures, we find that men do one-third of the world's work for 95 per cent of its income, and own more than 99 per cent of assets. This is the economic reality of male domination, which is vastly increased by the operation of the capitalist market economy.

Sen and Grown have described women as 'managers of human welfare', meeting 'survival and subsistence needs' (1987, p. 18). In addition women are responsible for securing the emotional needs of individuals and maintaining the functioning of the local community by minimising conflict in human relationships. In a patriarchal and capitalist system, women's work also reflects and reproduces the patterns of domination in which women are caught. Women's work provides free labour for capitalism in that it produces a healthy workforce and new generations of workers. It also provides physical and emotional support for men (Delphy, 1984). Because women's work is largely unrecognised and unpaid, it is carried out on top of the work women do in the waged economy. For most women, that means working a 'double shift' (Sharpe, 1984).

The importance of women's work is even more marked where subsistence economies are penetrated by the capitalist market. Wages paid to both male and female labourers are calculated *on the assumption* that their basic needs are being met by their own subsistence economy. Men are not given wages sufficient to sustain themselves, let alone their families. Despite this fact, women still get lower wages than men (Afshar, 1985, p. xv). This is the process that Maria Mies has described as super-exploitation:

> I define their exploitation as super-exploitation because
> it is not based on the appropriation [by the capitalist]
> of the time and labour over and above the necessary
> labour time, the *surplus* labour, but of the time and
> labour *necessary* for people's own survival or subsistence

production. It is not compensated for by a wage, the size
of which is calculated on the 'necessary' reproduction
costs of the labourer, but is mainly determined by force
or coercive institutions. This is the main reason for the
growing poverty and starvation of third world producers.
(1986, p. 48)

The invisibility of women and women's work goes right to the
heart of world decision-making systems. Most countries calculate
their wealth by using the United Nations System of National
Accounts (UNSNA), which explicitly excludes women's work from
its definition of 'production':

Producing and consuming entities in the economy
can be exhaustively and exclusively classified as either
enterprises or households . . . producers can be
identified with the former category. (Waring, 1989, p. 75)

Marilyn Waring describes herself as 'gasping for breath' when
she was told that women's subsistence work (defined as 'primary
work') had no value, 'since primary production and the consumption of their own produce by non-primary producers is of little or
no importance' (ibid., p. 78). As Waring points out, UNSNA embodies the blindness and arrogance of a patriarchy that enshrines the
invisibility and enslavement of women in the economic process.
The lack of recognition of women's subsistence, domestic or
caring work means that they are ignored in the allocation of
national and international resources by male decision-makers.

In her capacity as Chair of the Public Expenditures Committee
of the New Zealand Parliament, Waring 'found it virtually
impossible to prove . . . that child care facilities were needed.
Non-producers (house-wives, mothers) who are "inactive" and
"unoccupied" cannot, apparently be in need' (1989, p. 2). She
found that not taking account of women's subsistence work
had profound consequences for countries with large subsistence
economies, as their ability to benefit from aid or loans was

calculated on people's ability to earn cash incomes rather than the real productive capacity of the country. In trying to argue that women's work should be included in such calculations, Waring found that male statisticians placed all sorts of objections in her way, despite the fact that notional amounts are already included for such things as land values.

Women's invisibility means that aid programmes often ignore their needs for such fundamental things as access to clean water or sanitation (Rao, 1989; Dankelmen and Davidson, 1988). This is not a problem only for women in the South – women's domestic, health and sanitary needs were given an equally low priority, if not ignored, by state socialist production in Eastern Europe. In Western welfare systems, male and market interests also predominate in a way that excludes or marginalises women's 'claims' (Peattie and Rein, 1983). For example, in Britain, while there is no universal public transport system, particularly in rural areas, for those without private transport (mainly women), the right of every car driver to have a paved road to 'his' door is unquestioned. Although women as drivers and women and children as pedestrians use those roads, the safety of children and women is much less important than the right of the driver to proceed unimpeded. While women workers have to fight for childcare expenses, each family in Britain in 1991 paid the equivalent of £150 each year in tax relief for company cars, mainly driven by men.

As Lisa Peattie and Martin Rein point out, the male/market economy operates on the assumption that people produce and consume on the basis of free choice. In consequence, 'it has difficulty dealing with actions taken out of coercion or commitment' (1983, p. 16). This effectively excludes much of women's work, which is undertaken either in response to need or in response to fear of male violence. In Britain, one of the most critical policy areas where women's commitment is taken for granted is the euphemistically named 'community care', for the sick and elderly.

Who Cares?

The sick and elderly require care, which female relatives
are invariably expected to supply, and this is reinforced
by the stress on community care in current social service
policies.
(Sue Sharpe, 1984, p. 105)

In Britain there has been a great deal of discussion about the
'demographic time bomb' – that is, the fall in birth rate, leading
to a projected shortage of labour. Most, if not all, of the early
discussion of this problem was directed towards the labour needs
of the market sector. Only very belatedly was the question of who
would care for the elderly of the future addressed. By 1991 a fifth
of the population was already over sixty years old; this will rise to
a projected one million people over the age of eighty-five by the
year 2001.

In 1990 there were already signs of a crisis in care for the
elderly. Graham Pink, a Charge Nurse at Stepping Hospital,
Stockport, was accused of gross misconduct by his Health
Authority for his activities in publicising what he saw as inad-
equacy in staffing levels in geriatric wards. Age Concern reported
in October that the frail elderly in Greater London were finding
it difficult to keep themselves clean because of the withdrawal of
bathing services.

Caring for the mentally ill is equally problematic. In 1990 the
Mental Health Foundation reported that there were six million
people with clinically treatable mental illnesses in Britain, and
only 60,000 of them were catered for by the public services.
On the morning that I wrote the first draft of this chapter in
late 1990 I heard a woman on the radio say that she was caring
for her epileptic and schizophrenic husband without relief. He
was behaving so oddly that at times she had to lock away all
the knives.

At present the bulk of caring work in the home is carried

out by middle-aged to elderly women, although there are a substantial number of male carers (Arber and Gilbert, 1989). In 1990 the six million carers in Britain saved the British state £15–£24 billion a year. One study calculated that about 1.4 million people were spending more than twenty hours a week as carers, and that more than half of these carers had not had a break of more than one day since their responsibilities for caring began (Evandrou, 1990).

Although there are many male carers, care, particularly in old age, is mainly a problem for women. Women form the majority of carers and the majority of the aged who will need to be cared for – 75 per cent of the over-eighty-fives are female. A woman can find herself involved in a lifetime of caring: from family responsibilities as a child, to her own family, to care for her parents in their old age, to care for her partner in his old age and finally to the need to find care for herself in her own old age. The increasing number of women in paid work and the pressure on them to take jobs as the workforce shrinks mean that caring will be increasingly marginalised, or that carers will be even more pressured. Half of present carers already have jobs, and a third have children. If this type of work is not taken to the centre of our economic and political agenda, less-well-off women of the future may find themselves in paid work looking after the better-off elderly, with an unpaid second shift looking after the poor elderly.

Although this issue is slowly moving up the agenda for both the government and insurance companies, it goes deeper than just the question of financial resources. Dignity in old age and death must be one of the hallmarks of a civilised society. It is not just a case of one issue among many others, an afterthought when the cars have been produced, the computers programmed and the army equipped. It is not work that we can take or leave, that will be done only if the market can find it profitable or if the public services can 'afford' it. It makes little sense to try to solve this problem by 'market forces': by 1990, 56 per cent of people in private old people's homes were already dependent on state support.

The problem of caring makes a mockery of the arbitrary boundary between paid and unpaid work and profitable and unprofitable activities that pervades the male/market definition of the 'economy'. The real 'wealth-creating sector' for a society is not the production of 'something for the man who has everything', out of which a small amount of taxes may be extracted from profits and wages. The real wealth of a society is the work that is done, day in and day out, to build the quality of life for both individuals and communities. Marilyn Waring has argued (1989) that women can confront the male domination of economic structures only if we develop an alternative 'feminist economics' that sees the 'real wealth' of a nation as the well-being of all of its people. This the capitalist market cannot do, as inequality is essential to its functioning.

Marketing Inequality

If it had been the purpose of humanity on earth to bring
to the edge of ruin the planet itself, no more efficient
mechanism could have been invented than the market
. . . with its prodigious use of energy and materials in
the sublime mission of replacing as much of human
activity with commodities and the monetary transactions
that attend them . . . [We must] expel the market from
all those spaces it has inappropriately invaded, reclaim
autonomy and self-reliance . . . the market cannot create
social justice, it is powerless to distinguish between good
and evil.
(Jeremy Seabrook, 1990, p. 188)

The era of mass consumption in the North has pushed conspicuous consumption further and further down through society, from the rich to the poor. Consumption is sold to us as 'choice', as a celebration of our individual identities, despite the fact that we might be eating fast food that is standardised from New Zealand to Moscow. Consumption is fuelled by such a fierce commercial loyalty to brand names that some young people will kill for a pair of the latest 'box fresh' trainers with the 'right' label. Despite the superficial commonality of mass consumerism in the shopping mall shrines, the unfettered operation of market forces and the 'enterprise culture' have produced a grossly unequal society. Yuppie flats and up-market housing developments have burgeoned at the same time as 'cardboard city'.

In 1980s Britain the gap between the highest and lowest paid widened to the same ratio as in 1886. The rapid growth in retailing and services led to higher consumption but lower wages and less secure work. In ten years the number of McDonalds in Britain went from thirty to three hundred, while at the same time the number of people with an income of less than half the average wage doubled to ten million, many of whom were employed in the new consumer economy.

The consumer boom of the 1980s was built upon the sands of credit. In 1989 Britons were more personally indebted than the inhabitants of any other European country, paying commercial interest rates of up to 40 per cent (and much more to loan sharks). In 1991 consumers carried debts of £50 billion, six times higher than in 1979. During the 'Thatcher era' the number of households with credit facilities rose from 49 per cent to 73 per cent and by early 1990 200,000 were in serious arrears with loans and 500,000 in severe financial difficulties (*Guardian*, 7 February, 23 November 1990). The growth booms that got the Conservative government re-elected on successive occasions were based on what amounted to a 'privatised' Keynesianism. Unlike in Keynes's formula, it was not the government who borrowed money to stimulate the economy but private, and often very vulnerable, individuals. Nor did their borrowings produce a growth in infrastructure or productive capacity, as Keynes would have desired; most went on imported expendables.

The 'return to Victorian values' put 6.2 million families on the poverty line (*Independent on Sunday*, 30 September 1990). Reaganomics in America produced similar results. In the early 1980s the number of poor people in the United States rose by nine million in just four years. The worst effects were felt by ethnic minorities and women. More than one-third of all female-headed households and more than half of all Black and Hispanic households headed by women were living in poverty (Sen and Grown, 1987, p. 64).

Capitalism is the first economic system in history that does not give access to resources as of right to the citizens of a country. Resources, goods and services are available only to those who have money, not to those who live within the boundary of a national economy. The essence of the capitalist system is that it owes no one a living. Inheritance or success in the 'marketplace' as entrepreneur or worker is the only route to establishing a right to resources. If women/men find no work, or the income they receive for their produce is insufficient, in the absence of a welfare system, they starve. In Brazil more than half the population is 'outside' the market. The American privatised health system leaves substantial numbers of people without health cover.

In America, the unemployed – particularly the young – and ethnic minorities have been dubbed an 'underclass', people owing no allegiance to the wider society. Unlike the working class, this group has no economic clout; it cannot strike and in many cases does not vote. Similarly in Britain, many young people are 'disappearing' as citizens with no vote and little in the way of social rights. Faced with poor economic prospects, many find themselves forced into crime or take to the streets in protest. The dispossessed become a 'threat to law and order' and the police adopt an increasingly high-profile role as 'guardians of the state'. They are 'policing the crisis' (Hall, 1978; Gamble, 1988). Civil liberties become expendable as the government retreats behind iron grilles and the rich shelter behind security fences.

While the poor in the North are suffering the depredations of poverty, the crisis is much greater for the South. Every 'contrived demand' of the market economies of the North increases the gap between them and the poor South (Bahro, 1982; Redclift, 1991). However, both greens and market economists have come up with a possible solution to the problem of market inequality: give everyone the price of a ticket to ride the market merry-go-round.

A Ticket to Ride?

The Green approach is to abolish all welfare benefits, tax allowances and grants. Every citizen would receive instead a basic income sufficient for their essential needs. (Sandy Irvine and Alec Ponton, 1988, p. 70)

The green Basic Income Scheme is only one of a number of proposals to resolve the inequalities of capitalism by providing the poor with the 'wherewithal' to join the market on at least a limited level (Parker, 1989). One version based on a negative income tax has been put forward by one of the architects of the monetarist experiment that has plagued the world from Chile to Britain, Milton Friedman (1962, pp. 191–5). Similarly, some market socialists have suggested that a market system would be acceptable if wealth was comprehensively taxed and each person was given a 'poll grant' on reaching the age of maturity so that everyone was equal at the starting gate (Le Grand and Estrin, 1989). Unlike the two latter proposals, the green Basic Income Scheme is intended not to make the market work more effectively but to encourage people to drop out of it altogether by breaking the link between the right to resources and employment.

Such a scheme would certainly overcome the ludicrous situation where people are denied welfare benefits if they are deemed to be 'working', even for charity. It would break down the market-imposed boundary between paid work – i.e. employment – and unpaid work such as domestic labour. However, while the introduction of a Basic Income Scheme would enable people to work more flexibly, and could create access to the market for some people, it would do nothing to challenge the private ownership and control of resources, production and exchange upon which the capitalist market economy is based.

The levels of taxation that would be needed to fund a Basic Income of £60 per week per adult would be anything up to 86 per cent (Parker, 1989). The more modest £37 or so suggested by the British Green Party in 1991 would not really be sufficient to free people from waged work. The Basic Income Research Group gives figures to show that in 1989 all the current state benefits and income tax allowances combined would give each person around £38 per week. A 1991 study calculated that scrapping all income tax allowances and child benefit and adding 2p to income tax would produce a Basic Income of £11.89. For women, this level of Basic Income would not be sufficient to enable them to challenge the unequal allocation of work and income in the capitalist male economy (Voedingsbond FNV, nd).

While a Basic Income Scheme could go some small way towards redistributing resources, this would be effective in the long term only in a system in which resources were not in private hands and available only to the highest bidder; otherwise the benefits of a Basic Income could easily be wiped out by a rise in prices. This same problem affects David Pearce's suggestion (1991) that the higher costs of energy conservation could be ameliorated for the poor by giving them a financial subsidy or his argument for an international redistribution of wealth to resolve the environmental crisis while still retaining a capitalist world market economy. More importantly, a money redistribution within a market system would still depend on the capitalist economy to produce the 'wealth' to fund it (Ryle, 1988, p. 56).

The problem with the market system is not only the inequality it creates but the way it constrains and limits other aspects of social and political life. This is the crucial question of the relationship between the social principle and the market principle. Which is to have priority in the last resort – the needs of the market for profitability or the needs of the people for basic resources and services? As Michael Albert and Robin Hahnel have pointed out in their case for an alternative 'participatory economics':

> Anyone seriously interested in attaining a desirable
> economy (or polity, kinship sphere or culture) has to be
> interested in simultaneously attaining compatible equally
> desirable relations *throughout* society. (1991, p. 144;
> original emphasis)

The challenge we have to make is to the primacy of market ideology and the dominance of the market systems it represents – in particular the way they limit our social relations by undermining the non-economic basis of human relationships and discourage development of the non-material aspects of our lives.

Breaking the Boundaries of the Market

The market does not encourage me to relate to others
as fellow-citizens, members of the same community,
who have a multiplicity of goals . . . but only as factors
in production processes that have produced the goods
available to me to buy.
(Diane Elson, 1988, p. 16)

The purpose of the economy is to serve the people and
not the people to serve the economy.
(Manfred Max-Neef, 1989, p. 23)

The 'economy' that has been raised to such a high political profile under market capitalism is a totally man-made structure: 'the categories of the "economic" and "non-economic" are neither objective nor natural . . . they are culturally and historically specific' (Harding and Jenkins, 1989, pp. 175–6). Hilkka Pietilä argues that the market system which so dominates the politics of the globe reflects very little of our real lives. She has calculated that in Norway the export market sector dominated by international capitalism, which she calls the 'fettered sector', commands only 10 per cent of total working time (which she calculates as equivalent to 19 per cent of the worth of the whole formal and informal economy in money terms). Production for local use and the public sector accounts for 36 per cent of time (46 per cent in money terms). Finally, unpaid work, which she calls the 'free economy', accounts for 54 per cent of time (35 per cent in money terms) (1987, p. 9). Hazel Henderson sees the 'real' economy as a multilayered cake (see Figure 1), where the market economy is a fairly thin icing on a very deep cake that embraces the public sector, an informal underground economy, a 'social co-operative sector', the domestic sector and the wealth of the natural world.

Henderson sees the market economy as representing a one-dimensional 'flat-earth' approach to economics, which:

> . . . leads us to believe that we can 'afford' oversize
> private cars, thousands of brands of patent medicines,
> and billion dollar industries devoted to pet foods and
> cosmetics, while we cannot 'afford' nurses, teachers,
> police, fire and sanitation services . . . We . . .
> over-reward competition while ignoring co-operation and
> all the cohesive activities that bind the society together,
> which we have relegated to the status of unremunerated
> activities to be performed by women. It has caused
> us to overvalue property rights while undervaluing
> amenity rights and to overvalue individual freedom over
> community needs. (1978, p. 15)

The capitalist market economy can produce a third, fourth or fifth car for the rich, but not universal care for the frail elderly. It can deprive an Indian woman of her land and create a huge

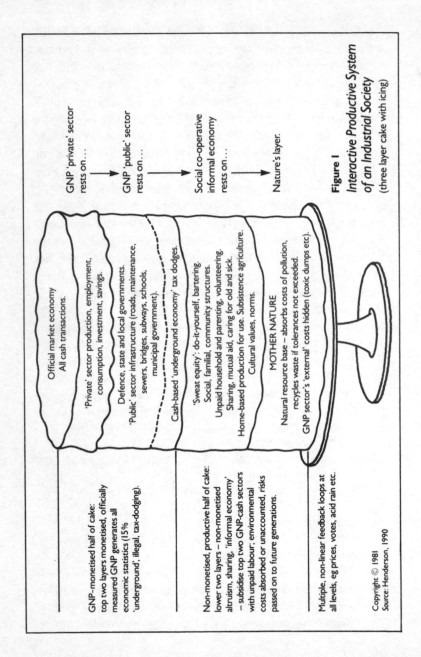

Official market economy
All cash transactions.

GNP 'private' sector
rests on....

'Private' sector production, employment,
consumption, investment, savings.

GNP 'public' sector
rests on....

'Public' sector infrastructure (roads, maintenance,
sewers, bridges, subways, schools,
municipal government).
Defence, state and local governments.

Cash-based 'underground economy' tax dodges.

Social co-operative
informal economy
rests on....

'Sweat equity': do-it-yourself, bartering.
Social, familial, community structures.
Unpaid household and parenting, volunteering.
Sharing, mutual aid, caring for old and sick.
Home-based production for use. Subsistence agriculture.
Cultural values, norms.

Nature's layer.

MOTHER NATURE
Natural resource base – absorbs costs of pollution,
recycles waste if tolerances not exceeded.
GNP sector's 'external' costs hidden (toxic dumps etc).

GNP-monetised half of cake:
top two layers monetised, officially
measured GNP generates all
economic statistics (15%
'underground', illegal, tax-dodging).

Non-monetised, productive half of cake:
lower two layers – non-monetised
altruism, sharing, 'informal economy'
– subsidise top two GNP-cash sectors
with unpaid labour; environmental
costs absorbed or unaccounted, risks
passed on to future generations.

Multiple, non-linear feedback loops at
all levels, eg prices, votes, acid rain etc.

Figure I
Interactive Productive System
of an Industrial Society
(three layer cake with icing)

Copyright © 1981
Source: Henderson, 1990

media empire for Rupert Murdoch on the income of which, it is claimed, he pays only 3p in the £ in tax (Channel Four, 20 December 1990). It can destroy the Amazonian rainforest and build a gambling 'Taj Mahal' for Donald Trump. It is a system that donates free baby milk to nursing mothers in the South to stimulate a worldwide baby food market of $5 billion, when UNICEF estimates that a bottle-fed baby is twenty-five times more likely to die than a breastfed one and one million babies die a year from unsafe bottle-feeding (Dally, 1990, p. 18; Palmer, 1988). It deluges each American household with five hundred items of junk mail each year and invades the privacy of nearly every citizen by keeping a commercial file on them. The deregulated and bloated financial market of the 1980s produced a 'junk bond king' and the 'politics of greed'. It was a sector whose operations 'came pretty close to usury, greed and straight theft' (Will Hutton, Economics Editor of the *Guardian*, 24 December 1990).

Despite these blatant abuses of economic power, socialists have not been able, or willing, to mount an adequate opposition to such an unjust and distorted economic system. It has been women, greens, excluded minorities and people of the South who have asked why we are living under an economic system that cannot meet the basic needs of nearly two-fifths of the world's people; that does not acknowledge women's work or needs and treats the environment as either a 'free resource' or someone's private property. The market system may offer 'choice' to a privileged few hundred million in the dominant centres of the world economy and the elites of the South, but at the same time it creates or sustains racism, colonialism, patriarchy and ecological destruction. The capitalist 'market' cannot be managed, adapted or reconstructed: we must be 'liberated from economics' (Bahro, 1982).

Praful Bidwai of the *Times of India* argues that the domination of the world by the capitalist market economy of the North has distorted our view of human geography and human history. It has led to a vision of the world that is antinature, antiwoman and antiSouth. Bidwai demands that we abandon the economic and political philosophies of the male industrial North in favour of a nature-orientated, female-orientated South. The South should now become the central focus of global politics, with the North as its periphery. He points out that the South represents the majority of the people in the world, the bulk of its natural resources, the breadth of its culture, civilisation and traditions. The North is the minority and exception to this natural and cultural wealth. Northern capitalism must be rejected in favour of:

> a shift from urban to rural, industrial to agricultural, high-cost to low-cost, inorganic to organic, modern to traditional, exotic to indigenous, processed to unprocessed, marketed to subsistence, quantitative to qualitative, standardised to vernacular, individual to community, male to female, light-skinned to dark-skinned (*New Ground*, Winter/Spring 1989, p. 10)

Under the capitalist world market, people across the globe are dying because they cannot afford the 'price' of survival. I would argue that we now face the choice between a personalised survivalism and a reconstructed socialism, informed by feminist and green principles.

CHAPTER 7

Towards a Feminist Green Socialism 1: Socialism or Survivalism?

We want a world where inequality based on class, gender and race is absent from every country, and from the relationships among countries. We want a world where basic needs become basic rights and where poverty and all forms of violence are eliminated. Each person will have the opportunity to develop her or his full potential and creativity, and women's values of nurturance and solidarity will characterize human relationships.
(Gita Sen and Caren Grown, 1987, p. 80)

The earth can no longer be owned; it must be shared. Its fruits, including those produced by technology and labour, can no longer be appropriated by the few; they must be rendered available to all on the basis of need.
(Murray Bookchin, 1989, p. 172)

This chapter and the next bring together my case for a feminist green socialism. As I pointed out in the introduction, it is not my intention to provide a blueprint or detailed policy recommendations for a future feminist green socialist society. What I want to do is argue the case for a feminist, green and socialist movement by drawing on the ideas of all three movements, showing how they must *necessarily* be integrated if we are to achieve a sustainable future for both humanity and the planet. In this chapter I want to argue the case for eco-socialism; in the next that a feminist analysis is also essential. Although none of these movements is new, it is socialism that has achieved the highest political profile and therefore, deservedly, the most criticism for its failure to combat inequality, racism and sexism and its contribution to the ecological crisis.

In contrast, the feminist and green movements are 'new' in the sense that their analysis and prescriptions have not become integral to existing political structures. While the green movement has put the ecological crisis firmly on to the political agenda, without a socialist perspective it lacks an effective politics of social justice. For many greens, particularly those who take an Earth-centred view, social justice is not even on the agenda. In a condition of scarcity, without a politics of social justice, there is nothing to prevent a deterioration into an individual struggle for survival. I would argue that if the predictions of the greens are correct, that is our choice: socialism or survivalism.

The Ecological Crisis: A Problem with No Politics

The environment does not exist as a sphere separate
from human actions, ambitions, and needs, and attempts
to defend it in isolation from human concerns have given
the very word 'environment' a connotation of naivety in
some political circles.
(Brundtland Report, 1987, p. xi)

The green movement has been very effective in getting the message across that an ecological crisis exists and is rapidly becoming worse. It has been much less effective in getting people to articulate their very widespread concern in political terms. Green Parties seem stuck on the very fringe of politics: a thorn in the side of traditional parties, but no immediate threat. I see no sign that this will change in the near future, but I would love to be proved wrong.

The problem for the green movement lies in the fact that *the ecological crisis has no inherent politics*. A 'green' crisis does not lead in any automatic way to a 'green' solution. This point has also been made by other eco-socialists (Gorz, 1980; Ryle, 1988; Williams, nd; Pepper, 1991). Eco-socialists challenge the assumption that underlies green politics in many quarters – that if we get our attitude to the natural world right, then our social arrangements will fall into place. This stems from a humanist reading of the natural world – that recognising our connectedness with the planet will put human society on the 'right' path. There is no reason why it should. We may read a political message into Gaia, but she tells us only of our *ecological* connectedness. There may well be a 'green' way of doing things and a 'green' way of life, but these have to be politically constructed. The search for the political message of Gaia has produced a reactionary as well as a progressive green politics (Bramwell, 1985, 1989). It has produced arguments for social justice alongside the 'lifeboat' ethics of national self-interest promoted by Garrett Hardin (1968, 1977). In any event, Gaia can have no 'natural' message, for as I have shown, the natural world is irrevocably social, having already been deeply influenced by human activity.

To say that the ecological crisis has no inherent politics is not to say that there is no green political thought. On the contrary, there has been a rich flowering of ideas in the green movement, but they are many-stranded, drawing on the ideas of other political perspectives: liberal, anarchist, conservative, feminist, socialist. Greens are not 'neither right nor left but in front', they are right and left and centre. David Pepper sees the environmental movement as representing various streams of radical and reformist thought. The radicals are made up of romantic conservatives, revolutionary socialists, anarchists and ecofeminists, while the reformists include market liberals, welfare liberals and democratic socialists. He also sees a distinct group of 'mainstream greens' who seek radical goals through reformist measures such as electoral or pressure-group politics or personal transformation. However, Pepper argues that all mainstream greens have a tendency towards reactionary conservatism in that they all to some extent embrace New Age irrationalism and mysticism as well as a rejection of 'politics' and industrialism (1991, p. 19).

The rise of green politics has not resulted in traditional political interests being thrown to one side, as some greens have suggested; instead, 'green issues' have been appropriated by other parties from socialists to the National Front. In response, greens have rightly argued that these parties have no conception of how revolutionary the ecological crisis is likely to prove. Socialists, in particular, have been very slow to grasp that the green issue must be central to any serious progressive politics (Ryle, 1988; Paehlke, 1989). Like the British Labour Party, they are still seeing it as a bolt-on option to 'business as usual'.

The ecological crisis has no inherent politics, but it has tremendous political implications. Even if only some of the ecological warnings of the greens are true, those who already suffer from domination, exploitation, oppression and exclusion from the wealth and resources of the planet will have their burdens made immeasurably worse, and the power of those who now own and control the resources of the world will be considerably enhanced. If the ecological crisis occurs without a confrontation with the present structures of power, life will be very bleak for countless millions. In many parts of the world a fascist response is as likely as a conservative, socialist, green or liberal one. If we are to avoid this possibility, we have to harness the challenge of the ecological crisis to a progressive politics. As Murray Bookchin has pointed out, the ecological crisis creates a greater opportunity for a mass mobilisation of public support than any other issue in human history:

> Our foremost need is to create a general human
> interest that can unify humanity as a whole. Minimally
> this interest centres around the establishment of a
> harmonious balance with nature (Bookchin, 1989,
> pp. 171–2)

Bookchin is pointing us in the right direction, but he is much too optimistic. There are a lot of boundaries and divisions between our present society and Bookchin's 'general human interest', not least the divisions of class, race and sex. Bookchin seeks for unity in our diversity, but this has to be politically forged, particularly in the face of a potentially divisive crisis. As I pointed out earlier, for poor people the ecological crisis is not new; it has been acknowledged as universal only because it has finally affected the rich and powerful nations. It is clear that the response of the latter is determined by self-interest rather than the needs of either humanity or the planet. *The ecological crisis may now be universal in its effects, but that does not mean to say that there will be a universal response.* The response in New York will differ from that in Nairobi; that in Canberra from that in Calcutta. Each class, national elite, ethnic group, sex or race will respond to the crisis within the framework of its own interests and in terms of its own claim on resources and power to determine events.

The benefits of the planet have been exploited by relatively few members of the human community, and there is no reason why such a deeply unequal world system should respond to an ecological crisis on the basis of social justice. If people within the green movement want to follow a progressive political direction, they will need to draw upon the insights of socialists and feminists in a far more systematic way than they have so far. In the case of socialists in particular, greens must stand on their shoulders and not on their necks. At the same time we can hardly blame greens for distrusting socialism's human-centredness when a socialist at the 1991 Socialist Scholars' Conference in New York declared that he would rather have a blasted earth with the human population living underground than a beautiful planet with no people on it.

Despite the fact that actually existing socialism has gone up many viciously corrupt blind alleys, at the centre of socialist philosophy there remains a fundamental vision of a just and equal society. It is a vision that any progressive green politics would need to embrace. The ecological crisis presents socialists with the opportunity to prove the superiority of collective egalitarianism over possessive individualism – to show that socialism rather than capitalism is the most appropriate political response in a world that is reaching, or has overreached, its natural boundaries.

Red without Green

Man *lives* from nature, i.e. nature is his body and he must maintain a continuing dialogue with it if he is not to die. To say that man's physical and mental life is linked to nature simply means that nature is linked to itself, for man is a part of nature.
(Karl Marx, 1975, p. 328; sexism in the original)

Let us not . . . flatter ourselves overmuch on account of our human conquests over nature. For each such conquest takes its revenge on us.
(Friedrich Engels, *Dialectics of Nature*, quoted in Parsons, 1977, p. 178)

The modern socialist movement's obsession with industry and growth is hard to square with the early ecological awareness expressed in these statements by Marx and Engels. Yet it is the Marxist influence on socialism that has driven it towards an obsession with 'productivism', seeing the producing and exchanging of commodities as the central pivot of political analysis and the industrial worker as the pivot of political action. Socialism has become 'industrial socialism', with preoccupations that are both antigreen and antifeminist. Its attention is focused on the political interests of 'real' workers in 'real' jobs, where 'real' workers are men in large-scale industry. Women's interests and their paid and unpaid work are largely ignored, and ecologically destructive forms of production like the nuclear, arms and car industries are not seriously challenged.

The limitations of these boundaries were clearly shown during the British miners' strike of 1984–5, when the National Coal Board's decision to close 'uneconomic' pits threatened to devastate the coal-mining communities. In fighting the closure of 'uneconomic' pits the miners were forced to argue within the parameters of capitalist economics: the relative costs of different kinds of power, the comparative price of coal around the world and the potential for new markets. Despite the miners' campaign for 'Pits, Jobs and Community', the last did not 'count' politically and the possibility of the conservation of coal stocks for future generations was not on the agenda at all. The sight of piles of unwanted coal pillaged from the Earth and from future generations was deeply depressing. This precious resource was being discussed only in terms of pounds and pence and men's jobs. The desire to 'save money' by closing pits was not abated by the possibility that future generations might have to expend huge amounts of energy reopening them, with – probably – only the difficult seams left to be worked.

Similarly, the pit communities could not be argued for as a 'good' in themselves, despite the fact that miners' wives stood 'side by side with their men' on the picket line. For the women it was not just a fight for employment, it was a fight for families, friends, a common culture and a way of life. The 10,000-strong women-led miners' support groups raised money from around the world to maintain basic subsistence for striking families. However, the work-based National Union of Mine-workers had no means of formally incorporating women into the struggle. The strike changed many individual women's lives, but did not break the patriarchal boundary between the 'breadwinner' and (his) family. When, after the strike, the miners' wives asked for associate membership of the NUM, they were refused. The sea of patriarchy closed over their heads once more, and their voices were drowned.

In the face of the miners' defeat, it seemed as if large-scale industrial struggle was no longer the way forward for socialism. We were in 'New Times' where global capitalism had slipped beyond the reach of class politics. One group of socialists turned away from productivism to embrace an equally ungreen alternative, the politics of consumption.

Bazaar Socialism in the New Times

New Times is a fraud, a counterfeit, a humbug. It
palms off Thatcherite values as socialist, shores up the
Thatcherite market with the pretended values of choice,
fits out the Thatcherite individual with progressive
consumerism, makes consumption itself the stuff of
politics. New Times is a mirror image of Thatcherism
passing for socialism. New Times is Thatcherism
in drag.
(A. Sivanandan, 1989, p. 1)

The birth of 'New Times' was heralded in October 1988 by the Eurocommunist magazine *Marxism Today*. In a series of articles it declared the death of traditional class politics through the arrival of new social movements, the changing nature of capitalism and the importance of cultural factors – in particular, the desire of individuals to celebrate their individual identities. Traditional industrial struggle had been rendered irrelevant by the way capitalism had managed to reorganise itself internationally beyond immediate political control and the way new technologies enabled it to operate without a large skilled workforce. The development of new industrial processes such as computer-aided technology meant that production was fluid and flexible, and a new politics was needed for these New Times (Hall and Jacques, 1989).

Politically, New Times socialism was in sympathy with the green movement and welcomed it, together with other new movements of women, Black people and peace campaigners. It also declared its support for expressions of grass-roots activity such as tenants' associations, co-operatives and community groups. However, it parted company with the greens in its 'politics of consumption'. The *Marxism Today* group saw a new political opportunity in the popular appeal of the Radical Right's celebration of the freedom of the 'marketplace'. Consumption had been raised to a seductive art form, leading to a 'manic compulsion to consume' with 'the hyper-eroticisation of a visit to the shops'. Shopping arcades were the new centres of worship, and to consume was to be. This appeal could not be ignored. The weapons for the new revolutionary were the credit card and the (designer label) shopping bag:

> Commodities and their images are multi-accented, they can be pushed and pulled into the service of resistant demands and dreams. High tech in the hands of young blacks or girls making-up are not simply forms of buying into the system, they can be very effectively hijacked for cultures of resistance, reappearing as street-style cred or assertive femininity. (Frank Mort, 1989, p. 166)

The dull, grey days of socialism as a bureaucratic, white brotherhood were over. Consumer choice was to be a 'source of power and pleasure'. Advertisers and marketers are 'not simply the slaves of capital' they:

> are the intermediaries who construct a dialogue between the market on the one hand and consumer culture on the other ... marketing taps something of our pleasures and aspirations as consumers. (ibid., p. 167)

Those who advocated New Times and the politics of consumption implicitly acknowledged that they were making a silk purse out of a sow's ear. They were trying to make the best of the triumph of market capitalism by advocating militant consumerism. According to Sivanandan, they ended up creating:

> A sort of bazaar socialism, bizarre socialism, a hedonist socialism; an eat, drink and be merry socialism

> because tomorrow we can eat again . . . a socialism for
> disillusioned Marxist intellectuals who had waited around
> too long for the revolution. (1989, p. 23)

Celebration of the market and the inevitability of 'flexible'
capitalist production is no basis for a green socialism. Rather,
we must go back to the roots of socialism and re-green it.

Greening Socialism

A 're-founded' socialism must . . . take up the challenge
of ecology and of the Green Parties and the green
movements. Both the negative, constraining limits of
ecological responsibility and the positive, utopian critical
thinking which that responsibility provokes are essential
aspects of any serious political reawakening.
(Martin Ryle, 1988, p. 100)

Tragically Marxism virtually silenced earlier revolutionary
voices for more than a century and held history itself
in the icy grip of a remarkably bourgeois theory of
development based on the domination of labour and the
centralization of power.
(Murray Bookchin, 1989, p. 169)

It is difficult to begin a greening of socialism without a greening
of Marx. Although Marx made a brilliant critique of the capitalist
system of ownership, production and exchange, his theory
became trapped within the web of capitalism by sharing its
definition of the 'economy', i.e. the sphere of production and the
allocation of value as defined by capital. Although he had early
reservations about the new industrial system and the alienating
effect of the division of labour, Marx could not help but be caught
up in the excitement of nineteenth-century industrialism and its
productive potential (Benton, 1989). He shared this optimism
with most socialists of his time, apart from notable exceptions

like William Morris and, rather earlier, Charles Fourier. For Marx, the new industrial system was there to be captured for the people. The agents of that capture were growing before his very eyes: the industrial proletariat. Little did Marx and Engels envisage that the impoverished and exploited worker they saw would eventually capitulate to the 'fetishism of commodities' and the 'politics of consumption'.

In their certainty of the inevitable collapse of capitalism and the revolutionary potential of the working classes, Marx and Engels dubbed their socialism 'scientific'. They denounced the moral criticism of capitalism made by the earlier 'utopian socialists' such as Robert Owen (1771–1858), Charles Fourier (1772–1837), William Thompson (1775–1833) and Anna Wheeler (1785–?). The utopian socialists not only criticised private property and the exploitation of workers but also attacked women's sexual and social inequality and the power of organised religion (Taylor, 1983). By limiting his analysis to the capitalist-defined boundary of the 'sphere of production', Marx ignored these wider questions as well as the way capitalism exploited both women and the planet.

Marx's theory explained the relationship between workers and capitalists *within* the capitalist system of production, but ignored the fact that capitalism does not just exploit the labour of workers in factories, it draws on two other sources of wealth: the natural world, which it has exploited virtually for free, and the unpaid labour of women, which it exploits through the much older system of domination, patriarchy. Marx did recognise the fact that capitalism exploited all three, but he did not build the latter two into his economic analysis and his programme for class struggle (Aronowitz, 1990). The weakness of industrial socialism is that it has been attacking only one leg of a three-legged chair (or a four-legged chair, if we include the exploitation of colonised peoples). This error was compounded by future generations of Marxists who were mainly white and male.

Despite the criticisms made by feminists and greens, socialist thinking is still limited by its concentration on the (male) working class and the industrial potential of the capitalist system. Women remain marginalised as workers; their sexual and reproductive rights, their unpaid domestic work as nurturers and carers, the violence they experience at the hands of men, are still secondary to 'economic' struggle. If women, people of the South and the natural world are to force themselves on to the political agenda they will have to overcome the dominance of the 'economic', not only in capitalist but in socialist thinking. Before socialism can confront capitalism, it will have to transcend it, get beyond its framework of reasoning. What Harriet Bradley has argued for sex equality is equally true for other forms of inequality and the exploitation of nature:

> there is no justification for the claim that socialism (even 'true' socialism) would, by itself, bring an end to sexual inequality, as long as socialism is defined as a type of economic arrangement. (Bradley, 1989, p. 228)

To criticise Marx's theory as limited is not to reject its essential critique of capitalism. As we have seen, capitalism is the predominant force in the exploitation of both people and planet. Nor, as I will argue later, can we reject class politics out of hand. However, we do need to begin again with the observation both Marx and Engels made: that human history and natural history are inextricably intertwined. Nature is part of human history, and humanity is part of natural history. We alter nature as nature alters us. Engels came very close to the position of present-day greens in his *Dialectics of Nature*:

> For in nature nothing takes place in isolation. Every thing affects every other thing and *vice versa*, and it is mostly because this all-sided motion and interaction is forgotten that our natural scientists are prevented from clearly seeing the simplest of things.
> (quoted in Parsons, 1977, p. 178)

He goes on to discuss the impact of the introduction of goats on forests in Greece and problems in the artificial breeding of plants and animals. He notes that the essential distinction between people and animals is that humans 'master' nature, but there will always be consequences. Only through a better appreciation of the unity of humanity with nature and a realisation of the interconnectedness of things will we be able to begin to get to know and control 'even the more remote natural consequences' of our activities.

In a later passage he echoes our present concerns with deforestation, noting that the Spanish planters in Cuba burned down the mountain trees to grow coffee but managed only one crop before the fertility of the soil was exhausted and the soil washed away in tropical storms. If only he had formed a green socialist party then! In fact he had set out his ideas as early as 1844 in his *Outlines of a Critique of Political Economy*:

> To make earth an object of huckstering – the earth
> which is our one and all, the first condition of our
> existence – was the last step toward making oneself
> an object of huckstering. It was and is to this very
> day an immorality surpassed only by the immorality of
> self-alienation. And the original appropriation – the
> monopolisation of the earth by a few, the exclusion
> of the rest from that which is the condition of their
> life – yields nothing in immorality to the subsequent
> huckstering of the earth. (quoted in Parsons,
> 1977, p. 172)

Unlike Engels, Marx did not foresee the problem of ecological limits to production (Benton, 1989). He argued that poverty and inequality were created by the artificial restriction on resources and production through private ownership in class society. Once workers seized control of the capitalist 'machine', there would be plenty for everyone. It is ironic that it is the revenge of nature rather than the working class that is now crying halt to capitalism.

The End of Nature and the Limits of Capitalism

Capitalist property rights are not an issue of freedom
versus equality, but of freedom for a few versus freedom
for everyone.
(John Baker, 1987, p. 80)

Since Adam Smith's *Wealth of Nations* in 1776 we have been promised that if each of us acts upon our own economic self-interest, a 'hidden hand' will guide us all to the capitalist 'Heaven on Earth'. Within the political systems of the North, 'market forces' have claimed the moral high ground; all non-market activity is by definition economically unprofitable and a 'drain' on the 'wealth-creating sector'. Supporters of capitalism argue that it is the fairest way to allocate scarce resources and guarantee individual freedom through the values of 'possessive individualism', with each individual taking personal responsibility for their economic well-being. If privately owned and controlled wealth, resources and production are allowed to circulate without hindrance in a profit-driven market system, economic benefits will eventually trickle down to all of humanity in some form.

The capitalist market economy is presented as a game that anyone can play and no one in the end will lose, although some may deservedly win more than others. Those who gain economic wealth and power are assumed to have exhibited more entrepreneurial flair, worked harder or sacrificed more than losers. Not only have they 'earned' their wealth, they have 'given other people jobs'. The system is limited only by the laziness and/or ignorance of those who are not willing to play the game, work hard, save, take risks. Poverty is the result of a lack of 'development' along the capitalist yellow brick road. This is an argument that has paralysed socialism, East and West.

The state-sponsored industrialism of the command economics of Eastern Europe could not match the efficiency of capitalism in Western Europe and North America, nor their democratic processes. In the West socialism became increasingly tied into capitalist industrial growth, waiting for the crumbs to drop from the entrepreneurial table.

For Marxist socialists, poverty was an artefact of the capitalist system. Capitalism needed economic inequality and the dread of the poorhouse or the dole queue to keep workers 'disciplined'. After the revolution the machinery of capitalism could be harnessed for the workers; there would be plenty for all: 'from each according to their ability, to each according to their need'. Socialism would mean 'levelling people up', not down. In making this claim, socialists have been locked into competing with capitalism in the promise of 'goodies', a race they were bound to lose. Capitalism could suck in resources from all over the world to feed its favoured markets, with no social or political obligation to those whose resources it had plundered or whose workers' health it had ruined.

When socialists challenged capitalism, pointing to its periodic economic crises and the deep inequalities it produced, capitalism could wave all criticisms and complaints away with its eternal promise, growth. Those who owned and controlled economic resources justified their privilege by claiming that the exploited and impoverished would get their turn when the development 'boat comes in'. The message from the green movement is that the boat will never come; instead, we are on a global lifeboat that is sinking.

Where socialism failed to puncture the capitalist illusion, the ecological crisis has succeeded in calling into question the 'mythic power' of the market (Seabrook, 1990). In a system with natural boundaries to production and consumption, it becomes clear that profits cannot be conjured out of thin air. Nothing is without cost – if not to other people, then to the planet itself. Without the promise of constant growth, there is no moral basis for the private accumulation of wealth. In a limited system, capitalism can no longer hide the fact that it is a mechanism for accumulating, rather than distributing, wealth. The ecological crisis exposes what Hazel Henderson has called the 'looking glass world' of flat-earth economics where 'money wealth' dominates our lives, as against the 'real' wealth of natural resources and the skills and creativity of human beings (1978, 1988).

When it becomes clear that 'economics is little more than politics in disguise' (Henderson, 1990), the question of the distribution of resources must be placed on the *political* rather than the *economic* agenda. In an ecologically boundaried economic system it would become clear that capitalism is inherently incapable of meeting even the basic needs of the world community; all it could offer would be a cruel and amoral survivalism.

Socialism versus Survivalism

There is no such thing as society, only individuals and the family.
(Margaret Thatcher, 1987)

In a situation of ecological scarcity . . . the individualistic basis of society – the concept of inalienable rights, the purely self-defined pursuit of happiness and laissez-faire itself all require abandonment if we wish to avoid environmental degradation and perhaps extinction as a civilization.
(Ophuls, 1977, p. 151)

An ecological crisis leading to a limit on consumption in a world driven by the values of individual, commercial and national economic self-interest can bring only one result: survivalism. Each person, group, organisation or nation will struggle mercilessly for its own continued existence. That must mean that those who are powerful now will use every ounce of their power to retain their position. The small gains that have been made towards international co-operation, eliminating absolute poverty or providing a foundation for women's economic independence will be lost. Moves towards intercultural understanding will be rapidly eroded as dominant cultures and races become less tolerant of those races and cultures they dominate.

The drive to control resources will lead to increased international conflict. The world market for raw materials has meant that capitalist economic growth and wealth do not necessarily relate to a country's riches in resources. Japan is the most obvious case, relying heavily on imports for most of its raw materials and energy. Even a resource-rich country like America is a net importer of oil. If capitalism is to survive even in a 'conservationist' form – that is, limiting wealth to those who already have it – sources of raw materials are going to have to be grabbed. The only way in which the resource-rich could keep the resource-poor at bay would be an increase in military control, both internally and externally. We have already seen eco-wars in the Middle East over the control of oil and water. In Africa the relationship between war and environmental degradation is extremely close, the one feeding the other. Already there are ten million displaced people in Africa, with another hundred million at risk, and this is likely to be increasingly echoed in other parts of the world. One major threat to international stability is the political collapse of the resource-rich USSR which leaves the danger of an economic, political or military struggle, internally or externally, over control of those resources. This is compounded by the fact that several of the newly independent republics have nuclear weapons.

The only possible alternative to the allocation of natural resources by economic or military muscle is socialism on a global scale – not the socialism of male-orientated industrialism but a socialism that expresses our collective recognition of ourselves as a global human *society*. Socialism has always had the aim of an egalitarian world without boundaries. In unity with the green movement, it now has a material as well as a moral basis for making that case. The material conditions of scarcity create a clear choice between socialism and survivalism. The ecological crisis creates the conditions for a reassertion of the moral values of the common good against the self-interested divisions of the nation-state and the marketplace. The 1991 British Attitude Survey showed that despite ten years of Thatcherism, collective values still hovered just below the surface. However, it will be a much bigger challenge to assert collective values that transcend boundaries of nation, race and culture.

A green socialism would, however, have to go even further and recognise that the future of the human race cannot be secured at the expense of other species. A socialism for the future must mean the realisation of a truly undivided world; it cannot be limited to one country, one sex, one generation or even one species. The starting point for green socialism must be to establish that the natural resources of the world cannot be divided either by private ownership or by national boundaries. If we are to have a sustainable and socially just future, we must hold that wealth in common.

Natural World as Common-wealth

common: land belonging to a community
(*The Concise Oxford Dictionary*)

My good friends, matters cannot go on well in England
until all things shall be in common.
(John Ball, quoted in Benn, 1984, p. 83)

Greens, particularly those who take a mystical turn, urge that we should realise our connectedness with the natural world as a change of consciousness. The assumption is that if we realise our connectedness, particularly in a spiritual, reverential way, we will see our responsibility and act upon it. This is to miss the point. Although we may not have *realised* our connectedness, with the planet, we have always been materially connected both with the planet and with each other. The problem has been that our connectedness with the planet and each other has been divisive and destructive. We cannot just change our consciousness, we have to find a way of overcoming the destructive material connectedness of our lives. As Marx said in his famous 'Eleventh Thesis on Feuerbach': 'philosophers have only *interpreted* the world in various ways; the point, however, is to *change* it' (1970, p. 30).

The green longing for the commonality of clan society is understandable, but misplaced. The reverence that earlier societies held for the Earth was not purely spiritual, it reflected a material reality that made the world seem literally boundless. It is not a case of re-creating a spiritual realisation of an unboundaried world but of finding a political route to achieving it as a material reality in a world boundaried by nation-states, private estates and individual plots. Any division of the global ecosystem is, in a sense, unnatural. The revolutionary potential of the ecological crisis lies in the challenge it makes to the boundaries and divisions within and between societies. We have divided our nations and communities in ways that pay no attention to our ecological connectedness. River basins are perhaps the most obvious example of an ecosystem that needs co-ordinated administration, yet in many cases they form the boundaries of nation-states. Local and national boundaries also cut across the river's downward flow. Without co-operation and collective management, each national or regional state will take what it can from the river and dump its effluent on those downstream.

Nation-states, private ownership and a profit-orientated economic system do not see the natural heritage of the planet as a common resource for the whole of humanity, now and in the future. They most certainly do not see the natural world as a resource for nature itself, for other species and the diversity of living things. The resources of the earth are not experienced as a 'common', as a source of wealth for all and the responsibility of all. The only 'wealth' that counts is money, and natural resources are turned into cash as quickly as possible. The seas are stripped of their fish, the hillsides of their trees, the rivers of their fresh water, the land of its fertility. Natural resources become a bounty for the nearest taker, directly depriving others, human and non-human, of those resources. Each logger or rancher is destroying the livelihood of a forest-dweller or contributing to the greenhouse effect. Each factory-ship is destroying the livelihood of other fishers. Each dam-builder is depriving river-dwellers further downstream of fresh water and alluvium. Under the logic of self-interest and survivalism there is nothing to stop the fisher fishing the last fish, the logging company taking the last tree, or the dam withholding the last drop of water.

The classic analysis of the problem of 'fishing the last fish' – or, rather, grazing the last blade of grass – is Garrett Hardin's 'Tragedy of the Commons'. Hardin based his influential article, written in 1968, on a parable set out in a neo-Malthusian pamphlet issued in 1833. The parable hypothesises a shared common grazing land with a finite carrying capacity, used by local herders to graze their cattle. On the assumption that the herders follow their own individual self-interest, each attempts to maximise self-interest by trying to graze as many cattle as possible, thus destroying the resource for everyone. According to the parable, each herder is aware of the damage overgrazing will do but still persists because it is in their self-interest to do so, as the net economic benefit to themselves of grazing one more head of cattle is less than the cost s/he bears for the decline of the common, which is shared with all the other herders. Hardin's solution is to put the commons into private hands or impose some kind of authoritarian control.

The fallacy in the 'tragedy of the commons' parable lies in the very concept itself. 'Common' land implies a community; it is something held in common. However, Hardin's parable assumes that the herders behave according to the principles of the individualised marketplace, on the basis of economic self-interest and possessive individualism. He does not consider the possibility that the common could be administered collectively, fixing a maximum number of cattle per herder. Certainly people pushed by need into marginal land all over the world are destroying their habitat, but the parable is talking about greed, not need. If the motivation is personal greed and the grazing land is treated as an 'ownerless' resource, then there is nothing to stop a herder grazing the last blade of grass. Hardin's case stands only if the grazing land is *not* being treated as a common. The concept of a 'common' is social by definition; it is understood as a boundaried and limited resource. When this breaks down there is certainly destruction, as when the 'Responsibility System' was introduced in China in 1983. The Responsibility System broke up collective herds and gave flocks to individual families, with consequent chronic overgrazing.

The tragedy of the commons occurs not just because each individual is trying to secure their self-interest but *because they know or fear that everyone else is doing the same*. It is not the presence of individual self-interest but the absence of a sense of commonality that is most crucial. If we are to prevent someone fishing the last fish, they must be assured that no one else will do so. We must *secure the commons* – that is, those resources essential to our mutual sustainability. The only way the commons can be secured is by persuading each individual that their needs will be met and they needn't grab and hoard for themselves.

Without doubt we face a future of increasing scarcity of clean air, water, raw materials, energy, food, space. We can meet this future as individuals driven by need or greed, or as a political community based upon sharing and mutual support. The only political philosophy that can 'secure the commons' by recognising the principles of equality and mutuality is socialism. Much more problematic in the light of the failures of state-sponsored industrial socialism is the mechanism by which it can be achieved. Re-establishing the common-wealth of the natural world will be one of the most difficult problems of the twenty-first century. Greens are quite rightly distrustful of the state-socialist approach to collective administration. They see it as sharing the very destructive, centralised and bureaucratic features of modern society that they seek to replace. Greens argue that we can unite globally only if we break up the nation-states into smaller self-managing communities. A true internationalism can be built only from the bottom up.

The Search for Community

We need a new Benedictine order. It can only flourish
in a socially effective way within a commune-type
framework.
(Rudolf Bahro, 1986, p. 90)

Stateless, decentralized, moneyless, small-scale
communes or other informal alternatives are not viable
without the complex administrative and social structures
necessary to guarantee democratic participation, civil
rights and egalitarian co-ordination of economic
resources.
(Boris Frankel, 1987, p. 270)

Not all greens share Bahro's ideal of the Benedictine commune, but decentralisation and local self-reliance are stressed in most green texts. Although the emphasis on local self-management is shared with anarchists and feminists, greens take the idea much further, equating communal life with both ecological and social harmony, drawing on evidence from clan societies. As I have already pointed out, while we may learn a great deal from clan societies – in particular their spiritual reverence for the Earth – it is hard to see whether this reflected a consciously constructed harmony with their environment or merely the fact that they lived in small-scale, relatively isolated bands. As Peggy Sanday has pointed out (1981), clan societies did live in relative harmony *if there were no environmental or other pressures.*

Those greens who advocate a 'return to the Stone Age' as a solution to the ecological crisis must necessarily take a harsh line on population control. While it is understandable that many greens, particularly deep ecologists, see 'civilisation' as the enemy of both nature and humanity, this is far too simplistic. It is undeniably true that human history has developed in ways that are to be deplored. European civilisation has many horror stories to tell, from Auschwitz to the abominable treatment of its migrant workers. However, modern society has not only enslaved us to militarism, science and technology, it has brought with it the ideals of citizenship and liberation. In particular it has established the basis for women's liberation, albeit limited by class and race inequality. Women must be absolutely certain that the green search for community is not taking them back to some atavistic patriarchal subsistence economy where they carry the bulk of the routine work while men pontificate in the 'men's house'.

Apart from the position of women, there are some difficult problems around the green idea of communal self-reliance. The compatibility of socialism with a green perspective depends upon whether the green idea of communal self-reliance gives an individual or a mutual meaning to the idea of 'self'. Sometimes self-reliance seems to mean local self-management, which is compatible with socialist ideas of local participation, but sometimes it seems to lean towards a more individualistic form of self-sufficiency. It is not always clear whether green communities are to be made up of groups of self-reliant people (peasant farmers, smallholders, nuclear family units, etc.) or a self-reliant collectivity. The first remains rooted in the ideals of possessive individualism; the second rests on the socialist ideal of mutual interdependence.

One of the problems in the green conception of community is the tendency to see communities as 'natural' structures, thereby ignoring the political implications of their formation. How are the communities of a united world going to be formed? On what basis will they coalesce: geography, culture, family relationships, like-mindedness? Will people be able to move freely between communities? Where will the currently disadvantaged or less able people go? What happens to disruptive people? How is the problem of the unequal geographic distribution of resources to be addressed? What will stop the most well-endowed communities becoming 'lifeboats', keeping resources for themselves while leaving other communities to 'drown'? 'Natural' communities can be disruptive of wider political relationships, as the re-emergence of community in Eastern Europe has shown, with its disturbing degree of racism and interethnic violence. In the absence of an avowedly socialist position, divisions of class, race and ethnicity will be the basis of inequalities between and within communities.

The evidence that greens can offer of the effectiveness of communal organisation comes from communities and communes that have been formed expressly to promote green ideals. The first limitation of such communities and communes is that they have tended to be created by white middle-class opt-outs and could hardly be replicated on a national, let alone a global, scale. As one English communard commented, 'it would be impossible for all society to live like this. There aren't enough seventeen acre houses to go around' (Pepper 1991, p. 181). David Pepper's sample of British communes found that there was a good deal of overlap with the experience of communards in the nineteenth century (Hardy, 1979; Mary Mellor *et al.*, 1988). The communes started with radical intentions and often with philanthropic sponsorship or personal savings/income. Communes reflected the 'privileged middle classes with a sense of awareness that they could do what they wanted, and the money to do it' (Pepper, 1991, p. 7).

Despite the original aims of the communes he studied, Pepper found very little evidence of continued revolutionary zeal. Most people had come to the commune to meet their own needs. As one put it: 'What we are about is making ourselves happier people: to look after the environment we first have to look after ourselves' (ibid., p. 87). People who were too needy were not welcomed, particularly single parents. As islands in the sea of conventional society, the communes either joined it in some way (becoming an alternative Disneyland or mental health farm for burnt-out executives) or bumped along the economic bottom. Pepper found that some of the communes he studied had reverted from co-operative ownership of housing to private ownership, from voluntary simplicity to the car and television. Even voluntary simplicity had had a depoliticising effect:

> The bulk of the work which goes on . . . is . . .
> gardening and cleaning. These things take over in
> communes, which is difficult for those of us who see
> more to life. You spend most of your lifetime keeping
> going, or having meetings to decide how to keep going.
> The place can attract people who aren't motivated to
> do much else, then it gets motiveless and goes round in
> circles. (ibid., p. 181)

The lesson that twentieth-century community formation shares with the experiences of the nineteenth is that change must be societal rather than communal. Communes can provide an exemplar of a future society, but they cannot exist over any period of time without failing or approximating to the wider society.

Some of the most hopeful recent developments in community formation have been in urban areas, and this would seem a way forward. Most people now live in cities or urban areas, and that is likely to be the pattern for the future. Local communities form sections of cities, suburbs or shanty towns. In ecological terms it would also be very destructive to spread the huge populations of cities back across the countryside – a 'house in every field', as one commune member put it. Even the building of small towns that many greens favour would cover yet more land with concrete.

Although greens have argued for decentralisation of society to the lowest level possible, this may not be practical for the management of the natural world. The idea of self-sufficient communities is a nice dream, but in practical terms the most appropriate way forward will be collectivised ownership with local self-management of delegated resources in various forms: local environment and infrastructure, local production, welfare and social services, leisure and culture. An ecologically sustainable human community will need to be both local and global, communal and social, locally and centrally administered. Effective social change needs both a green and a socialist perspective, involving the social and socialist construction of sustainable, self-managing communities.

In looking for new ways of constructing an ecologically sustainable and egalitarian world we must be careful not to fall victim to the 'structural fallacy' – that is, assuming that if the structure is right (be it collectivised control of the means of production or decentralised small-scale communities) then the rest will fall into place. We need to return to even more fundamental questions if we are to avoid survivalism: What do we need to survive? What will we need to do to 'secure the commons?'

Learning to Survive

The intellectual heritage for ecological survival lies
with those who are experts in survival. They have
the knowledge and experience to extricate us from
the ecological cul-de-sac that the western masculinist
mind has manoeuvred us into. And while Third World
women have privileged access to survival expertise, their
knowledge is inclusive, not exclusive. The ecological
categories with which they think and act can become
categories of liberation for all, for men as well as for
women, for the west as well as the non-west and for the
human as well as the non-human elements of the earth.
(Vandana Shiva, 1989, p. 224)

What the hell
Is a well?
I mean do you just dig a hole
And up it comes
Ready to drink?
And wheat
I've squashed bits of what I thought was wheat
But nothing came out
Looking at all like flour.
Sheep make wool
We all know that
And potatoes grow in the ground
But how do you stick woolly hairs together
And where do the seeds come from
Which make the potatoes grow?
You see
What I'm worried about
Alongside all those others
Returning to nature without knowing why
Is how to survive
(Nigel Mellor, 1989, p. 39)

Survival in a limited ecological system must begin with meeting basic needs (Bahro, 1982). The desire to achieve at least a basic standard of living for all humanity is the 'minimal utopia' shared by feminists, greens and socialists. For greens, a commitment to basic needs represents a move to a sustainable society; for socialists, it is the first step towards an egalitarian society. For women, it is the substance of their lives, and in the case of poor women, 'the fulfilment of basic needs is *the* priority issue' (Sen and Grown, 1987, p. 89).

Manfred Max-Neef has identified nine basic needs: subsistence, protection, affection, understanding, participation, leisure, creation, identity (or meaning) and freedom (in Ekins, 1986, p. 49). He asserts that these basic needs are the same in all cultures and historical periods but that they are met in different ways, by different 'satisfiers'. Very few of these needs relate to the market economy, and in fact they demand a very different definition of wealth. If political and social systems that will meet these basic needs are to be created, the boundary of the male-dominated market economy must be overcome. We can no longer be paralysed by the demands of profitability or private ownership, or the male demand for a 'family wage'. Needs, not profits or wages, must be the 'first call' on political and economic decision-making. The minimum standard of a dignified life and death for all can no longer be the by-product of an economic system, it must be the core of political life.

The starting point for survival and ecological sustainability is very different in the South and in the North. As Shiva points out, in the South many people, particularly women, are still connected with the Earth. They still retain their old skills and knowledge. The most important problem is the incursion of the capitalist market economy, with a consequent exclusion of poor women and men from land ownership. As the profit-orientated agribusinesses spread their monocultures over the landscape, the diversity of plant and animal species is lost.

In the North, knowledge, land and biodiversity have already been lost. Although our economic benefits are much greater than those of the South, our 'real wealth' is virtually nil – at least for the average person. We have skills that most of us can only sell as labour. We are almost entirely subject to what Marx called 'the fetishism of commodities', from prescription medicine to prepacked food. Our expectations and diets are geared to economic colonialism. Meat-eaters and vegetarians alike rely on imported grains and pulses for direct consumption or cattle feed. If we are to escape the massive level of commodification of our lives, we are going to have to reclaim the skills we have lost. None of us can learn everything, but it is important that some of us relearn particular skills in health, horticulture and appropriate technology (Carr, 1985). Only then can we begin to shake off the commodified products of the marketplace, where very simple ingredients are sometimes dressed up in elaborate names and packaging. Like the characters in Malcolm Bradbury's *Fahrenheit 451*, each of us must be a 'book' and share our knowledge with others. This would not represent the world of weekend survivalist courses, the person with the knife, box of matches and condom (to carry water) against the elements. It would be a collective relearning of our heritage.

While many of the basic needs that Max-Neef has identified lie outside the capitalist market and traditional 'economics', this is not true of basic resources. While forming self-help communities and relearning old skills will begin to re-empower us, it will not directly challenge the domination of capital. It has been calculated that by the year 2000 multinational companies will control more than 50 per cent of the exploitable resources of the world (Rifkin, 1987). The capitalist market will not 'wither away'. It is a force that is growing ever more powerful, and we are going to have to unite all our efforts in the struggle against it. Central to that struggle must be the traditional opponents of capitalism, the working class.

What about the Workers?

At the current stage of global industrial restructuring
... the strategy for participatory socialism is certain to
founder unless it reckons with grassroots organizations
representing women and black workers.
(Swasti Mitter, 1986, p. 161)

When you have pollution, the first to suffer are the
workers in the enterprises doing the polluting ... there
is no antagonism between the interests of labour, even
industrial labour, and ecology. Of course there are
difficulties in switching from one type of product to
another, from one stage of development to another ...
the problem is somehow to consolidate those interests.
(Boris Kagarlitsky, *Left Green Notes*, no. 3, 1990, p. 45)

The working class that services the capitalist market is Black and white, South and North, female and male, home-based and factory-based, part-time and full-time. Those who are sucked into the capitalist market are consumers: poor and rich, subsistence and industrial, rural and urban. Most people have their rights to basic needs determined in some way by private ownership of resources and the market. Curtailing or abolishing the market will not resolve all the divisions within human society, but it will at least give us back some control over our lives. Environmental struggles will take resources out of the market; women's struggles will put aspects of human society on the agenda that capitalism ignores; workers' struggles will reduce the level of exploitation that capitalism can achieve.

We must not get trapped into elaborating a hierarchy of struggles, or accepting that some divisions are irreconcilable: producer/consumer; full-time/part-time; race/class; gender/sexuality; nature/society. We are all linked into a destructive connectedness that is putting boundaries between people, but no boundary on our destruction of the planet. In this process it is important that feminists and greens do not neglect industrial struggle. Environmentalists may lie down in front of the tractor, but it would help even more to have the tractor driver on their side.

In practice it is becoming impossible to keep workers' struggles and environmental struggle apart, particularly in the South. Resistance to the incursion of capitalism, as industrial workers, agricultural workers or forestry workers, is equally dangerous. The international trades-union movement has reported that between January 1990 and March 1991 264 trades-union leaders were murdered worldwide, the majority of them in Latin America.

Lack of attention to environmental factors is putting workers' health at risk, particularly in export-orientated production in the South. One study found that 71 per cent of workers in a battery factory in Colombia had increased levels of lead in their blood, while in Brazil 86.8 per cent of workers in ninety-four electroplating plants had chromium-induced damage (Ives, 1985). Workers faced with unsafe practices with no other means of livelihood feel forced to accept working in a polluted environment in order to survive. The same is true of those people who work in destructive forms of production such as the nuclear or defence industries. In areas such as Cumbria there is very little alternative to working in nuclear reprocessing at Sellafield or the manufacture of Trident submarines at Barrow-in-Furness.

Ceasing ecologically destructive production will be achieved only in an economic system that both secures the commons and meets basic needs. Workers will not be moved to destroy their own livelihood by vague niceties about 'saving the planet' – only a social, economic and political programme that secures their future will be sufficient. If greens are to unite with the working class, it can only be on the basis of a socialist economic programme that offers workers an alternative to waged labour. If greens do not unite with the working class, they have little hope of effectively challenging capitalism. At the same time, greens are right to feel frustrated that the labour movement has been slow to take on board green issues.

Although industrial workers have conflicting interests, they are very well placed to have first-hand knowledge of dangerous forms of production and to expose environmental issues in industry. In Britain throughout the 1980s there was a growing Hazards movement involving workplace activists, trades-union officials, academics and health and safety practitioners (Jones, 1988). Some trades unions have shown themselves ready to get involved in green issues. In Britain the National Union of Seamen has played a key role in opposing the dumping of hazardous waste. In 1990 the British TUC, through its Environmental Committee, considered electing 250,000 'green' shop stewards. The Chair of that committee, John Edmonds, general secretary of the General, Municipal, Boilermakers' and Allied Trades Unions (GMBATU), accepted that there has been no real breakthrough as yet, but argued:

The TUC is trying to get ahead of the game, rather
than always being on the defensive, and if this means a
change in jobs, so what? The consequences of not acting
are going to be terrible. (*Tribune*, 8 February 1991)

Other indications of the potential for a closer relationship
between greens and trades unionists is the fact that David
Gee was recruited from the trades-union movement to head
Friends of the Earth.

However, the most important case for taking working-class
struggle seriously lies in the radical potential that the trades-union
and working-class movement has already shown. In searching
for alternative communities and economic programmes we
tend to forget that the working class has already created
its own alternative economic system. Women and men in
nineteenth-century working-class communities built a huge
co-operative movement in protest against the poor quality and
exorbitant prices they were being charged for food in the new
industrial system. From its origins in Rochdale's Toad Lane in
1844, the British consumer co-operative movement grew into a
massive organisation covering not only retailing but production,
housing, banking and insurance. By the 1950s twelve million
people were members of co-operative societies. It was a major
employer and channel of mobility for working-class people,
with its own education system. Co-operative societies formed
a democratically controlled, non-capitalist organisation linked to
the worldwide co-operative movement through the International
Co-operative Alliance.

The strength of the British co-operative movement was its
roots in working-class communities. It brought consumption
and production together by uniting producers and consumers in
one movement. Working-class savings were used to buy premises
and land, and to build houses. Integral to the co-operative society
was popular education and empowerment: the meeting room and
the reading room. Despite its achievements, the co-operative

movement has not been without its problems. As an economic organisation it was, for a time, swamped by the capitalist supermarket chains and, in trying to compete with them, lost a lot of its democratic base. It was also largely male-dominated and its high-price, high-dividend strategy excluded the poorer members of the working class (Mary Mellor, 1980).

Despite half a century of competition from the supermarket chains, the co-operative movement is still holding its own and even gained ground during the 1991 recession. The co-operative movement is also a major farmer and is using its unique farm-to-shop control of food production to introduce a 'farm-to-family' policy on the use of pesticides. Although the co-operative movement has had to reorganise into larger and more remote units of administration, it has not abandoned its co-operative status and is trying to maintain some elements of grass-roots democratic control. It is important that greens and socialists help it in this aim before it is too late and the co-operative movement goes the way of the TSB or the Abbey National. Neither socialists nor greens have tried to engage seriously with this still substantial alternative economic system to build a non-capitalist green system of production and consumption. Their failure to do so reflects the largely middle-class membership of the green movement and the middle-class domination of socialist thought.

Elements of a Green Socialism

The question that remains is whether we can create
an economic system that is efficient, equitable, and
ecologically sound based on the self-organization and
collective self-management of workers and consumers.
(Michael Albert and Robin Hahnel, 1991, p. 8)

The principles of a sustainable and equitable society must at least secure the commons and meet basic needs. The two cannot be separated. If we are to stop someone fishing the last fish, we need a society that prevents *anyone* fishing the last fish and makes sure there are enough fish, or fish substitutes, to go round. In a green socialist society there would be no distinction between politics and economics. There would be no tension between the social principle and the market principle. The social principle would prevail. The political priority would be to ensure sustainability of the resources of the community and that each person was born, lived and died in dignity and well-being. It may be that a market could achieve this end, but it would not be a male/capitalist one.

Michael Albert and Robin Hahnel have devised what they describe as a 'participatory economics'. For them, democracy lies at the heart of an egalitarian system of resource allocation. Instead of the amoral marketplace or the authoritarian central plan, they propose a system of workers' and consumers' councils where consumers' individual and collective demands and the ability of workers to supply at an acceptable price under agreed conditions are brought together into a gradually evolving production plan. Under this system wider principles can be brought into production decision-making, such as the interests of workers and consumers, ecological costs and the impact of individual production decisions on each other. Albert and Hahnel see information technology as overcoming the seemingly cumbersome nature of a participatory economy. Their basic message is that we should both empower and trust the people – something, they claim, that leadership of Eastern Europe never did and the market system cannot achieve:

> *Both* markets and central planning deny workers
> information about the situation of consumers and other
> workers and subordinate workers to powers beyond
> their reach . . . Both create competition, regimentation,
> inequality, coercion, experts, and instrumental decision-
> making. (1991, p. 67)

Albert and Hahnel see their system as carrying out 'economic allocation efficiently while promoting equity, solidarity, variety and collective self-management' (ibid., p. 67).

An example of the integration of producers and consumers are the Seikhatsu Clubs in Japan, which won an honorary award from the Swedish Right Livelihood Society (which presents the alternative Nobel Prize) in 1989. The Seikhatsu Clubs were started in 1965 when a woman in Tokyo organised two hundred other women into a group to bulk-buy milk and thereby reduce its price. By 1989 the Seikhatsu movement had grown to 170,000 members. It is now using its ability to guarantee bulk orders to determine the quality of the food that is produced by suppliers. This, in turn, gives the security of a certain market to producers like organic farmers, encouraging them to expand production.

The move towards a sustainable, egalitarian and participatory system of production and consumption cannot be achieved just by a change in personal values or the formation of co-operatives or collective buying systems, although all these are steps along the road. The capitalist market system is not just an ideology, it is a vast and powerful network of ownership and control backed up by economic, political and military force. A green socialist strategy will need to bring together many different forms of struggle: the campaigns of the peoples of the South to retain their traditional forms of production and control of their own resources; the struggle of workers against exploitation and hazards at the point of production; the struggles of people in their local communities around the quality of their 'social environment', representing not just the physical environment but their access to local resources and the decisions that affect their lives; attempts to build alternative forms of economic structure, be they co-operatives, work-brigades, local trading schemes or mutual aid organisations (Dauncey, 1988).

However, even if all these were achieved, none of them would necessarily meet the needs of women. As Albert and Hahnel acknowledge, no participatory system of production and consumption would be effective if the unequal relations between men and women had not been resolved:

> The effects of sexist kinship relations in home and families would subvert equality, self management, and variety at work and in consumption. (1991, p. 144)

If we are to achieve a green socialist society, it must also be feminist.

CHAPTER 8

Towards a Feminist Green Socialism 2: Caring for the World: Making and Taking Time

What men value has brought us to the brink of death.
What women find worthy may bring us back to life.
(Marilyn Waring, 1989, p. 11)

The world of nurturance and close human relationships
is the sphere where the basic human needs are anchored
and where models for *humane* alternatives can be found.
This world, which has been carried forward mainly
by women, is an existing alternative culture, a source
of ideas and values for shaping an alternative path of
development for nations and all humanity.
(Hilkka Pietilä, 1987, p. 26)

Socialists have long sought a world in which people offer mutual
support to each other without demanding cash payment or profit.
Greens look for a sustainable, decentralised world of face-to-face
interaction. Both decry the institutions of modern society for being
destructive, exploitative and alienating. Programmes and blueprints
for a new society are constructed to take us 'forward' or bring us
'back' to a green or socialist world. It is odd that they do not see
that this world exists already. Most of women's lives are spent in a
decentralised world beyond the market where basic needs prevail.
Women, particularly in subsistence economies, are rooted to the
Earth and the reproduction of life in their daily work.

The world that socialists and greens are seeking to escape
from is a male world. It is mainly male green and socialist writers
who seek a new autonomy for the individual (self-actualisation,

self-realisation) in the comfort of small-scale, mutual community life: Gorz, Bahro, Schumacher, Robertson, Trainer and even Marx. There may well be women who have written in a similar vein, but they are either 'hidden from history' or much less numerous. This latter is the more likely, for women are right to be suspicious of visions of greens and socialists that do not embrace an explicit feminism. The attack on modernity that has been launched with such passion from many quarters has rarely acknowledged that it is a modernity created by men from dominant cultures. It is a modernity that women have barely begun to share. Charles Fourier once said that women's liberation was the yardstick by which a civilisation should be judged; this was echoed by Lenin but subsequently sidelined by later Marxists and socialists. Equally, while greens applaud the feminine principle, they pay much less attention to the mechanisms by which men dominate women.

The task for a feminist green socialism is to move from a world built upon the interests and experience of men, a male-experience world, a ME-world, to a world built upon the interests and experience of women, a women's-experience world, a WE-world. A WE-world based upon women's experience would need to be both decentralised and safe, ecologically, physically and socially. Domestic life and paid work would have to be integrated, as women cannot move far from their homes because of their domestic and caring responsibilities. The boundaries between paid and unpaid work are in any event anachronistic from a woman's perspective. As all production would need to take place near the home, dangerous, polluting work could not be carried out, as it would affect the health of the local community. People would also not want their local environment disfigured by destructive forms of production. Shops and other social facilities would need to be within easy reach of the local community and not stuck on the edge of town, available only to the car driver. People, not traffic, would have priority on the roads. Public transport would be universally available.

A world based on women's experience would ensure people's physical and social safety. Personal violence would never be treated as a 'private' matter. Streets and public spaces would be patrolled if there was any danger to children, minority groups or women. A WE-world would see its primary role as producing well-rounded and creative human beings and a well-integrated community life. People would not be asked to uproot themselves every few years to chase promotion or to meet the needs of a transnational corporation. If someone were needed in a new location, a local person would have to be appointed and trained. People would not be forced to migrate hundreds or thousands of miles to look for work, never seeing their family or community for years on end. Emotional needs would be given equal priority with physical needs; people would listen to each other, sympathise and empathise.

The fact that women's experience prefigures many of the dreams of socialists and greens does not mean that women are superior beings. On the contrary, they are oppressed beings. Patriarchy has put a boundary around women's world in order to prevent women escaping from it. The division of society into a male/public and female/private world has been a central theme of feminist analysis (O'Brien, 1981). What is important about this boundary is the tasks and values that have been pushed into – or left behind in women's world. The patriarchal division of society has imposed on women responsibility for creating the basic conditions of human existence. In societies throughout the world it is women who fight to sustain some semblance of family and community life when all else has failed. When they can no longer find the strength or means to do so, we see children spilling on to the streets and society sinking to such a base level that adults begin to exterminate them.

By placing on women the major responsibility for nurturing and caring values and activities, a public world has been created in the one-sided, distorted and damaging image of male experience.

Imposed Altruism

Women's work, underremunerated and undervalued as
it is, is vital to the survival and ongoing reproduction of
human beings in all societies. In food production and
processing, in responsibility for fuel, water, health care,
child-rearing, sanitation and the entire range of so-called
basic needs, women's labour is dominant.
(Gita Sen and Caren Grown, 1987, pp. 23–4)

The main distinction of human virtue is ... *altruism* –
'otherness' – to love and serve one another, to feel for
and with one another ... the very existence of humanity
implies these qualities ... the development of humanity
is commensurate with their development.
(Charlotte Perkins Gilman, 1915, p. 523)

Although women experience their relationship with men and
with each other differently within and across races, classes and
cultures, we can rescue a common female experience. Women
throughout history and across cultures are overwhelmingly
responsible for the basic needs of their families: children,
siblings, husbands. Although in industrial economies a great
many physical needs are met through the formal economy (state or
market), it is women who fill the gaps. The necessity of women's
work is disguised by the male-orientated market economy, which
recognises work only if it is paid or makes a profit. If it is not
'economic' to care for the elderly or provide a well for a rural
village, the 'economy' washes its hands of the activity. The state
or a charity may offer this service, but only if 'the money' is
made available through taxes or donations. If neither appears, the
state/charity in turn washes its hands of the matter. This does not
mean that the elderly are not cared for or that water is not fetched;
in the last resort this work will be carried out by women.

Women's work is necessary for the survival of both individuals
and society. It is not work that 'needs' to be done to earn a wage,

it is work that 'needs' to be done if human life is to carry on in any meaningful sense. Women's work maintains minimal standards of health, food, love. We see it happening all over the world when women in gross poverty scrape together what they can, wash the rags, carry the water, cuddle the children. As mothers, daughters, wives, friends, neighbours, volunteers, women provide a huge support network to society.

Even where the state or a market economy meets most basic physical needs, women remain primarily responsible for nurturing and caring work. The essence of women's work is its 'immediate altruism' (Gilman, 1915). It cannot be 'put off' or slotted into a work schedule. It cannot be 'logically ordered' or 'rationally programmed'. The needs that women respond to are unignorable demands; if they are ignored, the social fabric of society begins to disintegrate. This work is altruistic in the sense that it is carried out for no reward other than pleasure at family relationships or through obligation, a sense of duty (Schreiner, 1978).

Why have women taken – or been forced to take – upon themselves the burdens of the essentials of life? Why do they feel themselves to be obligated? Why do men not feel it? In her study of professional couples (1990) Hochschild found that women carried with them the guilt and burdens of childcare in a way men did not. Women carried the home and family in their heads, remembered things that needed to be done or bought, and worried about the physical, social and emotional needs of children. Men were more likely to see their earnings as their 'gift' to the household. It is hard to explain this difference without falling into a biological explanation. Women 'feel' for the needs of others through their experience of motherhood or nurturing. Equally it can be seen as the burden of heterosexual domination: that throughout the world women are trapped into obligated labour through male-dominated family structures.

One of the most negative effects of male domination of

society is that it corrupts personal relationships and degrades and exploits caring and loving human activities. It is very difficult to separate out what is done as a gesture of love and affection from activities that support male domination. Patriarchy is perhaps the most unique form of power relation in this regard, where social relations of power are also experienced as personal relations of affection (hooks, 1989).

There is nothing intrinsic about women's work that means a woman should do it, but somebody has to. It is the altruistic work that keeps the whole of society functioning, it is the work that creates 'humanity' both as individuals and as a community. Woman's primary responsibility for this work is not inherent in her biology. Women give life and nurture, but the biological capacity to give life is so heavily influenced by the social context that it cannot be argued that women are 'naturally' altruistic, loving and supportive. Biology is reality, but it isn't destiny. Women can and do give birth, but they do so in many different contexts with many different attitudes and outcomes. Nor do all women do women's work or all men avoid nurturing and caring work. What is important is that male-dominated society has created a world which assumes that this is the case.

The imposition of altruistic behaviour upon women is, I would argue, the most destructive division in human society. It means that the public world based upon male experience is quite literally a ME-world, constructed on the false premiss of an independently functioning individual, with the nurturing, caring and supportive world hidden, unpaid and unacknowledged. Even when women carry their nurturing tasks into the public world, they are lower-paid and have less status than men. Central to women's caring work is 'emotional labour':

> Because emotional labour is seen as 'natural' unskilled women's work, because it is unpaid and because it is obscured by the privacy of the domestic domain where much of it takes place, the significance of its contribution

and value in social reproduction is ignored. (James, 1989, p. 22)

Although emotional labour is equally important in the public world, it continues to be largely ignored or undervalued. As a result, as James argues, 'there exists a distorting divisive conceit through which men are associated positively with rational thought and action while women are negatively associated with emotional reaction' (ibid., pp. 39–40).

Again, this association does not reflect a biological division. Women who do not have any caring responsibilities or anyone emotionally dependent upon them can operate independently according to the rational principles of the ME-world, although they will, in all probability, be disadvantaged in lacking the emotional support of a 'wife'. As David Puttnam put it when addressing a Women in Film Conference in 1990, it was an advantage as a film producer to have a wife to 'pick up the pieces'. Men who are engaged in caring and supportive relationships will equally find themselves disadvantaged if they cannot give their undivided time and attention to their job. The ME-world also makes social demands that women often do not find acceptable:

> There's a lot of emphasis on being a good chap, doing things like going to the pub, playing sport and generally being clubbable. But a lot of women don't want to go drinking and don't see that as part of their job. (Anthea Harrison, investment director of Lloyd's Development Corporation, *Guardian*, 3 August 1990)

What Anthea Harrison is describing are the social mechanisms of male bonding, an important support system in the ME-world.

The division between the ME-world and the WE-world is destructive in two important ways: first, the distorting effect it has on time; second, the distorting effect it has on men.

Taking Our Time

To speak of women and time is to speak of the ultimate theft . . .

Only free men can undertake to give up their time while women . . . don't have it to give.
(Frieda J. Forman, 1989, pp. 1, 5)

The most important element in woman's imposed altruism is the removal of her ability to control her time. It is not just that women do vast amounts of unpaid work (which they do) or that it is hard (which for many women it is) but that it constrains all of women's time. If a woman does not wish to live in Gilman's condition of 'immediate altruism', she must find someone else to do it, often another woman.

The world of immediate altruism is the world of biological time. Babies need to be fed when they are hungry, nursed when they are tired. The sick need treatment when they are in distress or pain. They do not cease their demands because it is 'outside working hours'. To the extent that women are responsible for biological time, they do not have time, they give time. They live in a world where time is unboundaried apart from the limits of physical exhaustion, and many women live even beyond those. A wife, mother, sister or daughter is on call twenty-four hours a day, seven days a week. As a result, women lose control over their own lives and have no way of creating 'time for themselves'. They create the time and thereby the space in which men – and children – live. Because her work is geared to biological time, time can never mean freedom for a woman. It is a resource to be juggled in order for her to fulfil her duties and obligations.

Despite this reality for women, the public world of modern industrial society has been created with boundaried time. Time is dictated by working time in paid work, which is fixed and limited, and all other activities have to fit in round that (Thompson,

1967). At the start of the Industrial Revolution the new factory owners found it very difficult to get workers to accept the new factory discipline. Many of the new business ventures failed because of the workers' reluctance to do a full day's labour. In the end industry resorted to using child labour, as 'it is found nearly impossible to convert persons past the age of puberty into useful factory hands' (quoted in Gorz, 1989, p. 21). Despite this initial reluctance, as the new industrial system developed it was men who predominated in paid work, while women found themselves divided between work and home.

Although the imposition of fixed working time meant that industrial workers lost the freedom to choose their pace of work, it did create a time that could be separated off as leisure. It created a space that men took for themselves, to develop hobbies, go to meetings, libraries and reading rooms or the pub. Throughout the nineteenth century men increasingly took advantage of this time and space to pursue their own needs and satisfactions; even the poorest could 'escape' their drudgery for a while in the gin shop (Hart, 1989). As well as commanding the best-paid employment and social space, men colonised political spaces as well. Trades unions and political parties became the new 'men's houses'.

For women, work outside the home brought problems of conflicting loyalties and obligations: 'In a world where time is money, and where money can mean time, women have little of either' (Forman, 1989, p. 3). In fact, going to work can be a way for women to escape for a short while from biological time (Deem, 1986). Even when women do paid work, however, they still retain overall responsibility for the household (Wheelock, 1990). Even if women are free of domestic responsibilities and have money for leisure activities, most organisations and public facilities are male-dominated or male-orientated. Male domination of the public world also creates a problem for women's safety, even if they have the time to attend leisure or political activities (Green et al., 1990).

It is important not to assume that all women have a common experience of biological time, the distinction between the public and the private worlds or the way public and private space is constructed. Feminism has quite rightly been criticised for falsely universalising the experience of the white middle-class housewife (hooks, 1982; Collins, 1990; Ramazanoglu, 1989). However, we have seen that even in the earliest pre-industrial societies, men seemed to claim public time for themselves.

Women's responsibility for biological time means that men have been able to create a public world that largely ignores it. As a result, two different time-worlds have emerged: the WE-time-world of immediate altruism and the ME-time-world of the person committed to the 'system' without regard to biological or emotional time. In the ME-time-world:

> Instead of working the conventional 9 to 5 . . . we worked from 5 a.m. to 9 p.m. . . . Since I started to work I've never taken a day off. I didn't have time to develop a single hobby, and I've never even had time for a drink. I gave up the joys of close-knit family life for the company. And I always have to live with the fact that I have never taken my kids on vacation. (Kim Woo Choong, a Korean businessman: *Independent*, 26 August 1990)

Kim Woo Choong is representative of many people in the whirlwind age. He has broken free completely from biological time, both physically and emotionally. Although he clearly works phenomenally hard in ME-world time, he is relying on others, and particularly his wife, to sustain his biological time and that of the rest of his family.

The ME-world, in breaking free of biological time, is no longer rooted in the physical reality of human existence. Instead, the ME-world sees:

> human life as something *un*conditioned and *un*limited. But we cannot destroy the limited and conditioned aspect

of human life without necessarily destroying that part of ourselves through which we remain related to nature and to all other living organisms: life itself. (McMillan, 1982, p. 156)

The ME-world is one in which people do not have to wash their clothes in water full of raw sewage or walk miles to find clean water, fresh fodder or fuelwood. Where people do not have to struggle with heavy shopping bags and small children in pushchairs on and off buses or dash across dangerous roads to get to the school. It is a world that does not have to walk at the pace of the toddling child or the elderly person with emphysema.

The ME-world is not one that liberates all men and restricts all women. It is a world that liberates some men and a few women at the expense of the rest of humanity and the planet. At the same time it has created an immensely powerful economic, political and ideological framework that insists that the different parts of human life are kept separate. Ecofeminists have argued that this false boundary runs deep into our lives. The boundaries are not only in society but in ourselves, dividing our minds from our bodies and the material and spiritual sides of our nature. Although the ME-world is one where very few people can realise their full potential, it still represents male priorities and male interests. The danger to the planet lies in the fact that in breaking free of their own physical reality in biological time, men also become distanced from ecological time and ecological reality.

Making Time for the Planet

Statistics tell the grim story of a civilization hell-bent on saving time on the one hand while eliminating the future on the other.
(Jeremy Rifkin, 1987, p. 12)

Because it is the labour of ensuring human subsistence,
the production time of domestic labour can never be
reduced, it can only be shared or redistributed.
(Meg Luxton, 1987, p. 172)

As Jeremy Rifkin has pointed out (1980), human society and the
planet are engaged in a 'time war'. The history of humanity has
seen it move away from the biological and ecological rhythms of
the planet at an ever-increasing pace. It took millions of years for
humanity to come to the boundary of hunter-gatherer resources,
thousands of years to do the same for agricultural resources, but
only a few hundred years to reach the limits of non-renewable
energy resources. We are now into the nanosecond culture of
the computer where the snap of a finger is equivalent to 500
million nanoseconds (Rifkin, 1987).

Paradoxically, in conquering ecological time we are in danger
of letting it slip beyond our control. Defence systems programmed to the nanosecond culture will have destroyed us all
before we even have time to reach for the abort button or the
hot line. Planes fly using computers with no mechanical means
of overriding their decisions or replacing them in the event of
failure. Financial transactions flash around the globe affecting
thousands, if not millions, of people's lives. The lack of human
control is shown in the stress, burn-out and tension-relieving
addictions of those who work the high-speed systems. It could
be assumed that a speeded-up existence would somehow save
us time, but this is not the case. The world computer culture
means a twenty-four-hour working day.

Those involved in the frenetic activity of production and
consumption seek relief by grabbing a few weeks' holiday in a
different climate where air-conditioned hotels, plentiful washing
and sanitation systems, swimming pools and golf courses play
havoc with the local ecology and divert resources from local
needs. In Hawaii and Barbados visitors use six to ten times as
much water as the local people. In Goa a five-star hotel gets

enough water to supply five villages, while the water pipe passes through villages without piped water (*Independent on Sunday*, 5 August 1990). With the constant search for 'unspoilt' places, the world is becoming littered with abandoned concrete strips as the great tourist steamroller passes through.

While the high-speed whirlwind catches up millions of people and whisks them to ever-increasing responsibilities and activities, it leaves many more outside, becalmed. The nanosecond culture is a divided culture. Ecological time is being destroyed by a minority while increasing numbers of people are flung aside, their personal life-histories and dreams an irrelevance. While I have argued that only a socialist approach can stop the ecological crisis bringing even more cruelties on the heads of those who are already suffering, traditional socialist theory has no adequate response to – or even awareness of – the dangers of the nanosecond culture. It is the greens who have alerted us to both the long-term and short-term effects of the ecological crisis. However, it is to feminism we must turn if we are to understand its fundamental cause. The conquest of time is the conquest of women.

In his book *Time Wars* (1987), Jeremy Rifkin asks us to pull back from the brink and realign human time to ecological time. He enjoins us to empathise with the biological and ecological pace of the planet and the needs of those who lie outside the whirlwind. What he does not see is that human time is gendered. It is men who are speeding up the whirlwind, but the fuel they are using is women's time. There is not just the gap between human (male) time and planetary time, there is the gap between human (male) time and human biological time. Human biological time is the missing link between the high-speed lunacy of the nanoculture and the speed of sustainability.

If we are to be in tune with ecological time, the false reality of ME-time will have to be abandoned. We will all have to live in biological WE-time where we share in the tasks of feeding, clothing and nurturing ourselves and others – where we share the care for the staging posts of human existence: youth, sickness, old age and death.

There is evidence that some Western workers and businessmen are becoming disillusioned with the rat race of the ME-world and the demands of ME-time. A report to the British Psychological Society in 1991 found a high level of stress in a sample of the estimated 100,000 employees who move around the country each year. A survey for the Institute of Personnel Management in 1991 also found that around a quarter of British and European executives were thinking of quitting the boardroom to spend more time with their families (*Guardian*, 15 April 1991). The pressure was greatest on younger executives, who tended to be in dual-career families. This confirms the findings of a report in 1990 that 23 per cent of top executives in European companies were thinking of quitting top management to spend more time with their families (*Independent on Sunday*, 4 November 1990). The danger is that those who remain will lead even more frenetic lives.

Both greens and feminists have questioned the quality of life that male-dominated competitive economies have created. They have challenged the basis of a society that rushes along at the pace of the fastest man, the man who has the most human and natural resources at his command – the man who has no time for personal relationships, to listen, to think, to reconsider. These men are in charge of governments, the military, business corporations and scientific establishments. Their ethic is the race – against time, against each other, against life itself. It is the death ethic, it is a race against mortality that creates death in its wake. Often it kills the winners themselves with stress-related diseases. Women who have joined the race can do so only as honorary men. Men who question its validity can only abandon it. To participate is to condone it. While the pace of economic life is driven by the fastest, least-encumbered man, at the other end of the social spectrum is the pace of life of the slowest and most needy person.

From the perspective of women's work, the well-being of society would not be determined by 'who is the most successful?' but by 'who cares the most?' The message for a feminist green socialism is that caring for each other and caring for the world cannot be dissociated. One cannot exist in any meaningful sense without the other.

Women Are Born, Men Are Made?

Woman creates naturally from within her own being,
whereas man is free to, or forced to create artificially . . .
through cultural means.
(Sherry Ortner, 1974, p. 77)

The recurrent problem of civilization is to define the
male role satisfactorily enough . . . so that the male may
in the course of his life reach a solid sense of irreversible
achievement, of which his childhood knowledge of the
satisfactions of childbearing gave him a glimpse.
(Margaret Mead, quoted in Sanday, 1981, p. 78)

As Rosalind Miles has pointed out, 'the renewal of the species has always been the sole, whole, unavoidable and largely unacknowledged gift to the future of the female sex worldwide' (Miles, 1988, p. xi). In the face of such inherent creativity, men have faced two problems: how to control women's reproductive powers and how to emulate them. According to Andrée Collard, the drive to control and constrain women's lives stems from 'the patriarch's fear of female autonomy . . . which must be held in check by compulsory heterosexuality and compulsory fertility' (1988, p. 106). It is a process that is destructive in two ways: it separates men from the nurturing and creative world of women and drives them towards 'worldly' achievements.

Some feminists attribute the male drive to achievement to the difference between the male and female transition to adulthood:

> One consequence of female mothering – virtually
> universal in human societies – seems to be that girls
> have an easier time becoming women than boys have
> becoming men. (Anderson and Zinsser, 1989, p. 11)

Menstruation 'signifies that a girl is ready to make her contribution to the continuation of the lineage through the bearing of children' (Sanday, 1981, p. 95). In traditional societies like the African Mbuti, it is publicly celebrated:

> The blood that comes for the first time to the young girl
> comes as a gift, received with gratitude and rejoicing,
> because she is now a potential mother. (Sanday,
> 1981, p. 24)

Male transition to adulthood is much more protracted, involving complex rituals which tend to mimic the onset of menstruation or the process of giving birth. Although initiation ceremonies for girls exist, they are not as common as those for boys and are generally much less elaborate (Bamberger, 1974; Cheater, 1989; Errington and Gewertz, 1987). As Sanday points out: 'perhaps because women have ways of signalling their womanhood, men must have ways to display their manhood' (1981, p. 78). Among the Arapesh of New Guinea the penis is incised at puberty to achieve symmetry with the female reproductive system (ibid., p. 96). While menstruation may mark a girl's movement into womanhood and motherhood, an equally important factor is the early socialisation she has had by helping with domestic tasks and looking after younger brothers and sisters. This represents a 'life-long process of learning' by which 'little girls are . . . taught to model themselves on their mothers' behaviour from a very early age'. On the other hand, 'in many cultures small boys enjoyed . . . a few years of relative freedom' before their social initiation to an adult role (Cheater, 1989, p. 143 f.).

Sherry Ortner has argued that men not only reject women's

mothering role because they fear it and the way it exposes the absence of a clear social role for themselves, they go on to associate women with the forces of 'nature' while they see themselves as the creators and guardians of 'culture' (1974). Although her analysis has been much disputed, particularly the male rejection of nature (MacCormack and Strathern, 1980), the division of society into female (nature, nurture, private family world) and male (public, culture, dominance and control) remains, as I have argued, the source of male destructiveness in human society.

Brian Easlea has argued (1983) that men suffer from 'insecure masculinity' throughout their lives. Lacking the creativity of a womb, men 'envy women their reproductive capacity' while at the same time denigrating them. In order to compensate, men engage in very public activities, often involving war and adventure. In earlier societies men risked only their own lives in derring-do, but with the development of modern technologies this drive in men has become a danger to the whole human community, and the planet itself. Easlea has shown how male scientists exhibit their 'uterus envy' through the language they use. The development of the nuclear bomb, which Easlea sees as a 'pregnant phallus', was described as 'Robert's baby' (Robert Oppenheimer). The first uranium bombs were named 'Little Boy' and 'Fat Boy' (later Fat Man) (1983, pp. 94–5). A male reporter described the successful nuclear tests as 'the first cry of a new-born world. It brought the silent, motionless silhouettes to life . . . the birth of a new force' (ibid., pp. 96–7). Scientific discoveries or technical developments are often described in the language of reproduction as someone's 'brainchild', or 'giving birth to an idea'.

It would be wrong to imply that all male achievements are destructive; many are quite the opposite and have greatly benefited humanity. What is important is the fact that men feel driven to achieve for good or ill. The importance of the construction of male identity is emphasised by the recent eruption of cults around the idea of masculinity, in particular the poet Robert Bly's call for a male-to-male process of initiation and personal development (1991).

The Perils of Not Being a Mother

Until male 'identity' does not depend on men's proving
themselves, their 'doing' will be a reaction to insecurity,
not a creative exercise of their humanity.
(Nancy Chodorow, quoted in Easlea, 1983, p. 10)

It seems reasonable to suppose that if men had felt all
along more closely identified with the first parent . . .
we would not now be so close to the irrevocable murder
of nature.
(Dorothy Dinnerstein, 1976, p. 103)

As Sara Ruddick has argued, mothering is not a biological imperative, it is a social process that either men or women could carry out. However, inherent in the process of mothering are a 'preservative love' and qualities of life-enhancement and life-preserving that could form the basis of a more peace-loving society (1990). The fact that most men are excluded, or exclude themselves, from the mothering role means that society is less life-orientated and less concerned with the preservation of life.

Feminists writing from a Freudian perspective have argued that men's exclusion from mothering damages both men and women. The primary responsibility of women for childcare traps them for ever in the emotionally dependent world of mothering and nurturing while male children, to achieve manhood, have to leave the nurturing, emotionally secure world of women to join the emotionally arid, non-nurturing world of men. It means leaving the love and tenderness of the mother for the more remote and elusive world of the father. Nancy Chodorow argues (1978) that this process is very traumatic for men and entails a male rejection of the feminine as represented in women and in their own personalities. Fear of women drives men to establish domination over them, while at the same time men remain psychologically dependent on women for emotional support. For Chodorow, psychologically insecure men with a drive towards domination are a danger to both women and society, a concern echoed by Dorothy Dinnerstein. Dinnerstein sees men as 'nature-killing' and declares that if the female monopoly over childcare is not broken, we risk the end of civilisation (1976).

Like Brian Easlea, John Stoltenberg sees men's problems as stemming from an insecure masculinity:

> You grow up to become a boy and you are terrorized into acting like a boy and you are rewarded for being a boy and you learn to dissociate from your mother by adopting a whole range of fears and hatreds of women and you learn what you need to learn to be accepted into the company of other men. Women shore up this identity; we look to women to confirm this identity. But we get the identity from other men; it is other men we look to as the arbiters of sex-class identity, the identity that gets inside of us, an identity so close to who we think we are that letting go of it scares us to death. (1990, p. 190)

Transcending the ME-*World*

Men must live in the ethics of a civilised, free, industrial democratic age, but they are born and trained in the moral atmosphere of a primitive patriarchate.
(Charlotte Perkins Gilman, 1915, p. 338)

For Gilman the boundary between the ME-world and the WE-world means that women have been 'tied to the starting post while the other half ran' (ibid., p. 330). Transcending the ME-world will mean reconstructing our ideas of what personal development means. The image of the independently functioning (male) individual has gone deep into our models of human development, such as Abraham Maslow's famous hierarchy of needs, first set out in 1942:

Understanding
and knowledge
Self-actualization
Self-esteem
Love and belonging
Safety
Physiological

At the base of the hierarchy is the need to be free from basic hunger, to feel safe and emotionally secure. Then self-esteem, which has two aspects, self-confidence and the respect of others. Maslow says that if the need for self-esteem is not met, people feel inferior, weak and helpless. Only when these needs are met can the process of self-actualising begin, the realisation of potential. Finally come knowledge and understanding (1970, pp. 35–51).

The question underpinning this hierarchy is: Who is fulfilling the basic needs that allow an individual to move towards self-actualisation, understanding and knowledge? Is each person securing them for themselves, or is 'society' doing it? Where there is no mutual and collective responsibility for meeting the basic needs of individuals, this burden falls mainly upon women. One man's self-esteem and self-actualisation is another woman's physical and emotional support. In the male-orientated ME-world, emotion becomes associated with weakness and the strength and centrality of women's nurturing role is denied. Women, in fact, are seen as the weak, dependent members of society, with men as the strong and independent nurturers in their role of 'breadwinners'. Nothing could be further from the truth. Women may appear fragile and clinging, but the reality is very different:

> Behind this outward façade is someone who, whatever
> the inner state, will have to deal with the emotional
> problems met in family relationships, a person who knows
> that others will expect to rely and lean on her, a person
> who fears that she will never really be able to depend
> on others or never feels content about her dependency.
> (Eichenbaum and Orbach, 1985, p. 21)

Eichenbaum and Orbach go on to point out that most men are looked after by women all their lives, from their mothers and other female relatives to female teachers, wives or partners. In addition, women play a supportive role as secretaries and assistants to men's professional lives, although many women are unhappy when this shades into the role of an 'office wife' (Pringle, 1989).

By meeting men's basic physical and emotional needs, women are effectively creating time for them to develop their own potential. In so far as men do not reciprocate by meeting the physical, emotional and safety needs of women, women have very little opportunity – certainly in heterosexual relationships – to develop their own potentiality, to engage in the process of self-actualisation. If women are judged by the male criterion of individualised success, lacking the basic supports Maslow thinks are essential, they are almost certain to experience low self-esteem and feelings of inferiority, weakness and helplessness. Women's experience is also ignored in Maslow's assumption that knowledge and understanding come at the end of the process of human development. This ignores the fact that knowledge and understanding are the primary elements of the WE-world.

For Carol Gilligan, the separation of the ME-world from the WE-world has meant two different visions of maturity in the process of moral and psychological development (Gilligan, 1982). Gilligan found that women saw their identity in terms of relationships based on an ethics of responsibility and care. Their moral judgement was inclusive and connected, reflecting the ethic of responsibility which saw fairness as resting upon equity and the recognition of differences of need. Men, on the other hand, saw their identity in terms of separation from others and personal integrity. Male morality reflects an 'ethic of rights' which balances the claims of individuals treated as equals in terms of universally applied criteria. Gilligan calls upon us to reclaim women's morality:

> As we have listened for centuries to the voices of men and the theories of development that their experience informs, so we have come more recently to notice not only the silence of women but the difficulty in hearing what they say when they speak. Yet in the different voice of women lies the truth of an ethic of care, the tie between relationship and responsibility.
> (1982, p. 173)

In the absence of women's voices, the interconnected nature of women's lives and the 'ethic of care' of the WE-world is rejected in favour of the 'bias of men' towards the separation, individualism and personal achievement of the ME-world. The origins of aggression lie in the 'failure of connection' in male experience.

In terms of personal development, a woman-orientated view of maturity would reflect the capacity to nourish others and help them develop their full potential. In the process, however, personal autonomy must necessarily be lost. If we are to transcend the ME-world we need to transcend the male-orientated view of personal development as independent self-actualisation. If we do not, those who are deemed to have achieved the highest levels of personal development according to the values of the ME-world will be the *least mature* in terms of the WE-world. In so far as men's lives are linear, single-path, discrete, emotionally distanced, it is *because* women's lives are multifaceted, intertwined and emotionally close. This does not imply that there is an essentially feminine or masculine way of thinking or being: rather, there is a male way of life and a female way of life. The former rests upon the oppression of the latter. Men can have a hierarchical, ordered and formalised view of the world because their lives are compartmentalised and unidimensional. The ME-world and the WE-world are not two complementary halves of a holistic world, they are the product of direct exploitation of women's time and labour by men. The two halves of the human world cannot be brought together without transcending the male dominance of women, so that women can 'put down the grown-up male children we have carried in our arms' (Rich, 1986, p. 215).

The ME-world is also a violent world for both men and women. The boundary between the ME-world and the WE-world is policed by the threat or reality of domestic violence and rape and by the institutions of militarism and war. Diana Scully has argued (1990) that it is men with the most rigid ideas of female 'virtue' who are most likely to rape. She also shares the conclusion of many feminists that rapists are acting in the interests of all men by controlling women through fear. It is ironic that Maslow identifies safety as one of the most basic needs in human development, yet the ME-world does not guarantee women's basic safety in public or in private.

The ME-world, because it *necessitates* the imposed altruism of women, cannot treat women with 'egalitarian consideration' (Collard, 1988). To do so would mean acknowledging women's vital contribution to male development and the central role of imposed altruism in human society. Imposed altruism cannot become part of the ME-world because it conflicts with the idea of individualised development. This does not mean that men as individuals have no emotions or don't care for anyone else, but they cannot act upon these feelings in the ME-world. For that reason the ME-world cannot be the basis of a green or socialist society. It is oppressive and exploitative, and by that token can never be egalitarian. Only a society that recognises the essential nature of nurturing and caring work will finally relieve women of the burden they have carried for so long. The only political philosophy capable of putting altruism at the heart of its political structures is feminist socialism.

Liberation? Whose Liberation?

Work less, live more!
(André Gorz, 1980, p. 134)

A future green socialist society can be liberating for women only if it recognises the centrality of the WE-world. Sadly, this does not appear to be the case, as there is a tendency within a good deal of green and socialist thought to see life and work as separate, as alternatives. Work is seen as an unnecessary imposition on human existence, rather than an integral and obligated part of life. Much of the writing is infused with a male-orientated view of freedom that can be traced back to the share owners of the Greek city-states, and possibly long before that.

In Greek thought, the 'free' world was the world of public affairs as against the domestic world of unfreedom, concerned with birth and production, populated by women and slaves (Elshtain, 1981). From this perspective freedom is achieved only when we are free of work, when our basic emotional and physical needs are met. In *Capital* Marx distinguishes between the realm of necessity and the realm of freedom. The realm of necessity is labour dictated by need and 'external purposes'. True freedom is 'outside the sphere of material production proper'. Where does women's work lie for Marx – in the realm of necessity or the realm of freedom? Neither realm takes account of women's work.

The green criticism of traditional economic structures, both socialist and capitalist, is that they trap people into unnecessary work (Ekins, 1986; Robertson, 1985; Schumacher, 1980; Osmond, 1986). The main criticism of waged work is not that it is exploitative, yielding profits for those who control it, but that it is meaningless with no room for personal expression or autonomy (Handy, 1989). For Ted Trainer, 'few people work at activities yielding them increased knowledge or valuable experience or personal growth' (1985, p. 197). People are trapped by the 'work ethic' into 'sorrowful drudgery' and endless wasteful production

(Porritt, 1984). According to André Gorz, most people waste their lives to earn their pay, and the most important political task now is to liberate ourselves from work (Gorz, 1980, 1985, 1989). Once free of unnecessary work we can engage ourselves in autonomous activities, 'activities one performs freely and not from necessity, as ends in themselves' (1989, p. 222).

Ted Trainer thinks it should be possible to get our paid work down to one day a week if we 'abandon affluence' by phasing out production of unnecessary things, making things more durable and easily repairable and in a way that uses minimum resources and labour. Like his nineteenth-century predecessors Charles Fourier and William Morris, Trainer argues that work would become indistinguishable from leisure or art: 'Work in these conditions might better be described as play or hobbies or pottering around'; daily life would involve 'planting seedlings, repairing tools, caring for animals, chairing a meeting, bottling fruit, glazing a window, soldering a solar panel, making group decisions, forging metal, helping to build a house, designing and planning, writing up records, teaching and explaining' (Trainer, 1985, p. 260). Little attention is paid to women's work, although Trainer suggests that the elderly could be looked after by children supported by a communal roster of adults. Another male writer offers a similar spectrum of exciting activities in post-industrial communities: 'learning, thinking, making music, writing, creating, gardening, painting, tinkering with engines [!], making our goods as we want them and building our local communities – instead of just working' (Wall, 1990, p. 95).

There tends to be a romantic haze in visions of a new green world based on craft work and small-scale technology (Schumacher, 1973). Trainer argues that we should aim for self-sufficiency, growing things in the back yard, producing many goods such as clothing and footwear in the neighbourhood. He even wants to get rid of technology like the domestic washing machine, arguing that 'we should look forward to doing the washing by hand in order to take advantage of the exercise it offers' (Trainer, 1985, pp. 262–3). It is not clear who the 'we' is here! Before we go back to keeping our own sheep and threshing our own corn, we should remember what a labour-intensive rural life was like for women. A 1555 'Boke of Husbandrye' demands that a wife should sow flax and hemp, weed, pull, water, wash, dry, beat, hatchell, spin, wind, wrap and weave it before using it to make sheets, tablecloths, towels, shirts and smocks, then starting the whole process again with wool (Miles, 1988).

Green criticisms of modern technology ignore the fact that a lot of the work it has relieved was traditionally women's work. Murray Bookchin pours scorn on those who put their 'emphasis ... on labour-intensive technologies, presumably to "save" energy by exhausting the working classes of society'. He sees it as a 'scandalous often self-indulgent middle-class affectation' by a 'salad of academics, students and professionals' who have 'never been obliged to do a day of onerous toil in their lives' (Bookchin, 1989, p. 196). I would add that the 'salad' is also almost exclusively male.

Advocates of the green 'new economics' see the choice as between alienating paid work in large-scale institutions and 'free', 'autonomous' 'own-work' in a decentralised economy. Is this the kind of world in which women will no longer be responsible for 'women's work'? Will it break down the boundaries between the ME-world and the WE-world? I doubt it; where domestic work is discussed, it tends to be something people will 'choose' to do with their newly 'freed' time. The work that the green visionaries are rejecting is male productivist work; they ignore the fact that much of women's work is not free, except in money terms! It is not autonomous, it is not 'own-work'. Women's work cannot be automated or abandoned as unnecessary consumption. There will always be children, routine domestic chores, people to nurse and care for. Women's work is by its very nature decentralised and localised, but that does not make it 'autonomous' or 'free'.

James Robertson is one of the few male green writers to put the sexual division of labour at the centre of his analysis, attacking the masculine and impersonal nature of employment and its separation from the unpaid work of women in the home (Robertson, 1985). In Robertson's SHE (sane, humane, ecological) future, paid work will be more evenly shared and redefined to include 'useful and valued' activities. Robertson acknowledges women's double burden of work and argues that their basic caring and nurturing role is the material basis of society, while a good deal of men's work is 'surplus' occupation. In fact, his view of the future is that everyone would share the patterns typical of women's lives now – a mix of part-time employment, family work at home, voluntary work and some full-time work (ibid., p. 88).

Nevertheless, there are still male-orientated individualist overtones in his concept of 'own-work' and in his view of work in the new SHE world as 'a balanced *freely chosen* sharing of work between men and women, perceiving each other as equal partners' (p. 86; emphasis added). Robertson sees a future in which work, leisure, learning and caring activities will be focused upon the home. New technology provides the opportunity for an 'electronic cottage' reuniting a pre-industrial relationship between home and work (Toffler, 1981; Robertson, 1990).

Rather pessimistically for Robertson's image of a sexually egalitarian green future, Dorothy Schwarz describes the frustration of life in her 'electronic cottage' as she jointly wrote *Breaking Through* with her husband, Walter Schwarz:

> Why, when this book is written together, does the male of the partnership claim a *jus prima nocte* over the word processor, while the female partner cooks the supper? (Schwarz and Schwarz, 1987, p. 190)

As Derek Wall has acknowledged, the 'feminisation of a green economy' would 'demand a cultural revolution that would make Mao's effort to re-educate urban intellectuals on the land look somewhat puny' (1990, p. 91).

While patriarchy is often explicitly rejected by male writers, there is usually an unquestioned assumption of family-based heterosexuality-as-usual. For Gorz 'the domestic community (the nuclear or extended family) is one in which life is based on *sharing everything*' (1989, p. 222). Gorz's view of women's emancipation is when 'man and woman voluntarily share the tasks of the private sphere as well as those in the public sphere and belong *equally* to one another' (1989, p. 164; original emphasis). Ted Trainer envisages a return to some form of tribal existence, with extended families possibly all living under one roof.

Do women want to turn their back on a modernity they have barely begun to share for a small-scale world circumscribed by the nuclear or extended family? Is the assumption of family-based heterosexuality-as-usual a Trojan Horse for patriarchy-as-usual?

Recovering the we*-World*

Seeking to promote a new vision of democratic
communities, with real resources for sharing the caring
... feminists dreamt of a world where relationships
beyond the couple would be invested with ... meaning,
commitment and passion.
(Lynne Segal, 1990, p. 279)

A feminist green socialism must be underpinned by the values that have hitherto been imposed upon women: altruism, selfless caring, the desire to help other people realise their potential. This will not be achieved unless women's sexual liberation is at the centre of a feminist green socialist politics. As Ann Ferguson has argued, the heterosexual family has played a central role in securing the 'sex/affective' labour of women (Ferguson, 1989). If the boundaries of the present destructive and distorted ideas of masculinity and femininity are to be broken, women must have control of their bodies both sexually and in terms of reproduction. However, sexual liberation is meaningless without economic liberation; to achieve their sexual and reproductive liberation, women must be economically independent of men. If men are to learn to live in the WE-world they will have to abandon the benefits and the constraints of both patriarchy and masculinity (Segal, 1990; Stoltenberg, 1990).

Ann Ferguson sees the elimination of what she calls the 'sex–gender' divisions in society through 'gynandry'. She prefers this word to androgyny. Both mean transcending the boundaries of the sexes, but androgyny implies the priority of male values and experience, whereas gynandry stresses the importance of women's values and experience. If we are to move towards gynandry, men must acquire women's skills of 'sex/affective labour', that is 'nurturance, emotional sensitivity, receptivity to the desires of others, skills in the healing arts' (1989, p. 231). Ferguson argues that gynandrous people could develop only under a society run on the basis of 'council socialism', where decision-making was decentralised to the lowest possible level. Types of work would not be segregated on any basis, and everyone would receive an equal income or a basic income if they were too old or young to work. All workers would work two fifteen-hour 'blocks' each week: one in what Ferguson calls 'standard sector work' (construction, factories, doctoring, teaching, skilled clerical and white-collar work) and a second in service work (garbage collection, recycling, cleaning, physical care of young, sick and elderly and educational support work). Service work would be rotated. Education would be a free and lifelong process, and everyone would be required to share in caring for the next generation.

Children would not be segregated from the adult world and would have rights to income and care. These would be provided by the adults who share the child's home, no matter what form the household may take. With a high level of communal support for childcare, this should not be an onerous burden. Ferguson suggests that there should be the equivalent of the Cuban Domestic Family Code, whereby both men and women are held responsible for housework and providing an income for children. Ann Ferguson's ideal community reflects many of the attributes of bell hooks's description of a Black neighbourhood:

> Many people raised in black communities experienced this type of community-based child care. Black women who had to leave the home and work to help provide for families could not afford to send children to day care centers and such centers did not always exist. They relied on people in their communities to help. She did not need to go with her children every time they walked to the playground to watch them because they would be watched by a number of people living near the playground. People who did not have children often took responsibility for sharing in childrearing. In my own family, there were seven children and when we were growing up it was not possible for our parents to watch us all the time or even give that extra special individual attention children sometimes desire. Those needs were often met by neighbors and people in the community. (hooks, 1989, p. 144)

Most working-class communities would provide a similar support system, although almost always provided by women. bell hooks claims that in her community caring was not taken for granted, it was valued and appreciated. When she went to university, hooks was surprised by the way in which white students rejected the care they had received as they prepared themselves for a competitive, affluent, individualised society. Emotional and physical support was pushed below the surface, out of sight. People pretended they had 'got there on their own'.

A feminist green socialism would recognise the essential values of care and nurturing in human development, and our mutual responsibility for them. However, we do not just need to build ourselves as individuals, we need to build a supportive social environment and a sustainable relationship with the natural world.

Caring for the World

As we face slow environmental poisoning . . . we can
hope that the prospect of the extinction of life on the
planet will provide a universal impetus to social change.
(Ynestra King, 1983, p. 125)

We do not have much time if we are to avoid increased human
suffering and ecological destruction on a global scale. The present world system is driven by the competitive and individualistic
values of patriarchal capitalism, based on private ownership,
profit and self-interest, sustained by militarised nation-states.
It is a system that has produced tremendous developments as
well as tremendous destruction. It is not a system of organisation
or values appropriate for a sustainable future. Only a feminist
green socialism is equal to this task. Feminist, because it
acknowledges the centrality of women's life-producing and
life-sustaining work and focuses upon the predominance of
men in destructive institutions. Green, because it argues that
we should act and think globally to regain a balance between
the needs of humanity and the ability of the planet to sustain
them. Socialist, because it recognises the rights of all peoples of
the world to live in a socially just and equitable community.

We need to deconstruct from above and reconstruct below.
We need to free ourselves from the structures and institutions
that divide us, while building our connectedness with each other
and the natural world. For some people that will mean difficult
and dangerous struggles with powerful institutions. Workers'
struggles with multinational companies, forest-dwellers' and
forestry workers' struggles against landowners who are willing
to use murder as a weapon of repression. Poor women's daily
struggle for livelihood and in defence of their land. The violence
women face at the hands of men. Environmental and peace
campaigners who risk their lives and liberty. Some people may
be able to break away completely from modern industrial society

to become green 'Benedictines' in small-scale communities, as Rudolf Bahro has suggested. This will not be a solution for the mass of the population; most of us will be able to change things only in little ways, using small spaces, possibly only within ourselves and our own lives. Even now, in the shantytowns of Brazil, Colombia and Mexico, women are pooling their resources into a 'common pot'; in Kenya women are drawing on traditional mutual aid networks to obtain supplies of fuel and water. bell hooks records a similar experience in poor Black communities where a co-operative value system emerged:

> that challenged notions of individualism and private property so important to the maintenance of white-supremacist, capitalist patriarchy. Black folk created in marginal spaces a world of community and collectivity where resources were shared. (hooks, 1989, p. 76)

Within the richer societies there are possibilities in consumer action, through boycotts or selective consumption. People can begin to free themselves from total dependence upon the wider economy through more flexible approaches to work and income, such as a Basic Income Scheme or local production and trading schemes; by joining alternative organisations such as producer or consumer co-operatives or forming local mutual aid networks. Local authorities could be empowered to act more creatively to stimulate local autonomy, through using local savings and labour. As well as finding marginal spaces locally to create a world of community and collectivity, we must reach out to those who are struggling for their livelihood across the globe and work with them to break down the boundaries that are destroying us all. We must build multicultural and international alliances that will be 'bridges of power' and solidarity (Albrecht & Brewer, 1990). If we can do nothing else, we must constantly push and question: push at boundaries and question authorities. What is being done, in whose interest, to whose benefit? What will be the cost in ecological, social and personal terms? By our pushing and questioning we must reclaim time. The world is being hurtled to oblivion at the pace of the fastest man, the man who is least personally encumbered, who is most nurtured and who takes account of the fewest restraining factors. There is a destructive conflict between the need of the individual to achieve as much as possible before (he) dies and the need of the planet to move as slowly as possible towards its inevitable death. For most women, sustaining the future generation is more important than personal achievements. Women, moving at the pace of the slowest child or the most needy adult, are closer to the sustainable pace of the planet.

At the same time, we must not reject modernity out of hand. If we stop development now, we are freezing it at the present levels of advantage and disadvantage. The many benefits of science, technology and large-scale organisation have not yet passed down to the majority of the people of this planet; that is the cruelty of the patriarchal, racist, capitalist system. The majority of people in the world have never had the chance to determine the way in which the benefits of human knowledge and creativity are used. It is not for the well-heeled white male middle class of the North to cry halt. It is fine for a well-educated person with the whole of Western (or Eastern) culture in their heads to go and whittle wood on a Welsh hillside, but communing with nature will not have the same meaning for those who have never had those advantages.

A sustainable egalitarian society will not be achieved if we abandon the ideals of progress and rational control of human history for an irrational and atavistic attachment to a mythical or mystical past or future. What is needed is a change of priorities: from men to women, from rich to poor, from North to South, from nature exploitation to nature stewardship. However, none of these will be achieved on its own; that is the reality of our interconnectedness. And that is why we need a feminist green socialism.

Last Thoughts

I imagine, but I do not know, that the universe has an
intelligence, a Great Spirit, that it cares as we care . . .
Sometimes I feel that I hear the universe weeping or
laughing, speaking to me. But I do not know . . .

What I do know is that whether the universe has a center
of consciousness or not, the sight of a field of flowers in
the colour purple, the rainbow, must be enough to stop
us from destroying all that is and wants to be.
(Carol P. Christ, 1990, p. 69)

A world order that commits planetary suicide in the
search for profit while driving the majority of human
beings into despair and poverty is a killing/producing
machine without spiritual centre . . . spirit creates a new
sense of the possible.
(Joel Kovel, 1991, pp. 12–13)

This book began with my fear in going through the wire at
Greenham Common: a fear of authority, soldiers, prisons,
uncertainty, being 'outside' society, of losing career, family
and other cocooning structures. My fear resulted from a lack
of vision, which in turn represented a fragmentation of my self
and my life imposed by patriarchy, capitalism, militarism, racism
and the separation of human society from the natural world. All
these things still exist, but I am beginning to lose my fear.
This book has been about tearing down the boundaries that
isolate us and make us feel powerless and afraid. That is the

beginning of our re-empowerment, putting back together the fragments of our lives that capitalism, militarism, racism and patriarchy have pulled apart.

The tearing down and reconstruction of boundaries is both a personal and a political process, and I am sorry when personal transformation is seen as opposed to wider political struggle. I do not think it is possible to have one without the other. I do not see personal change having a 'ripple effect' throughout society without direct political struggle. Equally, although there is tremendous empowerment in the solidarity of collective struggle, it will not always be there. We need to have some internal sense of strength, a strength of the spirit. I think this comes in two forms. One lies in a political vision, a trust in others and in the future – a knowledge that we are not alone in our struggle, and that it will not be in vain. The second lies within ourselves – an inner sense of cohesiveness and control.

I agree with Joel Kovel that in strengthening our inner selves, our spirit, we need not reject out of hand either modernity or rationality. It is not abandoning reason to 'get in touch with our feelings'. What we need to do is use our feelings to regain control of both modernity and rationality.

My personal empowerment has come through Taoism. For me the Taoist idea of Chi, internal energy, does not represent a religious sense of supernatural forces. I see it as a human-based strengthening of the spirit that is within all of us; an emancipatory and empowering humanist spirituality. I do not see Taoism as the only source of empowerment; there are many other ways of strengthening the spirit. Nor does spiritual empowerment offer us a morality; it does not tell us how to use that strength for good or ill.

I do not reject the emancipatory force of human reason because I am certain that there is no supreme being guiding us or any dynamic of nature that we can discover and follow. I see the human race as an accidental development on an accidental planet in an accidental universe. This does not imply randomness and chaos; everything that comes into existence has its own rationality and range of choices, and that is my source of hope. The existence of life on this accidental planet may be unique in the universe, but it has created a natural world of incredible beauty. It has created in human beings, and possibly some sea mammals, the capacity for love, understanding and reason. Human beings have not always used these wonderful gifts very wisely, but we haven't yet lost them. Every time I see an act of love or kindness, a beautifully constructed human creation, or look at a tree or see a dolphin swimming I feel empowered. I feel equally empowered by the collective strength of those who would be powerless as individuals.

Our task now is to replace the fragmented and external forms of knowledge and power that control us by our collective strength and wisdom and our inner strength of spirit. We must transform both society and ourselves by breaking down the false boundaries within ourselves and within our lives, between each other and between our societies, between the human race and the natural world. We must create necessary boundaries in our lives that enable us to treat each other and the natural world with respect, tolerance, equity, care, consideration and reverence. That would be a feminist green socialism worth having.

Bibliography

Adams, W.M. (1990) *Green Development*. Routledge, London

Afshar, Haleh (1985) *Women, Work and Ideology in the Third World*. Tavistock, London

Albert, Michael and Robin Hahnel (1991) *Looking Forward: Participatory Economics for the Twenty First Century*. South End Press, Boston

Albrecht, Lisa & Rose M. Brewer (1990) *Bridges of Power: Women's Multi-cultural Alliances*. New Society Publishers, Philadelphia

Alic, Margaret (1986) *Hypatia's Heritage*. Women's Press, London

Anand, Anita (1983) 'Saving Trees, Saving Lives: Third World Women and the Issue of Survival', in Leonie Caldecott and Stephanie Leland (eds) (1983) *Reclaim the Earth*. Women's Press, London

Anderson, Bonnie S. and Judith P. Zinsser (1989) *A History of their Own*, vol. 1. Penguin, London

Anderson, Karen (1987) 'A Gendered World: Women, Men and the Political Economy of the Seventeenth-Century Huron', in Heather Jon Maroney and Meg Luxton (eds) (1987) *Feminism and Political Economy*. Methuen, London

Arber, Sara and Nigel Gilbert (1989) 'Men: The Forgotten Carers', *Sociology*, vol. 23, no. 1, pp. 111–18

Ariès, Philippe (1962) *Centuries of Childhood*. Penguin, Harmondsworth

Ariffin, Rohana and James Lochhead (1988) *Issues Related to the Participation of Women in Trade Unions in Malaysia*. Pub. authors, Kuala Lumpur

Armstrong, Pat and Hugh Armstrong (1988) 'Taking Women into Account', in Jane Jenson, *et al. Feminization of the Labour Force*. Polity, Cambridge

Aronowitz, Stanley (1990) *The Crisis in Historical Materialism*. Macmillan, London

Asian and Pacific Women's Resource Collection Network (1989) *Asian and Pacific Women's Resource and Action Series: Health*. Asian and Pacific Development Centre, Kuala Lumpur

Bahro, Rudolf (1982) *Socialism and Survival*. Heretic Books, London

Bahro, Rudolf (1986) *Building the Green Movement*. Heretic Books/GMP, London

Baker, John (1987) *Arguing for Equality*. Verso, London

Bamberger, Joan (1974) 'The Myth of Matriarchy', in Michelle Z. Rosaldo and Louise Lamphere (eds) *Woman, Culture and Society*. Stanford University Press, Stanford, CA

Barrett, Michèle and Mary McIntosh (1982) *The Anti-Social Family*. Verso, London

de Beauvoir, Simone (1968) *The Second Sex*. Random House, New York

Benn, Tony (1984) *Writings on the Wall*. Faber, London

Benton, Ted (1989) 'Marxism and Natural Limits: An Ecological Critique and Reconstruction', *New Left Review*, no. 178, pp. 51–86

Beresford, Meg (1988) 'We are all connected', in Felix Dodds (ed.) *Into the 21st Century*. Green Print, London

Biehl, Janet (1988) 'What is Social Ecofeminism?', *Green Perspectives*, no. 11, reprinted in *Green Line* no. 70 (1989) pp. 16–17

Biehl, Janet (1989) 'Separating Fact and Fiction in the Green Goddess Myth', *Green Line*, no. 70, pp. 17–19

Biehl, Janet (1991) *Rethinking Ecofeminist Politics*. South End Press, Boston, MA

Black, Anthony (1984) *Guilds and Civil Society*. Methuen, London

Bly, Robert (1991) *Iron John: A Book about Men*. Element Books, Bath

Bookchin, Murray (1982) *The Ecology of Freedom*. Cheshire Books, California

Bookchin, Murray (1988) *Green Perspectives*. Green Programme Project, Burlington, VT

Bookchin, Murray (1989) *Remaking Society*. Black Rose Books, Montreal

Boserup, Ester (1970) *Women's Role in Economic Development*. St Martin's Press, New York

Boulding, Kenneth (1973) 'The Economics of the Coming Spaceship Earth', in Herman E. Daly, *Toward a Steady State Economy*. W.H. Freeman & Co., San Francisco

Bowlby, John (1953) *Childcare and the Growth of Love*. Penguin, Harmondsworth

Bradley, Harriet (1989) *Men's Work, Women's Work*. Polity, Cambridge

Bramwell, Anna (1985) *Blood and Soil: Walther Darre and Hitler's Green Party*. Kensal Press, Bourne End, Bucks

Bramwell, Anna (1989) *Ecology in the 20th Century*. Yale University Press, London

British Association of Nature Conservationists (1990) *Economics of the Environment: The Conservationists' Response to the Pearce Report.* 23 Donnerville Gardens, Admaston, Telford

Brown, Lester R. (1981) *Building a Sustainable Society.* W.W. Norton, New York

Brown, Lester R. (1990) *State of the World.* Unwin Hyman, London

'Bruntland Report' (1987) *see below.* World Commission on Environment and Development

Business in the Environment (1990) *Your Business and the Environment.* London

Caldecott, Leonie and Stephanie Leland (eds) (1983) *Reclaim the Earth.* The Women's Press, London

Cameron, Anne (1989) 'First Mother and the Rainbow Children', in Judith Plant (ed.) *Healing the Wounds: The Promise of Ecofeminism.* Green Print, London

Capra, Fritjof (1983) *The Turning Point.* Flamingo, London

Carr, Marilyn (1985) *The AT Reader.* Intermediate Technology Publications Ltd, London

Carson, Rachel (1962) *Silent Spring.* Houghton Mifflin, Boston, MA

Cartwright, J. (1989) 'Conserving Nature, Decreasing Debt', *Third World Quarterly*, no. 11, pp. 114–27

Chambers, Robert (1983) *Rural Development: Putting the Last First.* Longman, London

Cheater, Angela (1989) *Social Anthropology.* Unwin Hyman, London

Chodorow, Nancy (1978) *The Reproduction of Mothering.* University of California Press, Berkeley, CA

Christ, Carol P. (1990) 'Rethinking Theology and Nature', in Irene Diamond and Gloria Feman Orenstein (eds) *Reweaving the World.* Sierra Club Books, San Francisco

Clarke, John (ed.) (1990) *Renewing the Earth: The Promise of Social Ecology.* Green Print, London

Collard, Andrée (with Joyce Contrucci) (1988) *Rape of the Wild.* The Women's Press, London

Collins, Patricia Hill (1990) *Black Feminist Thought.* HarperCollins, London

Commoner, Barry (1971) *The Closing Circle.* Knopf, New York

Coontz, Stephanie and Peta Henderson (1986) *Women's Work, Men's Property.* Verso, London

Coote, Anna and Beatrix Campbell (1982) *Sweet Freedom.* Picador, London

Corea, Gena (1988) *The Mother Machine: Reproductive Technologies from Artificial Insemination to Artificial Wombs*. The Women's Press, London

Costello, Alison, Bernadette Vallely and Josa Young (1989) *The Sanitary Protection Scandal*. Women's Environment Network, London

Costello, Nicholas, Jonathan Michie and Seumas Milne (1989) *Beyond the Casino Economy*. Verso, London

Crosbie, Liz (1988) 'Creating the New Economic Orthodoxy' in Felix Dodds (ed.) *Into the 21st Century*. Green Print, London

Dahlberg, Frances (ed.) (1981) *Woman The Gatherer*. Yale, New Haven, CT

Dally, Ann (1982) *Inventing Motherhood*. Burnett Books, London

Dally, Kathryn (1990) 'Milking the Third World', *Green Line*, no. 80, p. 18

Daly, Herman E. (1973) *Toward a Steady State Economy*. W.H. Freeman, San Francisco

Daly, Mary (1979) *Gyn/Ecology*. The Women's Press, London

Daly, Mary (1986) *Beyond God the Father*. The Women's Press, London

Dankelman, Irene and Joan Davidson (1988) *Women and Environment in the Third World*. Earthscan, London

Dauncey, Guy (1988) *After the Crash: The Emergence of the Rainbow Economy*. Green Print, London

Deem, Rosemary (1986) *All Work and No Play*. Open University Press, Milton Keynes

Delphy, Christine (1984) *Close to Home*. Hutchinson, London

Devall, Bill (1990) *Simple in Means, Rich in Ends*. Green Print, London

Devall, Bill and George Sessions (1985) *Deep Ecology*. Peregrine Smith Books, Layton, UT

Diamond, Irene and Gloria Feman Orenstein (eds) (1990) *Reweaving the World*. Sierra Club Books, San Francisco

Dinnerstein, Dorothy (1976) *The Mermaid and the Minotaur*. Harper & Row, New York

Dobson, Andrew (1990) *Green Political Thought*. Unwin Hyman, London

Dodds, Felix (1988) *Into the 21st Century*. Green Print, London

Doubiago, Sharon (1989) 'Mama Coyote Talks to the Boys', in Judith Plant (ed.) *Healing the Wounds*. Green Print, London

D'Souza, Corinne Kumar (1989) 'A New Movement, A New Hope. East Wind, West Wind and the Wind from

the South' in Judith Plant (ed.) *Healing the Wounds*. Green
Print, London

Easlea, Brian (1983) *Fathering the Unthinkable*. Pluto Press, London

Ecologist (1973) 'Blueprint for Survival', *The Ecologist*, vol. 2, no. 1,
pp. 1–43

Ehrenreich, Barbara and Deirdre English (1979) *For Her Own Good*.
Pluto, London

Eichenbaum, Luise and Susie Orbach (1985) *Understanding Women*.
Penguin, Harmondsworth

Eisler, Riane (1987) *The Chalice and the Blade*. Harper & Row,
New York

Eisler, Riane (1990) 'The Gaia Tradition and the Partnership
Future: An Ecofeminist Manifesto', in Irene Diamond and Gloria
Feman Orenstein (eds) *Reweaving the World*. Sierra Club Books,
San Francisco

Ekins, Paul (1986) *The Living Economy*. Routledge & Kegan
Paul, London

Elgin, D. (1981) *Voluntary Simplicity*. William Morrow, New York

Elkington, John and Tom Burke (1987) *The Green Capitalists*.
Gollancz, London

Elshtain, Jean Bethke (1981) *Public Man, Private Woman*. Martin
Robertson, Oxford

Elson, Diane (1988) 'Market Socialism or Socialization of the
Market?' *New Left Review*, no. 172, pp. 3–44

Elson, Diane and Ruth Pearson (1984) 'The Subordination of
Women and the Internationalisation of Factory Production',
in Kate Young, Carol Wolkowitz and Roslyn McCullagh
(eds) *Of Marriage and the Market*. Routledge & Kegan
Paul, London

Elton, Ben (1989) *Stark*. Penguin, Harmondsworth

Engels, Friedrich (1884) *The Origin of the Family, Private Property and
the State*, in Marx and Engels (1970) *Selected Works*. Lawrence &
Wishart, London

Erlich, Paul (1972) *The Population Bomb*. Ballantine, London

Erlich, Paul R. and Anne H. Erlich (1970) *Population, Resources,
Environment*. W.H. Freeman, San Francisco

Erlich, Paul R. and Anne H. Erlich (1987) *Earth*. Thames
Methuen, London

Errington, Frederick and Deborah Gewertz (1987) *Cultural
Alternatives and a Feminist Anthropology*. Cambridge University
Press, Cambridge

Evandrou, Maria (1990) *Challenging the Invisibility of Carers*. STICERD, London School of Economics, London

Ferguson, Ann (1989) *Blood at the Root*. Pandora Press, London

Ferguson, Marilyn (1981) *The Aquarian Conspiracy*. Paladin, London

Firestone, Shulamith (1979) *The Dialetic of Sex*. The Women's Press, London

Forman, Frieda Johles (ed.) (1989) *Taking our Time*. Pergamon, Oxford

Frankel, Boris (1987) *The Post-Industrial Utopians*. Polity, Cambridge

Freeman, Jo (1970) *The Tyranny of Structurelessness*, reprinted in *Untying the Knot, Feminism, Anarchism and Organisation* (1984) Dark Star/Rebel Press, London

Friedman, Milton (1962) *Capitalism and Freedom*. University of Chicago Press, Chicago

Frobel, F., J. Kreye and O. Heinrichs (1980) *The New International Division of Labour*. Cambridge University Press, Cambridge

Fruzzetti, Lina (1985) 'Farm and hearth: rural Women in a Farming Community', in Haleh Afshar (ed.) *Women, Work and Ideology in the Third World*. Tavistock, London

Fuss, Diana (1989) *Essentially Speaking: Feminism, Nature and Difference*. Routledge, London

Gahrton, Per (1990) 'Diary of a Swedish Green in North America', *Green Line*, no. 82, pp. 8–9

Gamble, Andrew (1988) *The Free Economy and the Strong State*. Macmillan, London

Gardner, Don (1988) *Mianmen Women: Myth and Reality*, in D. Gewertz (ed.) *Myths of Matriarchy Reconsidered*. University of Sydney Oceania Monographs, Sydney

George, Susan (1988) *A Fate Worse Than Debt*. Penguin, Harmondsworth

Gewertz, Deborah (ed.) (1988) *Myths of Matriarchy Reconsidered*. University of Sydney Oceania Monographs, Sydney

Gilligan, Carol (1982) *In a Different Voice: Psychological Theory and Women's Development*. Harvard University Press, Cambridge, MA

Gillison, Gillian (1980) 'Images of Nature in Gimi Thought', in Carol MacCormack and Marilyn Strathern (eds.) *Nature, Culture and Gender*. Cambridge University Press, Cambridge

Gilman, Charlotte Perkins (1915) *Women and Economics*. G.P. Putnam's Sons, London

Goodale, Jane C. (1980) 'Gender, Sexuality and Marriage: A Kaulong Model of Nature and Culture', in Carol MacCormack

and Marilyn Strathern (eds) *Nature, Culture and Gender*.
Cambridge University Press, Cambridge

Gorz, André (1980) *Ecology as Politics*. South End Press, Boston

Gorz, André (1985) *Paths to Paradise*. Pluto, London

Gorz, André (1989) *Critique of Economic Reason*. Verso, London

Green, Eileen, Sandra Hebron and Diana Woodward (1990) *Women's Leisure, What Leisure?* Macmillan, London

Griffin, Susan (1978) *Women and Nature*. The Women's Press, London

Grow, Richard (1990) 'Decolonising the Language of the Green Movement'. *Green Line*, no. 76, pp. 4–5

Hall, Stuart (1978) *Policing the Crisis*. Macmillan, Basingstoke

Hall, Stuart and Martin Jacques (eds) (1989) *New Times*. Lawrence & Wishart, London

Handy, Charles (1989) *The Age of Unreason*. Business Books Ltd, London

Hardin, Garrett (1968) 'The Tragedy of the Commons'. *Science*, vol. 162, pp. 1243–8

Hardin, Garrett and John Baden (1977) *Managing the Commons*. Freeman, San Francisco

Harding, Philip and Richard Jenkins (1989) *The Myth of the Hidden Economy*. Open University Press, Milton Keynes

Hardy, Dennis (1979) *Alternative Communities in the Nineteenth Century*. Longman, London

Hardyment, Christina (1983) *Dream Babies*. Oxford University Press, Oxford

Harris, Olivia (1980) 'The Power of Signs: Gender, Culture and the Wild in the Bolivian Andes', in Carol MacCormack and Marilyn Strathern (eds) *Nature, Culture and Gender*. Cambridge University Press, Cambridge

Harrison, Paul (1987) *The Greening of Africa*. Paladin, London

Hart, Nicky (1989) 'Gender and the Rise and Fall of Class Politics'. *New Left Review*, no. 175, pp. 19–47

Hartsock, Nancy (1984) *Money, Sex and Power*. Northeastern University Press, Boston.

Hays, Terence (1988) 'Myths of Matriarchy' and the Sacred Flute Complex of the Papua New Guinea Highlands', in Deborah Gewertz (ed.) *Myths of Matriarchy Reconsidered*. University of Sydney Oceania Monographs, Sydney

Henderson, Hazel (1988) *The Politics of the Solar Age*. Knowledge Systems Inc., New York

Henderson, Hazel (1983) 'The Warp and the Weft: The Coming

Synthesis of Eco-Philosophy and Eco-Feminism', in Leonie Caldecott and Stephanie Leland (eds) *Reclaim the Earth*. The Women's Press, London

Henderson, Hazel (1978) *Creating Alternative Futures*. Perigee Books, New York

Henderson, Hazel (1990) *Evaluation for Accountability*. Paper presented to the European Seminar on Evaluation Approaches and Methods, Aldeia Da Acoteias, Portugal, 6–8 December 1990

Hochschild, Airlie (1990) *The Second Shift: Working Parents and the Revolution at Home*. Piatkus, London

hooks, bell (1982) *Aint I a Woman?* Pluto, London

hooks, bell (1989) *Talking Back*. Sheba, London

Hülsberg, W. (1988) *The German Greens*. Verso, London

Icke, David (1990) *It Doesn't Have to be Like This*. Green Print, London

Icke, David (1991) *The Truth Vibrations*. Aquarian–Harper Collins, London

Ikanan, Evaristo Nugkuag (1990) 'The Myth of Amazonian Development'. *Green Line*, no. 82, pp. 12–13

Irvine, Sandy and Alec Ponton (1988) *A Green Manifesto*. Optima, London

Ives, Jane H. (ed.) (1985) *The Export of Hazard: Transnational Corporations and Environment Control Issues*. Routledge & Kegan Paul, Boston, MA

Jacobs, Michael (1991) *The Green Economy*. Pluto, London

Jacobson, Jodi (1990) *The Politics of Abortion*. Worldwatch Institute, Washington, DC

James, Nicky (1989) 'Emotional Labour: Skill and Work in the Social Regulation of Feelings'. *The Sociological Review*, vol. 37, no. 1, pp. 15–42

Jenson, Jane, Elisabeth Hagen and Ceallaigh Reddy (1988) *Feminization of the Labour Force*. Polity, Oxford

Jones, Kath (1988) 'The Hazards Movement Blossoms'. *New Ground*, no. 17, pp. 8–9

Kagarlitsky, Boris (1990) *The Dialectic of Change*. Verso, London

Kapp, K.W. (1978) *The Social Costs of Business Enterprise*. Spokesman, Nottingham

Kelly, Petra (1984) *Fighting for Hope*. Chatto & Windus, London

Kelly, Petra (1988) 'Towards a Green Europe and a Green World', in Felix Dodds (ed.) *Into the 21st Century*. Green Print, London

Kemp, Penny and Derek Wall (1990) *A Green Manifesto for the 1990s*. Penguin, Harmondsworth

Kheel, Marti (1990) 'Eco-feminism and Deep Ecology: Reflections on Identity and Difference' in Irene Diamond and Gloria Feman Orenstein (eds) *Reweaving the World*. Sierra Club Books, San Francisco

King, Ursula (1989) *Women and Spirituality*. Macmillan, London

King, Ynestra (1983) 'Toward an Ecological Feminism and a Feminist Ecology', in Joan Rothschild (ed.) *Machina ex Dea*. Pergamon, Oxford

King, Ynestra (1989) 'The Ecology of Feminism and the Feminism of Ecology', in Judith Plant (ed.) *Healing the Wounds: The Promise of Ecofeminism*. Green Print, London

Kitzinger, Sheila (1978) *The Experience of Childbirth*. Penguin, Harmondsworth

Koonz, Claudia (1986) *Mothers in the Fatherland*. Methuen, London

Kovel, Joel (1991) *History and Spirit*. Beacon Press, Boston, MA

Kropotkin, Peter (1955) *Mutual Aid*. Extending Horizon Books, New York

LaDuke, Winona (1990) 'Racism, Environmentalism and the New Age'. *Left Green Notes*, no. 4, pp. 15–18/32–4

Lambert, Jean (1988) 'Moves Towards a Green Future', in Felix Dodds (ed.) *Into the 21st Century*. Green Print, London

Large, Martin (1981) *Social Ecology*. Self-published, Gloucester

Le Grand, Julian and Saul Estrin (1989) *Market Socialism*. Clarendon Paperbacks, Oxford University Press, Oxford

Lee, Richard Borshay (1979) *The !Kung San*. Cambridge University Press, Cambridge

Leland, Stephanie (1983) 'Feminism and Ecology: Theoretical Considerations', in Leonie Caldecott and Stephanie Leland (eds) *Reclaim the Earth*. The Women's Press, London

Leonard, Anne (1990) 'Robber Barons of the Rainforest.' *Green Line*, no. 79, pp. 14–15

Lidz, R. and L. Lidz (1977) 'Male Menstruation: A Ritual Alternative to the Oedipal Transition'. *International Journal of Psycho-Analysis*, vol. 58, no. 17, pp. 17–31

Lovelock, J.E. (1979) *Gaia*. Oxford University Press, Oxford

Luke, Tim (1988) 'The Dreams of Deep Ecology'. *Telos*, no. 76, pp. 65–92

Luxton, Meg (1987) 'Time for Myself: Women's Work and the "Fight for Shorter Hours"', in Jan Maroney and Meg

Luxton (eds) *Feminism and Political Economy*. Methuen,
London

MacCormack, Carol and Marilyn Strathern (eds) (1980) *Nature,
Culture & Gender*. Cambridge University Press, Cambridge

McKibben, Bill (1990) *The End of Nature*. Penguin, Harmondsworth

McLuhan, T.C. (1971) *Touch the Earth*. Simon & Schuster,
New York

McMillan, Carol (1982) *Women, Reason and Nature*. Blackwell,
Oxford

Malthus, T.R. (1973) *An Essay on the Principle of Population*. Dent &
Sons, London; first published 1803

Manes, Christopher (1990) *Green Rage*. Little Brown, Boston, MA

Manifesto for a Sustainable Society (MFSS) 1987 British Green
Party, London

Mann, Mick (1986) *The Sources of Social Power*, vol. 1. Cambridge
University Press, Cambridge

Maroney, Heather Jan and Meg Luxton (eds) (1987) *Feminism
and Political Economy: Women's Work and Women's Struggles*.
Methuen, London

Marshall, Lorna (1967) '!Kung Bushman Bands' in Ronald Cohen &
John Middleton (eds) *Comparative Political Systems* Natural History
Press, New York

Marx, Karl and Friedrich Engels (1970) *Selected Works*. Lawrence &
Wishart, London

Marx, Karl (1844) 'Economic and Philosophical Manuscripts',
in Lucio Colletti (ed.) *Marx – Early Writings*. Penguin,
Harmondsworth

Maslow, Abraham H. (1970) *Motivation and Personality*. Harper &
Row, New York

Max-Neef, Manfred, Antonia Elizade and Martin Hopenhayn (1989)
'Human Scale Development'. *Development Dialogue*, no. 1, CEPAUR
Dag Hammarskjöld Foundation, Uppsala

Maycock, Barry (1989) 'Arms, Cold War and Third World'. *Green
Line*, no. 75, pp. 14–15

Meadows, D.H., J. Randers and W.W. Behrens (1972) *The Limits to
Growth*. Universe Books, New York

Meillassoux, Claude (1981) *Maidens, Meal and Money*. Cambridge
University Press, Cambridge

Mellor, Mary (1980) *Motivation, Recruitment and Ideology: A Case
Study of the Co-operative Movement in North East England*. PhD
thesis, University of Newcastle upon Tyne

Mellor, Mary, Janet Hannah and John Stirling (1988) *Worker Co-operatives in Theory and Practice.* Open University Press, Milton Keynes

Mellor, Nigel (1989) *For the Inquiry.* Dab Hand Press, Ruislip

Mendes, Chico (1989) *Fight for the Forest.* Latin American Bureau, London

Merchant, Carolyn (1980) *The Death of Nature.* Harper & Row, New York

Merchant, Carolyn (1983) 'Mining the Earth's Womb', in Joan Rothschild (ed.) *Machina ex Dea.* Pergamon, Oxford.

Mernissi, Fatima (trans. Jo Lakeland) (1988) *Doing Daily Battle.* Women's Press, London

Mies, Maria (1982) *The Lace-makers of Narsapur: Indian Housewives Produce for the Worldmarket.* Zed Books, London

Mies, Maria (1986) *Patriarchy and Accumulation on a World Scale.* Zed Press, London

Miles, Rosalind (1988) *The Women's History of the World.* Penguin, Harmondsworth

Mitter, Swasti (1986) *Common Fate, Common Bond.* Pluto, London

Mitter, Swasti (1991) 'Socialism out of the Common Pots', *Feminist Review*, no. 39, p. 113–118

Moore, Henrietta L. (1988) *Feminism and Anthropology.* Polity, Cambridge

Morgan, Elaine (1985) *The Descent of Woman.* Souvenir Press, London

Mort, Frank (1989) 'The Politics of Consumption', in Stuart Hall and Martin Jacques (eds) *New Times.* Lawrence & Wishart, London

Myers, Norman (1990) *The Gaia Atlas of Future Worlds.* Robertson McCarta, London

Naess, Arne (1973) 'The Shallow and the Deep, Long Range Ecology Movement: A Summary'. *Inquiry*, no. 16, pp. 95–9

Naess, Arne (1990) 'The Basics of Deep Ecology', in John Button (ed.) *The Green Fuse.* Quartet, London

Norberg-Hodge, Helena (1990) 'A Culture Under Threat', in John Button (ed.) *The Green Fuse.* Quartet, London

O'Brien, Mary (1981) *The Politics of Reproduction.* Routledge & Kegan Paul, London

O'Connor, James (1989) 'Uneven and Combined Development and Ecological Crisis: A Theoretical Introduction'. *Race and Class*, vol. 30, pp. 1–11

O'Connor, James and Barbara Laurence (nd) *The Nature of Construction and Construction of Nature: Fall Creek, Felton, California 1860 to 1990*. Unpublished paper, Santa Cruz, CA

Odent, Michel (1984) *Birth Reborn: What Birth Can and Should Be*. Souvenir Press, London

O'Laughlin, Bridget (1974) 'Mediation or Contradiction: Why Mbum Women do not Eat Chicken', in Michelle Z. Rosaldo and Louise Lamphere (eds) *Woman, Culture and Society*. Stanford University Press, Stanford, CA

Ophuls, William (1977) *Ecology and the Politics of Scarcity*. W.H. Freeman, San Francisco

Ortner, Sherry (1974) 'Is Female to Male as Nature is to Culture?', in Michelle Z. Rosaldo and Louise Lamphere (eds) *Woman, Culture and Society*. Stanford University Press, Stanford, CA

Osmond, John (1986) *Work in the Future*. Thorsons, Wellingborough

Paehlke, Robert (1989) *Environmentalism and the Future of Progressive Politics*. Yale University Press, New Haven, CT

Palmer, Gabrielle (1988) *The Politics of Breastfeeding*. Pandora Press, London

Parker, Hermione (1989) *Instead of the Dole*. Routledge, London

Parkin, Sara (1989) *Green Parties*. Heretic Books, London

Parsons, Howard L. (1977) *Marx and Engels on Ecology*. Greenwood, London

Pearce, David (1991) *Blueprint 2: Greening the World Economy*. Earthscan, London

Pearce, David, Anil Markandya and Edward B. Barbier (1989) *Blueprint for a Green Economy*. Earthscan, London

Peattie, Lisa and Martin Rein (1983) *Women's Claims: A Study in Political Economy*. Oxford University Press, Oxford

Pepper, David (1984) *The Roots of Modern Environmentalism*. Croom Helm, London

Pepper, David (1991) *Communes and the Green Vision*. Green Print, London

Pietilä, Hilkka (1987) *Alternative Development with Women in the North*. Paper given to Third International Interdisciplinary Congress of Women, Dublin, 6–10 July; previously published in Johan Galtung and Mars Friberg (eds) *Alternativen*. Akademilitteratur, Stockholm 1986

Plant, Judith (ed.) (1989) *Healing the Wounds: The Promise of Ecofeminism*. Green Print, London

Plant, Judith (1990) 'Searching for Common Ground: Ecofeminism

and Bioregionalism' in Irene Diamond and Gloria Feman
Orenstein (eds) *Reweaving the World*. Sierra Club Books, San
Francisco

Porritt, Jonathon (1984) *Seeing Green*. Blackwell, Oxford

Porritt, Jonathon and David Winner (1988) *The Coming of the Greens*.
Fontana, London

Pringle, Rosemary (1989) *Secretaries Talk*. Verso, London

Programme of the German Green Party (PGGP) (1983) Heretic
Books, London

Ramazanoglu, Caroline (1989) *Feminism and the Contradictions of
Oppression*. Routledge, London

Randall, Margaret (1981) *Sandino's Daughters*. Zed Press, London

Rao, Brinda (1989) 'Struggling for Production Conditions and
Producing Conditions of Emancipation: Woman and Water in
Rural Maharashtra'. *Capitalism, Nature Socialism*, no. 2, pp. 65–82

Raquisa, Tonette (1987) 'Prostitution: A Philippine Experience', in
Miranda Davies (ed.) *Third World, Second Sex*. Zed Press, London

Razak, Arisika (1990) 'Towards a Womanist Analysis of Birth',
in Irene Diamond and Gloria Feman Orenstein (eds) (1990)
Reweaving the World. Sierra Club Books, San Francisco

Reay, Marie (1988) 'Man-made Myth and Women's Consciousness',
in Deborah Gewertz (ed.) *Myths of Matriarchy Reconsidered*.
University of Sydney Oceania Monographs, Sydney

Redclift, Michael (1991) *Environment and Development*. Manchester
University Press, Manchester

Reed, Evelyn (1975) *Women and Evolution: From Matriarchal Clan to
Patriarchal Family*. Pathfinder, New York

Reed, Evelyn (1978) *Sexism and Science*. Pathfinder, New York

Rich, Adrienne (1986) *Of Woman Born*. W.W. Norton, New York

Rifkin, Jeremy (1980) *Entropy*. Viking, New York

Rifkin, Jeremy (1987) *Time Wars*. Holt, New York

Ritchie, Jean (1991) *The Secret World of Cults*. Angus & Robertson,
London

Rivers, Patrick (1988) *The Stolen Future*. Green Print, London

Robertson, James (1983) *The Sane Alternative*. Self-published,
Cholsey, Oxon.

Roberton, James (1985) *Future Work*. Gower, Aldershot

Robertson, James (1990) *Future Wealth*. Cassell, London

Rowbotham, Sheila (1989) *The Past is Before Us*. Pandora, London

Rubin, Gayle (1975) 'The Traffic in Women: Notes on
the "Political Economy" of Sex' in Rayna Reiter (ed.)

Toward an Anthropology of Women. Monthly Review Press, New York

Ruddick, Sara (1990) *Maternal Thinking*. Women's Press, London

Ryle, Martin (1988) *Ecology and Socialism*. Radius, London

Sagoff, Mark (1988) *The Economy of the Earth*. Cambridge University Press, Cambridge

Sahlins, Marshall (1974) *Stone Age Economics*. Tavistock, London

Sale, Kirkpatrick (1991) 'Bioregionalism' in Andrew Dobson (ed.) *The Green Reader*. André Deutsch, London

Sanday, Peggy (1981) *Female Power and Male Dominance*. Cambridge University Press, Cambridge

Schreiner, Olive (1978) *Woman and Labour*. Virago, London; first published 1911

Schumacher, E.F. (1968) 'Buddhist Economics' *Resurgence*, vol. 1, no. 11, reprinted in Schumacher (1973) *Small is Beautiful*. Blond & Briggs, London

Schumacher, E.F. (1973) *Small is Beautiful*. Blond & Briggs, London

Schumacher, E.F. (1980) *Good Work*. Abacus, London

Schwarz, Walter and Dorothy Schwarz (1987) *Breaking Through*. Green Books, Bideford

Scully, Diana (1990) *Understanding Sexual Violence*. Unwin Hyman, London

Seabrook, Jeremy (1988) 'Green Values' in Felix Dodds (ed.) *Into the 21st Century*. Green Print, London

Seabrook, Jeremy (1990) *The Myth of the Market*. Green Books, Hartland

Segal, Lynne (1990) *Slow Motion*. Virago, London

Sen, Gita and Caren Grown (1987) *Development, Crises and Alternative Visions*. Monthly Review, New York

Shanmugaratnam, N. (1989) 'Development and Environment: A View from the South'. *Race and Class* vol. 30, no. 3, pp. 13–30

Sharpe, Sue (1984) *Double Identity*. Penguin, Harmondsworth

Shiva, Vandana (1989) *Staying Alive*. Zed, London

Shuttle, Penelope and Peter Redgrove (1978) *The Wise Wound: Menstruation and Everywoman*. Paladin, London

Simon, J. (1981) *The Ultimate Resource*. Princeton University Press, Princeton, NJ

Simon, J. and H. Kahn (1984) *The Resourceful Earth*. Oxford University Press, Oxford

Sivanandan, A. (1989) 'All That Melts into Air is Solid: The

Hokum of New Times'. *Race and Class*, vol. 31, no. 3, pp. 1–30

Slocum, Sally (1982) 'Woman the Gatherer: Male Bias in Anthropology', in Mary Evans (ed.) *The Woman Question*. Fontana, Oxford

Smith, Joan (1989) *Misogynies*. Faber, London

Spelman, Elizabeth V. (1990) *Inessential Woman*. Women's Press, London

Spretnak, Charlene (1982) *The Politics of Women's Spirituality*. Doubleday, New York

Spretnak, Charlene (1985) 'The Spiritual Dimension of Green Politics', in Charlene Spretnak and Fritjof Capra, *Green Politics*. Paladin, Glasgow

Spretnak, Charlene and Fritjof Capra (1985) *Green Politics*. Paladin, Glasgow

Spretnak, Charlene (1990) 'Eco-feminism: our roots and flowering' in Irene Diamond & Gloria Feman Orenstein (eds) (1990) *Reweaving the World*. Sierra Club Books, San Francisco

Starhawk (1990) 'Power, Authority and Mystery: Ecofeminism and Earth-based Spirituality', in Irene Diamond and Gloria Feman Orenstein (eds) (1990) *Reweaving the World*. Sierra Club Books, San Francisco

Stivens, Maila (1985) 'The Fate of Women's Land Rights: Gender, Matriliny, and Capitalism in Rembau, Negeri Sembilan, Malaysia', in Haleh Afshar (ed.) *Women, Work and Ideology in the Third World*. Tavistock, London

Stoltenberg, John (1990) *Refusing to Be a Man*. Fontana, London

Stone, Merlin (1979) *The Paradise Papers*. Virago, London

Stretton, H. (1976) *Capitalism, Socialism and the Environment*. Cambridge University Press, Cambridge

Swimme, Brian (1990) 'How to Heal a Lobotomy', in Irene Diamond and Gloria Feman Orenstein (eds) *Reweaving the World*. Sierra Club Books, San Francisco

Tanner, Nancy (1974) 'Matrifocality in Indonesia and Africa and among Black Americans', in Michelle Z. Rosaldo and Louise Lamphere (eds) *Woman, Culture and Society*. Stanford University Press, Stanford, CA

Taylor, Barbara (1983) *Eve and the New Jerusalem*. Virago, London

Thiam, Awa (1986) *Black Sisters, Speak Out*. Pluto, London

Thompson, E.P. (1967) 'Time, Work-Discipline and Industrial Capitalism'. *Past and Present*, no. 38, pp. 56–97

Tickell, Oliver (1989) 'Killing the Goose that Lays the Golden Eggs'. *Green Line*, no. 75, pp. 21–2

Todd, N. (1986) *Roses and Revolutionists*. People's Publications, London

Toffler, Alvin (1981) *The Third Wave*. Pan Books, London

Tokar, Brian (1987) *The Green Alternative*. R. & E. Miles, San Pedro, CA

Tokar, Brian (1990) 'Eco-Apocalypse'. *New Internationalist*, no. 210, pp. 14–15

Trainer, Ted (1985) *Abandon Affluence*. Zed, London

Truong, Thanh-Dam (1990) *Sex, Money and Morality*. Zed, London

Voedingsbond FNV (nd) *No Frontiers to a Basic Income*. Utrecht, The Netherlands

Walby, Sylvia (1990) *Theorizing Patriarchy*. Basil Blackwell, Oxford

Wall, Derek (1990) *Getting There*. Green Print, London

Wallerstein, Immanuel (1983) *Historical Capitalism*. Verso, London

Ward, Barbara and René Dubos (1972) *Only One Earth*. André Deutsch, London

Waring, Marilyn (1989) *If Women Counted*. Macmillan, London

Weston, Joe (ed.) (1986) *Red and Green*. Pluto, London

Wheelock, Jane (1990) *Husbands at Home*. Routledge, London

Williams, Raymond (ed) *Socialism and Ecology*. SERA, London

World Bank (International Bank for Reconstruction and Development) (1990) *World Development Report: Poverty*. Oxford University Press, Oxford

World Commission on Environment and Development (1987) *Our Common Future*. Oxford University Press, Oxford

Yankelovitch, D. *et al.* (1983) *Work and Human Values*. Aspen Institute for Humanistic Studies, New York

Index